THE JEWS OF NORTH AMERICA

THE JEWS OF NORTH AMERICA

EDITED AND INTRODUCED BY
MOSES RISCHIN

Wayne State University Press   Detroit   1987

Library of Congress Cataloging-in-Publication Data

The Jews of North America.

Proceedings of a conference sponsored by the Multicultural History
Society of Ontario, held at the University of Toronto Apr. 24–26,
1983.

Includes bibliographies and index.

1. Jews—United States—History—Congresses.
2. Jews—Canada—History—Congresses. 3. United
States—Ethnic relations—Congresses. 4. Canada—
Ethnic relations—Congresses. I. Rischin, Moses,
1925–   . II. Multicultural History Society
of Canada.

E184.J5J67 1987   971'.004924   87-10110
ISBN 0-8143-1890-8
ISBN 0-8143-1891-6 (pbk.)

To
the Pioneer Historians
of
Ethnic North America
Marcus Lee Hansen
(1892–1938)
and
John Bartlett Brebner
(1895–1957)

Contents

Contributors

Irving Abella, professor of history at Glendon College, York University, Toronto, is co-author of *None Is Too Many.*

Pierre Anctil, a researcher at l'Institut québécois de recherche sur la culture in Montreal, where he studies aspects of ethnicity in Quebec society, has served as president of the Canadian Ethnic Studies Association.

David J. Bercuson, professor of history at the University of Calgary, specializes in modern Canadian political and diplomatic history and the history of the Arab-Israeli conflict. He is the author of *The Secret Army, Canada and the Birth of Israel: A Study in Canadian Foreign Policy,* and *A Trust Betrayed: The Keegstra Affair.*

Lloyd P. Gartner, holder of the Abraham and Edita Spiegel Family Foundation Chair in European Jewish History at Tel Aviv University, is the author of *History of the Jews of Cleveland, Jewish Education in the United States: A Documentary History* and other publications.

Gerald L. Gold, associate professor of anthropology, York University, Toronto, a specialist on French-speaking minorities in North America and on inter-ethnic relations, is the author of *St. Pascal, Changing Leadership and Social Organization in a Quebec Town* and *Minorities and Mother Country Imagery.*

Arthur A. Goren, professor of history in the Institute of Philosophy and History at the Hebrew University of Jerusalem, is the author of *The American Jews* and *New York Jews and the Quest for Community* and editor of *Dissenter in Zion: From the Writings of Judah L. Magnes.*

Barbara Kirshenblatt-Gimblett, chair and professor of performance studies at New York University's Tisch School of the Arts and a research associate at the YIVO Institute for Jewish Research, is co-author with Lucjan Dobroszycki of *Image before My Eyes: A Photographic History of Jewish Life in Poland, 1864–1939.*

Fred Matthews, associate professor of history and humanities at York University, Toronto, writes on intellectual history, including the development of the social sciences, and is the author of *Quest for an American Sociology: Robert E. Park and the Chicago School* and other works.

Deborah Dash Moore, chair of the Department of Religion at Vassar College, where she teaches Jewish studies and American culture, is the author of *At Home in America* and *B'nai B'rith and the Challenge of Ethnic Leadership.*

Marc Lee Raphael, professor of history and director of the Melton Center for Jewish Studies at Ohio State University, is the author of *Jews and Judaism in a Midwestern Community: Columbus, Ohio, 1840–1975* and other works.

Robert M. Seltzer, professor of history at Hunter College and at the Graduate School of the City University of New York, is the author of *Jewish People, Jewish Thought: The Jewish Experience in History,* articles on modern Jewish intellectual history and studies of Simon Dubnow's life and ideas.

Mark Slobin, professor of music at Wesleyan University, has published books on the music of Afghanistan, Central Asia, and the Eastern European Jews in Europe and America.

William Toll, the author of *The Resurgence of Race, Black Social Theory from Reconstruction to the Pan-African Conferences* and *The Making of an Ethnic Middle Class: Portland Jewry Over Four Generations,* resides in Eugene, Oregon.

Harold Troper, professor of history at the Ontario Institute for Studies in Education in Toronto, is co-author of *None Is Too Many.*

Gerald Tulchinsky, professor of history at Queen's University at Kingston, Ontario, has written extensively on Canadian Jewish history.

Preface

The last quarter century has witnessed the ushering in of a new American and Canadian history vitalized in good part by a growing appreciation for the role of ethnicity in the development of the two great neighbouring countries and in the lives of their peoples. Important new journals, most notably the *Journal of American Ethnic History,* which has taken North America for its province, an impressive and variegated historical literature, regional, national, and international conferences and symposia, and the maturing of a whole new generation of scholars in ethnic history and kindred disciplines have lent freshness and vigour to a scholarly enterprise that has begun to recast our understanding of the North American experience and of the American and Canadian peoples.

In this transformation, American Jewish historians for some time and more recently Canadian Jewish historians as well in their own new journal and elsewhere have shown remarkable vitality and contributed impressively to a growing public consciousness of a complex Jewish ethnic individuality.[1] The bountiful harvest of provocative scholarship that accrued over two decades clearly called for a critical assessment of the total North American field.

It was most timely therefore for the academic director of the Multicultural History Society of Ontario, itself a product of the publicly-endowed ethnic nascence and a potent vehicle for its wide dissemination and explication, most conspicuously in its journal, *Polyphony,* to convoke a conference where scholars in both American and Canadian Jewish studies would be able for the first time to present their work before the larger community of learning. On 24–26 April 1983 Professor Robert F. Harney and his associates sponsored a landmark international event at the University of Toronto which brought scholars from Canada, Israel and the United States together in a first joint effort to explore the Canadian and American Jewish experience as a North American totality. It was my great privilege to be invited to assist in the planning of the conference and in the editing of this volume.

At the conference, the variety and range of papers presented by historians and other historically minded scholars projected the expansive horizons of ongoing research, inspiration and understanding that have become emblematic of the field in the final decades of the twentieth century. *The Jews of North America* reflects therefore the most vital and original scholarship of our time.

In preparing this volume for publication, it has been my privilege to work with a most varied and talented array of scholars without whose cooperation and patience this book would not have been possible. All of us are especially grateful to the academic director of the Multicultural History Society of Ontario for playing a catalytic role in organizing the conference on the North American Jewish experience, as he has in so many other Canadian American ethnic convocations. The graciousness, tact and wit of the society's staff in working with so diverse a company of scholars may well serve as a model for international sensitivity and politesse in a world where interethnic filaments link nations in ways that ever continue to unfold.

Also, I should like to express my appreciation to Jonathan D. Sarna for his perceptive reading of the manuscript.

NOTE

1. See Jeffrey S. Gurock, *American Jewish History: A Bibliographical Guide* (New York, 1983), the most comprehensive appraisal of the impressive scholarship of the past generation. For Canadian Jewish history, see Jonathan D. Sarna, "The Value of Canadian Jewish History to the American Jewish Historian and Vice Versa," *Canadian Jewish Historical Society Journal* 5 (Spring 1981), pp. 17–22; Gerald Tulchinsky, "Recent Developments in Canadian Jewish Historiography," *Canadian Ethnic Studies* 14 (February 1982), pp. 114–125; Tulchinsky, "Contours of Canadian Jewish History," *Journal of Canadian Studies* 17 (Winter 1982–1983), pp. 46–56; and Michael Brown, "The Americanization of Canadian Zionism, 1917–1982" in Geoffrey Wigoder, ed., *Contemporary Jewry: Studies in Honor of Moshe Davis* (Jerusalem, 1984), pp. 129–158.

Introduction

I n the twentieth century in both the United States and Canada, the
Jews of the great migration came to shape the Jewish community and
its culture. The effect, therefore, of this migration, primarily between
1881 and 1924, on the history and present condition of the Jews of North
America is the focus for this volume of provocative essays on some of the
most salient aspects of the Jewish experience.

The great migration that brought so many millions of European immigrants to North America and the world's other continents as well beginning in the 1820s did not embrace eastern Europe for another half century
or more. Until then, the countries to which Jews were to migrate in great
numbers lured only a few thousand of them, except for the United States
where by 1880 there were already a quarter of a million Jews. These newcomers, however, came primarily from western and central Europe, from
regions where their numbers had been relatively small. Also, they were
devoid of the religious intensity and deep Jewish learning cultivated in
eastern Europe's vaunted Jewish heartland, where after more than four
hundred years nearly two thirds of the world's Jews had come to reside
and where in Poland-Lithuania in the sixteenth and early seventeenth
centuries Jewish life had attained its golden apogee. Subsequently, mas-
sacres and persecutions and the successive partitions of the kingdom of
Poland had led to the incorporation of the great majority of Poland's Jews
into Tsarist Russia, the most backward and oppressive of all Europe's

empires. Impelled by fear and superstition, the Tsar confined the so-called enemies of Christ to the Pale of Settlement. There, except during the episodic liberal era of Alexander II, their condition became progressively more desperate, setting the stage for the great Jewish migration of Russian, formerly Polish-Lithuanian, Jewry, as Simon Kuznets insistently has designated the Jews of Russia, so as to place them within the true framework of their total social and economic history.[1]

The coming of well over two and one-half million Jews from eastern Europe to North America, like the great migrations from the Old World to the new during the nineteenth and early decades of the twentieth century, proved inseparable from the effects of modernization and industrialization on the societies from which the immigrants came. From one end of the European continent to the other, a new social economy was undermining century-old habits of farmers and artisans, of village tradesmen and town merchants, of landed nobility and former serfs. At the same time, an unprecedented population explosion, especially energized by abruptly declining infant mortality rates, drove millions of the young and even some of the old to look abroad for new opportunities.

The subject peoples of Europe's underdeveloped empires were particularly prone to make the journey. For Jews living in the Russian Pale of Settlement, formerly the kingdom of Poland, the pressure of numbers was without parallel. In 1880 the Jewish population of four million was four times greater than it had been in 1800. From White Russia and Lithuania where the economy proved especially sluggish, prohibitive restrictions throttling and population pressures unrelenting, displaced village and small-town Jews streamed eastward and southward within the Tsarist empire to the beckoning Ukraine and westward to Poland's booming industrial cities. But they moved in greatest numbers to the lands beyond the seas, a continent and an ocean or more away, to countries which beckoned to them as did no others. Sophisticated new transportation and communication networks, the replacement of the sailing vessel by the steamship, the horse, wagon and stagecoach by the railroad and telegraph, the declining costs of travel and the reduced time for the trip, combined to make mass immigration overseas one of the central phenomena of the modern age. As contagious as the idea of progress, as dizzying as the dream of liberty, and more exhilarating than the feats of technology, was the freedom to migrate. If often undertaken with heavy heart and with grim foreboding in the face of the unknown, there was ever present, with each new wave of immigrants, better prospects for those who followed. Between 1900 and 1914, for the first time in nearly a century, Russia's Jewish population failed to grow, as even the ever high natural increase failed to keep pace with the vast exodus overseas.

The immigration fever that crested in the early years of the twentieth century was to send the Jews of eastern Europe to the far corners of the globe: to western Europe, particularly to England, France and Germany, at least as points of transit; to all the world's continents, primarily Argentina in South America; to South Africa, Australia and to Palestine. But they were to go in greatest numbers to North America, where horizons seemed broadest and prospects most promising.

Between 1901 and 1914, in the peak immigration years, over 1.6 million Jews migrated overseas, the huge majority coming directly or indirectly from eastern Europe. Ninety per cent of them went to North America, eighty-four per cent going to the United States and six per cent to Canada. Subsequently, World War One, restrictionist immigration policies and inexorable barriers in eastern Europe virtually brought the great Jewish migration, after a final spurt between 1920 and 1924, to a close.

No people in the modern world, except the Irish in the mid-nineteenth century and the Norwegians some decades later, felt as impelled to migrate in such proportions as did the Jews of eastern Europe, most especially Russia. The immigration of no other immigrant group was so permanent or comprised so high a proportion of children and of older persons, reflecting the family character of the migration, and only the Irish counted a higher percentage of women.

So vast, cohesive and permanent a migration between 1881 and 1914 virtually recast the whole structure of the Jewish population of the United States and the historical literature by Arthur Goren, Irving Howe and Moses Rischin, particularly, leaves no doubt as to what this meant for Canada as well.

Only the State of Israel from the date of its founding on 14 May 1948 through the early 1960s experienced a migration comparable in numbers and in its impact on the total society as did the Jews of the United States and Canada a half century earlier. For Israel, the return of a people to its homeland after the passing of nearly two thousand years was without compare in the history of the nations of the world. Just three years after the end of World War Two and the horrors of the Holocaust, the founding of the State of Israel came at the lowest point in Jewish history since the fall of Jerusalem in A.D. 70. The incandescent magnetism of the ancient Jewish homeland for Jews driven not only from the lands of Europe, but also from those of north Africa and the Middle East as well gave historic Zionism new dimensions. The nation's commitment to "the law of return," to the "ingathering of exiles," transformed Israel within fifteen years from a country of 650,000 Jews to one with nearly three and one-half times that number, as the one million new immigrants came to make up one-half the country's Jewish population and along with their native-born children came to comprise more than two-thirds of its inhabitants. With nearly three and one-half million Jews in the 1980s, Israel ranked second only to the United States as a Jewish center of population and stood first as the cultural and religious center of world Jewry. Sorely needed is a full-scale portrait of the place of North America, no less than of the place of Palestine-Israel, and the other countries of Jewish migration, as they appeared in the imagination of the Jews of eastern Europe in the era of the great migration and beyond. Only then will it be possible to fully appreciate the vast transformation set in motion by the forces of migration.

The study of the Jews of two countries with a shared border, cultural tradition and political heritage second to none is intended to add a new dimension to Jewish group understanding. Seen not only as Americans and Canadians but also as Ha-Americani, as Israelis have aptly designated Canadian and American Jews in their midst, they appear as a vital collectivity sharing in a larger North American history no less than in the epic of Jewish migration and in one of the world's foremost religious traditions. The passage of threescore decades and more since the end of the great Jewish migration has seen the sudden, tragic and inspired relocation, after World War Two, in the historic locus of the Jews from Europe to North America and to Israel. Except for France, which has succeeded Germany as western Europe's pre-eminent Jewish population center, and England, Europe has become a continent almost without Jews, as it had not been for nearly two thousand years. The liberalization of American and Canadian immigration policies, the heroic surfacing of the lost Jews of the Soviet Union and a new cultural climate that has sanctioned ethnic individuality in the lives of all North Americans could not but help elicit new perspectives on the past. For the first time as well, the Canadian and American Jewish experiences must be viewed against the backdrop of what are the two most transforming synchronous events in all of postexilic history. The genocidal murder of six million Jews and the founding of the State of Israel after a near two thousand-year lapse in Jewish territorial sovereignty have been events that bear momentous intimations for an understanding of North America's Jews, for their new sense of themselves and for the perception by others of the Jewish past.

In 1910, just a few years before the great Jewish migration neared its close, almost half the world's 11.5 million Jews still lived in Tsarist Russia, the Austro-Hungarian Empire accounted for 2 million more and the United States with slightly less ranked third. With the redrawing of the map of eastern Europe after World War One, the United States for the first time became the home of the greatest number of Jews in the world. So it has continued to be, with but one eerily all-too brief interlude when in 1940 the Soviet Union annexed parts of Poland and the Baltic states and the Jewish populations of the Soviet Union and the Russian-occupied border nations may together have approached six million—on the eve of the Holocaust.

After World War Two, with the murder of six million Jews, primarily those inhabiting Poland and Russia, the countries of origin of a great majority of the parents and grandparents of North America's Jews, the United States emerged as the greatest Jewish center in the long history of this ancient people, numbering nearly half the surviving Jews in the world. Canada, which as late as the 1930s counted relatively few Jews, ranking nineteenth among the nations of the world, by the 1980s stood sixth, as its Jewish population almost doubled after World War Two, in contrast to the United States whose Jewish population had grown only by twenty per cent. Also, thirty per cent of Canada's Jews consisted of Holocaust survivors or their descendants. A generation closer to Europe in their origins, culture and sensibilities, Canada's Jews were overwhelmingly concentrated in the Montreal and Toronto areas where the Canadian-Jewish community had crystallized almost two generations after its American counterpart, whose Jewish population, by contrast, was dispersed among a dozen or more metropolitan regions. Yet despite their divergences, the Jews of Canada and the United States, like the two nations of which they are a part, have become more alike in the final decades of the twentieth century than ever before. Canada's mounting independence from England, the growing world-centeredness of both countries, and the unifying forces of technology, trade and a higher self-interestedness all have had their effect. In addition, a new ethnic mentality has linked the two nations as post-modern society has not only legitimated diverse ethnic groups as never before, but has accepted their representatives, irrespective of their ethnic origins, on their own individual merits.

Divided into four parts, *The Jews of North America* focuses on several critical themes central to our concern with the meanings and the realities of Jewish immigration and ethnicity in Canada and the United States: modern migration; continuity and tradition; the fathers of Jewish ethnic culture; and Jews, community and world Jewry. Each part consists of a series of original essays that examine a particular trend, institution, idea, ideology, community or personality that sheds light on some aspect of the larger experience. Taken together the essays in this volume open the way to that larger understanding of the North American totality which we all seek.

NOTE

1. Simon Kuznets, "Immigration of Russian Jews to the United States: Background and Structure," *Perspectives in American History* 9 (1975), pp. 35ff.

I

MODERN MIGRATION

Introduction

Nearly half a century ago, two pioneer historians of Canadian-American intermigration patterns wrote glowingly of the free movement of peoples across the Canadian-American border as "one of those great natural phenomena . . . taken for granted in the lives of the two nations . . . that constitutes the largest single reciprocity in international migration history."[1] If given our present awareness of immigration policies and patterns, we wince at Marcus Hansen's and John Brebner's rhapsodic sentiments, we may yet grant that they still convey a residual truth. Historically, the peoples of Canada and of the colossus to the south continuously have sustained a more intimate symbiotic relationship one to another at many levels than have the peoples of any two genuinely independent nations in the world. If their migration policies were guided by shared assumptions that for many decades were directed against Jewish and other less-favored immigrants, surely their inauguration of the world's most liberal immigration policies in recent decades, by whatever standard, has been an earnest reaffirmation of both nations' best selves.

In the opening paper, Lloyd P. Gartner, a historian of modern Jewry, if not quite taking a cue from Hansen and Brebner, faithfully places the North American Jewish immigration story within a broad framework. In a sweeping analysis of the sources of the great Jewish immigration to North America, he points to the vagueness of our knowledge, particularly of the

European background, and to the myriad unplotted microhistories and chain migrations that gave the whole process a specificity that is only beginning to be detailed. Gartner also calls for research into shifting attitudes to emigration, precise places of origin, cyclical migration patterns and age, sex, vocational and other important demographic indexes that might provide us with a more discriminating understanding of the great Jewish migration as a complex and variegated process no less than a great epic. By way of example, he makes note of the differential impact across half a century, first of non-Hasidic, and later, of Hasidic immigrants on American Jewish educational, religious and institutional life.

Unlike Jewish immigration to the United States, Jewish immigration to Canada has yet to generate the range and depth of historical study that would allow for ready comparisons, doubtless because the immigration myth in Canada, at least until recently, failed to capture the imagination of historians and the general public as it long has in the United States. Jewish immigrants, surmises Harold Troper, were prone to see Canada simply as an extension of the American republic, rather than as a distinct country of destination, a hypothesis that needs to be elaborated and its implications probed and spelled out. We know, however, that immigration to Canada, despite increasing difficulties, continued to be important in the 1920s, a critical transition decade, when restrictive immigration legislation brought mass Jewish immigration to the United States to a halt. As a consequence, Canada received a small but disproportionately important infusion of newcomers whose most gifted representatives, imbued with an intensely modern Jewish outlook, helped vitalize North American Jewish life, a theme that has yet to be pursued with the attention that it merits. But, as Troper stresses, Canadian immigration policy, rigorously weighted to select immigrants with agricultural skills who might readily be dispersed to the rural west, proved particularly unfavourable to urban-oriented Jewish immigrants. It was to show itself at its worst and most rigid between 1933 and 1948 when the largest nation in the Western world admitted the smallest number and the lowest percentage of Jewish refugees of all.

NOTE

1. Marcus Lee Hansen and John Bartlett Brebner, *The Mingling of the Canadian and American Peoples* (New Haven, 1940), p.v.

I

Jewish Migrants en Route from Europe to North America

Traditions and Realities

LLOYD P. GARTNER

J ewish emigration within Europe is as old as the diaspora, and Jewish
emigration from Europe to the Americas commenced not long after
Columbus. The earliest transatlantic movement was that of Sefardim,
including Marranos returning to Judaism, and it dwindled by the eighteenth century, about the time Ashkenazim from central and eastern Europe began to migrate westward in increasing numbers. Gradually, the
geographic sources of European Jewish emigration moved further east
and south from Germany and the province of Posen, reaching deep into
Russia and the Ukraine during the late nineteenth century. Emigrants
came from further east, and they went farther west. During the eighteenth
century they moved mainly into Germany, Holland and England, but by
the beginning of the twentieth century they were settling en masse in
South Africa, Canada, Argentina and, above all, the United States. By
then international migration had begun also among Oriental Jews. Here
was the demographic revolution of the Jewish people which was to bring
cultural and economic transformation, and it was in large measure completed by the "ingathering of the Exiles" (*kibbutz galuyot*) in the State of
Israel.

The peak years of Jewish migrations lie between 1881 and 1914, when
approximately two and a half million Jews crossed national borders. They
sought liberation from poverty and autocracy, mainly in liberal countries
undergoing large-scale economic development. Statistically, Eretz Israel

was one of the less important lands of Jewish migration during this period, with no more than 45,000 immigrants settling there permanently. Also, the proportion of Jews who left was higher than for any other country, mainly because of the absence of large-scale economic development and a liberal regime, for which even Zionist fervour could not compensate. Obviously the importance of Eretz Israel in Jewish migration has to be measured by other standards.

Throughout the era of massive Jewish emigration from Europe, a huge migration of European peoples was likewise under way. Over 35 million Europeans crossed international boundaries between 1881 and 1914, and nearly 23 million of them came to the United States. Jews travelled aboard the same ships and were subject to the same laws as gentile emigrants. However, the causes of their emigration differed. Most Gentiles who sought the fabled free land of America were peasants whose livelihood was cramped by overpopulation and landlord oppression. There were also craftsmen displaced by industrial change. Virtually no Jews belonged in the first group, and few in the second. Minority nationalities, or those like the Poles and the Irish who lived under alien rule, had a generally higher rate of emigration than the national majorities. The annual emigration rate of the Russian Jews was about 12 emigrants annually per 1,000 population between 1881 and 1914, and in the decade before 1914 it reached approximately 21 per 1,000. Thus, one-fifth of Russian Jewry left the country in the ten years ending in 1914. Only the Irish emigrated at a higher rate.[1]

The year 1881 does not signify a new beginning or a change of direction in Jewish migrations, but the beginning of a great intensification of existing trends. In many countries there had been a lengthy period of small-scale immigration which unknowingly prepared the ground for mass immigration after the critical year of 1881. Before 1870 German Jews had emigrated on a large scale to the United States preceded in good part by a perceptible number of Dutch and British Jews. After 1870, the means of migration had been revolutionized by the railroad and the steamship and the great source of emigration now became eastern Europe.

Emigration occurred in vaster proportions than ever before, for, under the Czarist regime, few could see any hope for improvement or emancipation. To give the reasons why two and a half million Jews emigrated, mainly from eastern Europe, would require a history of the Jews in those areas. The governing facts must suffice:

1. The Jewish population of the Russian empire increased from approximately one million in 1800 to 5,189,000 in 1897. The latter figure does not include, of course, the more than half a million who had already left;

Galician Jewry went from about 250,000 in 1800 to 811,000 in 1900. The 135,000 Roumanian Jews of 1859 numbered 266,000 in 1899, to a large extent because Roumania was a country to which Jews emigrated from Russia and Galicia.[2]

2. Of the restrictions on Russian Jewry, probably the most harmful were those on residence. The Jews were driven off the land and, except for a privileged few, were forbidden to settle in the growing Russian cities. By preventing the Jews from participating in Russian economic growth and hobbling their efforts to develop an economic structure adequate to their immense numerical increase, the Russian regime practically forced the Jews to emigrate.[3]

3. The Hapsburg rulers of Galicia kept that province in colonial subordination to the western part of their dominions. Although the Jews of Galicia enjoyed the political advantages of the emancipation of 1867, the economic backwardness of the impoverished province drove a high proportion of them to emigrate.[4]

4. Roumanian Jewry was kept in a state of rightless alienhood, subject to expulsion from trades and livelihoods and to violent popular agitation. In that country political oppression, more than economic privation, caused emigration.[5]

5. General conscription of Russian Jews replaced in 1874 the abandoned cantonist system initiated by Nicholas I. The prospect of two years' service in the army of the Czar provoked thousands of young men to leave Russia. The three-hundred-ruble fine imposed on their parents in such cases did not have to be paid if the youths were inducted into the army but then deserted. Some communities secretly maintained an elaborate system to employ substitutes for their sons, according to a fixed schedule of priority.[6]

6. Russian pogroms, and such cruel episodes as the expulsion from Moscow in 1891, were regarded in the West as the particular causes of Jewish emigration. However, the causes already given are more basic and pervasive. Galicia was relatively free of pogroms, yet its Jews emigrated in greater proportion than those in Russia. Pogroms were a symbol of the determination of the Russian regime to degrade its Jews, and to use them as scapegoats for deep faults of the regime itself.

Only slowly was it realized in western Europe and America that a mass movement was in progress, which was not just a terror-stricken response to pogroms and disabling decrees. Jewish emigrants from eastern Europe could no longer be regarded in the West as drifters or unattached individuals. Yet not before 1900 did western Jews genuinely recognize that mass settlement in their lands was a permanent fact of Jewish life.

EMIGRANTS' DESTINATIONS

Migration included not only the movement across national frontiers but within them, usually from little towns and the countryside to large cities. The experience of Kovno in the 1880s was typical of many other districts during that economically depressed decade. In earlier times "each town was a center unto itself. A town situated upon a river where boats plied prospered greatly." When the railroad came, "the entire province was as one city, whose metropolis obviously would devour all its sisters," and businessmen and paupers alike "abandon[ed] their localities and trek[ked] to the big city." The Lithuanian city, most of whose inhabitants were Jews, drew more settlers than it could support. "Many of them go to America, and whoever is master of a trade does not regret his intention of crossing the ocean."[7]

This was all possible thanks to the ready availability of safe, scheduled mass transportation on land and sea, and the nearly untrammelled right to leave one country and enter another. This combination of circumstances never existed before, and it has not occurred since.

The emigration routes before 1914 took the emigrant from home to a junction on the railroad network, such as Kiev, Warsaw or Brody. From there he travelled to a depot city in mid-continent, usually Vienna, Berlin or Breslau, and thence to a port city. The main ports of embarkation for emigration from eastern Europe were Hamburg and Bremen. Of special importance was the emigrant traffic through England, which usually brought migrants from Hamburg to England at Grimsby or Harwich, or London. They then crossed to Liverpool for the voyage to America. The journey from a continental port to America by way of England cost less than did the direct route for emigrants who circumvented the high fixed prices of the North Atlantic shipping ring by purchasing transatlantic tickets in England under an assumed name.[8]

The riskiest step in the journey was passing the border from Russia, usually into Germany. After 1882 Russia issued passports. However, to secure a passport required months and an appreciable sum of money, and it was not issued to a man subject to conscription. Hence, most Jewish emigrants were smuggled across the frontier guided by professional border-runners. Rather strangely, the stringent immigration regulations of the German government applied only to emigrants who left Russia with a passport, and let alone the far greater number who reached its territory by a stealthy crossing under the indifferent or bribed eyes of Russian guards. After 1906, however, the Russian port of Libau became available for emigration, enabling large numbers to sail directly overseas with a minimum of complications.

During the 1880s and 1890s a complete system had been evolved in Germany that removed most of the uncertainty in emigrant travel. Sailings were frequent and regularly scheduled, and travellers were protected from being cheated as they passed through the country. The arrangements by which German shippers paternalistically controlled migration were developed largely through the efforts of Albert Ballin (1857–1918), the German-Jewish shipping magnate and confidant of Kaiser Wilhelm II.

The transition from sail to steam was under way about 1870, and almost all transatlantic migration after 1881 took place on steamships. A crossing took about ten days, and a regular schedule of sailings was generally maintained. Compared with the terrors of the Atlantic passage in the first half of the nineteenth century, the days aboard ship were uneventful if not quite pleasant. Steerage accommodations were crowded and uncomfortable, but sanitary control made outbreaks of disease rare. The major lines provided kosher kitchens which Jewish passengers could put to use. The majority of emigrants crossed the ocean between March and October, and avoided the winter months. The danger of shipwreck and loss at sea was small.

While British ships enjoyed a slightly better reputation than German vessels, British protection of emigrant passengers cannot be compared with the precautions taken by the German lines. From the early 1890s steamship rivalries were neutralized by the North Atlantic shipping ring, which parcelled out passenger traffic between British and German lines. Another reason for England's importance is its role as a midway point en route to America or the British Empire. The testimony of 1886 held true for twenty-five years more:

> their goal is America, and they stop en route in London. Sometimes they spend all they have in coming to London, and have no means to travel farther. Hence they remain here a short while until they learn a trade and save enough money to journey to the land of their choice. As I know, more Jews have left London for America than come here from Russia. All in all, Whitechapel is the corridor for the Jews in which they prepare to enter the hall.[9]

It cannot be known how many Jews used England as a "corridor," for periods ranging from weeks to years. They numbered several times more than the 120,000 alien Jews who settled permanently in England between 1880 and 1914, forming the largest East European immigrant group outside the United States; in 1914 more than two-thirds of England's 300,000 Jews consisted of post-1880 immigrants and their children.[10]

The vast stretches of the Dominion of Canada lay open to Jewish immigration, but they did not receive large numbers of Jews until after

1900. There were 2,443 Jews living in Canada in 1881, most in Montreal, and no more than 16,401 in 1901, with 6,941 of them in the metropolis. Toronto and Winnipeg ranked a distant second and third. The prosperity that began in 1902 helped bring mass immigration to Canada, aided by the Jewish Colonization Association which actively promoted Jewish settlement in western Canada. By 1911 there were 74,564 Jews in the Dominion, thanks to the net increase of 56,055 by immigration during the preceding decade.

A peculiarity of Jewish immigration to Canada was movement back and forth across the open border with the United States, paralleling the mingling of the two countries' peoples. The 18,043 Jews who crossed into the United States between 1900 and 1914 meant comparatively little in the gigantic Jewish immigration to that country. However, the 37,670 Jews who emigrated in the contrary direction yielded a net Canadian gain of 19,627 Jewish immigrants, which represented 30 per cent of the net immigration between 1900 and 1914. Practically all the immigrants in this exchange were originally from eastern Europe. The census of 1921 counted 125,197 Jews in Canada, an increase due to a net accession of 42,029 Jewish immigrants during the preceding decade. Most of them were in Canada by 1914.

Immigration to Canada was unrestricted, and immigrants had only to pass a medical examination upon their arrival. However, administrative rules against the admission of nearly penniless immigrants were enforced with rigour during the economic setback of 1908–1909, which came during the otherwise prosperous period from 1902 to 1914. The port of arrival was generally Quebec City, and Halifax and Saint John served during the winter when ice closed the St. Lawrence River. As mentioned above, the Jewish Colonization Association took particular interest in Canada. It aided thousands of immigrants to go there and also subsidized the London Jewish Board of Guardians to despatch many of its immigrant clients across the Atlantic. In Montreal, to which immigrants proceeded from the port city, the Baron de Hirsch Institute, under JCA sponsorship, received newcomers, sought jobs for them, despatched them to other cities or, in some cases, to JCA agricultural colonies far to the west. Children and adults remaining in Montreal were also taught English under its auspices.[11]

The United States of America dwarfed all other countries for Jewish as well as general immigration.[12] Argentina and South Africa each enjoyed the reputation of lands of promise only for limited periods. The United States, however, was regarded at all times as the "golden land." The difficulties of adjustment, periodic economic depressions and extremely hard work never seem to have clouded America's lustre in the minds of millions of Europeans, including Jews. Of more than 2,500,000 Jews who crossed national frontiers in the thirty-four years following 1880,

2,056,600, (Kuznets's figure), or more than eighty per cent, entered the United States. The approximately 280,000 Jews who lived in America in 1880 numbered about 3,500,000 in 1914.

About 85 per cent of all Jewish immigrants entered the United States through the port of New York. Other significant points of entry were Baltimore, Boston and Philadelphia, and Rouse's Point in New York State, where most transmigrants from Canada entered. An attempt by the Baron de Hirsch Fund, subsidized by the Jewish financier and communal leader Jacob H. Schiff, began in 1907, to make Galveston, Texas, a port of entry. The purpose was to encourage Jewish immigrants to settle in the western United States, far from the congestion of New York City and other eastern and middle western cities. Before the Galveston Movement ceased in 1914, almost 10,000 Jews arrived in the United States at that port.

American immigration was regulated by the states where the ports were located, until a Supreme Court decision of 1876 removed the power from the states and placed it entirely in the hands of the federal government. However, not until 1882 did the federal authority fill the vacuum, when an act of Congress responded to the repeated pleas arising from the overburdened port of New York.

The basic pattern of immigration control was set by the statute of 1891. At the same time, the outmoded Castle Garden was replaced by an elaborate new terminal in New York harbour, the famous Ellis Island, where federal inspectors examined immigrants for signs of contagious or "loathsome" diseases, and attempted to weed out criminals, contract labourers and, after 1900, anarchists. Persons "likely to become a public charge" were also barred, but this was interpreted with latitude. Although United States consuls at the ports of embarkation were supposed to certify the absence of contagious disease among passengers, their examinations were perfunctory. Occasionally they conducted their own examinations and turned aside some who would have sailed in vain; Fiorello H. LaGuardia, the young American consul at Fiume from 1904 to 1908, was such a rare exception. Since steamship lines were obliged to return at their own expense any immigrants who were rejected for medical reasons, some companies examined their passengers before sailing. Organizations assisting emigration sometimes did likewise. This explains in part the low rate of rejection at Ellis Island, which seldom exceeded 1 per cent and never reached two per cent of Jewish arrivals. There is no means of knowing how many Jews were turned away in Europe or decided not to try their chances.

Jewish immigrants constituted but one of the many ethnic groups pouring into the United States between 1880 and 1914. The earlier preponderance of English, Irish, Germans and Scandinavians began to shift during the 1880s to peoples from southern and eastern Europe as Italians, Greeks, Slovaks, Poles, Russians and Bohemians entered the American republic by the million, and Canadians poured across the open northern border. After 1896 most immigrants came from southern and eastern Europe. Most of them became industrial workers who provided the manpower for industrialization in large and small cities east of the Mississippi and north of the Ohio rivers.

Jews were 9.4 per cent of immigrants to the United States between 1881 and 1914. They were permanent settlers, unlike those who came only to make money and to return to their homelands with improved fortunes. After 1908, when the United States government began taking statistics, the percentage of immigrants who departed was 32.2 per cent, while that of Jews was only 7.1 per cent. (Jewish departures in earlier years were probably more numerous, however.) Some came back after visiting their family or taking a bride, or after finding themselves so "Americanized" that they no longer fitted in their native land. Aboard one returning vessel in 1912 "almost all [except those rejected for medical reasons] said they would not remain long in Russia."[13] Once departures are taken into account, Jewish immigrants account for 12.6 per cent of total American immigration between 1881 and 1914. Another sign of the permanence of Jewish immigration is the proportion of children under 15, about one quarter, and women, about 44 per cent. Although Jewish immigration was made up largely of families, few families had the means to travel together. The husband and father usually went first, saved money and then sent for his wife and children. In older families the eldest son might go first, and send for his younger brothers and sisters one by one; perhaps the parents, too, would ultimately come to America.

Jewish immigration made New York City the largest urban Jewish community in history. Its 80,000 Jews of 1880 grew to about 1,400,000 by 1914 and the centre of immigrant life, the lower East Side of Manhattan, sheltered 450,000 inhabitants in its two square miles. Once Jews established themselves, even modestly, they generally quit the East Side and spread out to such neighbourhoods as Harlem, Williamsburg and South Bronx. Second to New York was Chicago, followed by Philadelphia, Boston, Baltimore, Cleveland, Detroit and other cities. Cincinnati and San Francisco, second and third after New York in 1870, fell far behind the other cities as they failed to draw large numbers of East European Jews.

Jewish immigrants often came to inland Jewish communities after spending months or years in coastal cities such as New York, Boston or Philadelphia, frequently moving west to join relatives or former townsmen already settled there. This chain migration often gave rise to concentrations from particular East European towns. For example, in Milwaukee,

Jews from Slutsk and nearby Kapulye were heavily represented, and immigrants from Grodno and Kovno were predominant in Atlanta.[14]

Jews were aided to quit overcrowded New York, and to a lesser extent Boston and Philadelphia, by the Industrial Removal Office, which was financed by the Baron de Hirsch Fund and administered by B'nai B'rith and Jewish charities in each city. The IRO commenced operations in 1900 and ultimately assisted over 72,000 Jews to move to western cities where suitable work and Jewish communities already existed. It was similar in its objectives to the much smaller, if better known, Galveston Movement.

EMIGRATION AT THE CLIMAX

Jewish migration proceeded despite repeated warnings from every official Jewish source. Word went forth that a Jewish emigrant could expect only grief and trouble:

> In order to avoid trouble in the coming days we beseech every right-thinking person among our brethren in Germany, Austria, and Russia to place a barrier to the flow of foreigners, to persuade these voyagers not to venture to come to a land they do not know. It is better that they live a life of sorrow in their native place than bear the shame of famine and the disgrace of the missionaries and perish in destitution in a strange land.[15]

This and other innumerable warnings emphasized a few key points: an immigrant could not earn a living nor uphold his Judaism, and would encounter an anti-Semitic atmosphere. The British consul general in Odessa, in conformity with his instructions, "always warned those who are proceeding to England to settle there that England is over crowded with unemployed workmen and that it is most undesirable that people should proceed there."[16]

Nidhey Yisrael ("Dispersed of Israel"), written in Hebrew and Yiddish by R. Israel Meir Kahan (1838–1934), the "Hafez Hayyim," was published in 1897 as an immigrant guide to pious observance. The book exhorted immigrants to maintain a life of rigorous religious observance at whatever cost, although here and there its author relaxed some requirements during periods of urgency. He observed that migrants needed divine aid more than any other group:

> You should know, my brother, what we know—that persons wandering in distant lands require God's mercy more than anyone. The hint of danger occurs at times on rivers and seas, or on the road. How strong must one be, not to depart from even one commandment of the Torah, in order to possess fortitude on the day of trouble (p. 40).

He warned immigrants against eating forbidden foods, neglecting their children and shaving beards, always emphasizing the supremacy of eternal religious values over making money. Sabbath observance was the main test of a Jew's fidelity:

> It happens that their instinct leads them altogether astray, telling them that during their brief period in America or other distant lands, it is impossible to conduct themselves religiously, in Sabbath observance and so forth. "When I return to my ancestral dwelling place, there I shall return to true religion." How mistaken are these people! (p. 193).

To this revered leader of East European Judaism, dangers to piety appeared so serious that Jews were advised not to emigrate, or at least not permanently.

> The true and correct way for anyone desiring to acquire genuine merit with God is to have the fortitude not to settle in one of these countries. (Unless it be a God-fearing man who strengthens Jewish religious life; we are not speaking of such a person.) If he is compelled to go there on account of need, then once God helps him he may return home, and trust in God, who provides bread for all flesh, to sustain him also at home. Let him not listen to the seduction of his instinct, that he should stay there until he amasses a fortune, for then he is exchanging the Everlasting World for the transient world. . . . (Whoever is unable for some reason to return home and must bring over his wife and children, should not in any case keep control over his older sons whom he no longer supports. They can sustain themselves without him, and it is certainly right and proper that they remain in their own country and walk in God's ways.) Truly, the heart of any righteous man will shake within him once he arrives in those countries, at the sight of the breakdown of religion among many people there. He will curse the day he had to see this with his own eyes, and will put all his hope in fleeing the place. . . . But free choice is granted to all, and every man who is in awe and trembling at God's word should take strength from God who will aid him to return to his country and bring up his sons in Torah and piety (pp. 288, 290, 291).

The counsel of the "Hafez Hayyim" was that of the religious leaders of East European Jewry generally, although no one else is known to have written as he did.

There is no way to tell how strongly this concerted opposition and lack of information swayed East European Jews contemplating emigration. If two and a half million Jews disregarded such advice, there is no way of knowing how many pious Jews did not risk living in countries whose Jewish inhabitants were largely "religiously dissolute."

One reaction to the warnings against migration was expressed in the words of a Jewish peddler in the English Midlands: "Those brethren of ours will not be frightened by this announcement as they are not frightened by the many announcements heard from America and France."[17]

At the objective level, a negative factor in Jewish migration was the absence of emigrant guides, such as the English, Germans and Scandinavians possessed in abundance. Moreover, not until 1904, when the Jewish Colonization Association and Hilfsverein der deutschen Juden entered the scene, did a prospective emigrant have reliable advice and information available before he left home.

Voluntary JCA representatives served in every Russian community of any significance; in 1906 there were already 360. To these local representatives, who were mostly maskilim and somewhat Russified Jews, went a steady stream of literature for distribution, such as *Algemayne Yediyes far di Vos Villen Foren in Fremde Lender, Amerikanishe Shtet* (General Information for Those Desiring to Travel Abroad, American Cities), and brochures on travel routes, passports, medical requirements and other essential data. *Der Yudisher Emigrant* was published by the Information Bureau at St. Petersburg twice monthly. All were published in small Russian and large Yiddish editions. Placards for posting in synagogues and public places also were produced. After twenty-five years of mass emigration, Russian Jews could secure at last accurate, distinterested information. The Centralbureau für jüdische Auswanderungsangelegenheiten, whose headquarters in Berlin opened at the same time as the Information Bureau in St. Petersburg, sought to provide protection to emigrants from the time they entered Germany until their embarkation for America.[18] The array of organizations on both sides of the Atlantic was occupied with aiding and protecting the Jewish immigrant.

These organizations did not openly encourage emigration, but this was hardly necessary during the climactic period beginning with the Kishinev pogrom of 1903 and the outbreak of the Russo-Japanese war in 1904. Jews who left because of the pogrom were followed by tens of thousands of Jewish reservists who fled the prospect of military service in Siberia. The revolution which erupted in 1905 was suppressed in 1906, to the accompaniment of the greatest wave of pogroms yet seen. The next year recorded the onset of economic depression in Russia. A mood of despair oppressed Russian Jewry, and no comforting words counselled it to wait patiently for emancipation.

From 1904 until the outbreak of war in 1914 was the greatest period of migration in Jewish history. A total of 1,195,000 Jews entered the United States, and 67,000 arrived in Canada. Among them were many emigré revolutionists, Russified Jews, Hebraists and Yiddishists, as well as rabbis, who were to play significant roles in the lands of their adoption. The mood of the masses of emigrants is suggested by JCA reports of economic depression from one hundred localities:

the main cause of emigration is simply that they can't earn a piece of bread. They write from 34 cities that one does not hear of emigration after the pogroms. In 84 cities the larger proportion of the emigrants is workmen and from 46 cities a mass of traders and shopkeepers emigrates.

In the Ukraine "there is not a single household among us where there is no one aspiring to go to America," and the report from Warsaw could apply to all of eastern Europe: "obviously, emigration has already become a natural and steady fact in our life."[19]

Emigration overseas did not depend only on conditions at home. The North American economic depression which began late in 1907 affected immigration, particularly in 1909—a typical example of the delayed impact of economic events on the flow of immigration. While 115,000 Russian Jews entered the United States in 1907, and 72,000 in 1908 (still a "normal" figure), only 39,000 came in 1909, before turning upwards sharply to 60,000 in 1910; the 15,300 Galicians of 1908 declined to 8,400 in 1909, before ascending to a normal 13,000 in 1910. The Jewish Colonization Association, which was kept well informed by its network of correspondents, reported that emigration resumed at full speed in July 1909. American statistics show the change by early 1910.[20]

The year World War One began bade fair to be the greatest year of Jewish immigration to the United States, Canada and Argentina. Even before emigrant movement out of Europe virtually ceased in September 1914, 138,000 Jews had reached the United States, and net immigration to Canada exceeded 15,000. Except for a few years just after World War One, 1914 concludes the greatest age of Jewish, as well as western, migration. The full consequences for the Jews were to become clear during World War Two.

LEADERS AND IMMIGRANTS

The great Jewish migration was a genuine people's movement. In the countries which Jews left en masse, the ideologists and publicists of the day paid it relatively little attention. They were largely concerned with anti-Semitism and government policies toward the Jews, Zionism, socialism and revolution, or with the maintenance of the traditional religious way of life. One reason emigration was neglected is merely geographic. Emigrants usually left small cities and villages, far from the main centers of public discussion in the large, growing cities. Emigration, undertaken in response to manifest pressures at home and inspired by hopes and rumours from abroad, held little ideological content, and it was ideology that ruled contemporary thinking. Finally, a class bias appears to underlie the neglect of the subject. The emigrants came from the obscure masses, precisely the people whom the ideological programs were intended to serve, rather than from the middle class or the intelligentsia, which did the speaking, writing and agitating. Emigration constituted an immense blind spot in their world view. Only during the dramatic episodes of the revolutionary year 1881–1882, or when Baron de Hirsch's project for Argentine colonization was unveiled, or during the Roumanian *fusgayer* movement of 1900, did the subject come to the forefront of public discussion.[21]

The traditional rabbinic leadership was also inattentive to emigration, although as published collections of responsa show, it was common for them to receive halakhic questions from immigrant communities abroad. But most rabbis did not participate as leaders in the worldly affairs of the Jewish community. We have already noted the counsel offered by R. Israel Meir Ha-Kohen ("Hafez Hayyim"). It might be added that R. Isaac Elhanan Spektor (1819–1896) of Kovno appears to have exercised patronage in placing numerous rabbis, especially younger men from his *kolel*, in rabbinic positions abroad.

Almost all Jewish emigrants settled in English-speaking countries and this fact alone had vast implications. So dramatic a demographic shift not only emancipated the Jews but also opened the way to large-scale assimilation into new societies and their cultures. It was probably the fastest and easiest assimilation the Jews have ever experienced. Emigration therefore meant new forms of Jewish identity under conditions of personal freedom and voluntary communal association.[22] As East European Jewry spread to the most distant countries, it also made world Jewry more homogeneous than it ever had been. Mass migration emphasized the minority position of Sefardi and Oriental Jewry, who then constituted only 10 per cent of world Jewry, and likewise that of the few western Jewish communities, such as the Netherlands and Italy, which received few immigrants.

A price was paid for these accomplishments, not only by the group as a whole but also by individuals and families. The separation between husbands and wives, for example, was often long and painful, and marriages were disrupted, and there were many cases of deserted wives (*agunot*). Immigrant parents who were attached to the traditional ways and language frequently came into conflict with their children who were rapidly assimilating into their new environment. A streak of crime, including an international Jewish traffic in prostitution,[23] accompanied migration and the adjustment to the new lands.

Migration was a process of extraordinary dynamism. Placid, staid Jewish communities vastly enlarged their sphere of activity and their pace on account of the huge number of immigrants, for whom they felt somehow responsible. The immigrants generally left behind their religious and economic elite, for, as usual with elites, few would voluntarily leave the society where they enjoyed high status in order to take their chances in a new one. Hence new elites were quickly established among the immigrants, based largely on the acquisition of wealth (none was inherited) and recognition in the general or the native Jewish community. Such traditional values as piety and learning played almost no role in the formation of the new elites. "Those below are on top, and those on top are below," lamented those who recalled fondly (but not everybody's recollection was fond) the social order of the Jewish communities from which they had emigrated. Distress, very hard work and difficult times were the lot of all immigrants, and illness and failure befell many who never achieved even their most modest goals. An impressively high proportion, however, did attain the freedom and prosperity they sought. If they did not, their children almost always did.

THE IMMIGRANT'S OWN HISTORY

The subject of immigration history is the immigrant. Laws and the men who enacted and administered them, communal institutions and political and religious leaders all derive whatever importance they possess for immigration history from their impact on the immigrant. However, what we know of Jewish immigration is weighted too heavily toward its legal, institutional and communal aspects with insufficient attention to the immigrants themselves. This may be truer for the Jews than for others, since the network of organizations which functioned to control or to serve Jewish immigration was denser than for any other immigrant group. It is all too easy to emphasize the organizations' unquestionably important role, especially because they produced an impressive volume of records. Yet more can be done to illuminate our subject, the immigrant. To cite a few examples: there are numerous collections of immigrant letters of different peoples, but none yet for the Jews. The folklore and belles lettres bearing on migration, especially those written in Europe, have been little noted. There are large collections of rabbinic responsa which contain many queries deriving from the migration experience, particularly on the subject of marriage. The Hebrew Immigrant Aid Society in New York, the Poor Jews Temporary Shelter in London and other immigrant aid institutions kept registers of arrivals, many of which have been preserved. Demographers and social historians have shown how immigrant nuptiality and fertility patterns reaching back to Europe can be analysed from census and other records which exist in western countries.[24]

The lower east sides of western Europe and the Americas have been the starting points for immigrants, and Jewish immigration historians have begun from this classic district. Moses Rischin, Arthur Goren and

Irving Howe have shown that the Lower East Side of New York throbbed with economic vitality, and its political and cultural pulse beat vigorously—while traditional Judaism, hard beset, also attempted to establish itself.[25] Historians Deborah D. Moore and Jeffrey Gurock have recently examined areas of second settlement in New York City. Various works about smaller cities have also shown how repeated neighbourhood changes created distance from the immigrant experience.[26]

The future of Jewish immigration historiography lies in the story of Jewish emigration, or in what is somewhat languidly called the European background. We have yet to learn the fundamentals: from which regions did the East European Jews come, and how and when did these geographic origins shift? Since Galicia was a province of the Austro-Hungarian Empire and Roumania a sovereign state, we are better informed about them than we are about the 80 per cent of the immigrants who came from the empire of the Czars. What was the social level and cultural character of the immigrants? Is there any means of determining how an emigrant chose his country of destination? The answers have largely been guess-work, but religious and literary works are full of hints, as are memoirs and the press. We have divisions by sex, but even relatively equal proportions does not prove families emigrated together. Nor have we much idea about age levels, because the division at the United States end is merely tripartite: until age 15, 15 until 45, 45 and older. Finally, the occupational classifications collected by the United States authorities from arriving immigrants, which have been used skilfully by Kuznets, appear less reliable than those collated from Anglo-Jewish sources.

The conceptions of historians regarding the economic sources of migration tend to be very simplistic: so much push and so much pull. But their relative weight and variations, and exactly who was pushed and who pulled, must bring us into the realm of the economists. Brinley Thomas' great work exists at least to show us the possibilities: the reciprocal relations between long and short cycles on both sides of the North Atlantic and the movement of emigrants. Had we only the statistical riches he has used for England and the United States during the nineteenth century! We have not but we do have his exemplary work, together with the older classics by Marcus L. Hansen and Robert F. Foerster.

Lest these remarks remain arid proposals, I shall suggest an example which combines geography, religion and communal life. A Galician Jew was probably a Hasid, and a Lithuanian Jew was probably not. Under the surface of their common Orthodoxy, substantial differences existed in their conception of individual religiosity and, in what concerns us, communal life. The Hasid-Galician had replaced attachment to the local community (Kehillah) where he lived, with total devotion to his rebbe, who might live far away, and to whose court he would travel for extended stays during the holidays, leaving his family to fend for itself. The effects of this sort of attachment to a distant rebbe included a weaker family structure than non-Hasidism, and a sense of orphanhood by immigrant Hasidim. No rebbe is known to have come to North America before 1914, although some quasirebbes apparently came. The initiative in establishing Orthodox schools, synagogues and other religious institutions in lands of immigration came not from Hasidim, whose communal skills had atrophied, but from Litvaks, accustomed to communal life in their small towns and cities. The Hasid–non-Hasidic division reaches deep into pre-World War One immigrant Jewry. It is notable, moreover, to observe the transformation once major Hasidic rebbes began arriving in the United States, starting with Lubavich in 1941.

Perhaps we shall yet turn the history of Jewish immigration into the history of immigrants?

NOTES

1. No satisfactory study of Jewish migrations exists. Jacob Lestschinsky, "Jewish Migrations, 1840–1956," in Louis Finklestein, ed., *The Jews: Their History, Culture and Religion,* 3d ed., 2 vols. (Philadelphia, 1960), pp. 1536–1596, summarizing the author's lifetime of pioneering work, is inadequate and out of date, and Mark Wischnitzer, *To Dwell in Safety: The Story of Jewish Migration since 1800* (Philadelphia, 1949), deals largely with organized migration and is not very good. An important study, especially for the demographic and economic data, is Simon Kuznets, "Immigration of Russian Jews to the United States: Background and Structure," *Perspectives in American History 9* (1975), pp. 35–124. Walter F. Willcox and Imre Ferenczi, eds., *International Migrations,* 2 vols. (New York, 1929, 1931) is a standard work with a serviceable chapter on the Jews by L. Hersch (II, pp. 471–520). Brinley Thomas, *Migration and Economic Growth: A Study of Great Britain and the Atlantic Economy* (2d. ed., Cambridge, 1973) is a major study, and Marcus L. Hansen, *The Atlantic Migration 1607–1860* (Cambridge, Mass., 1940; new ed., 1961) a classic. Philip Taylor, *The Distant Magnet: European Emigration to the U.S.A.* (N.Y., 1971) is an excellent up-to-date account.

2. Arthur Ruppin, *Soziologie der Juden,* 2 vols. (Berlin, 1930), I, pp. 114–115; Jacob Lestschinsky, "Das jüdische Volk im Wandel der letzten hundert Jahre," [YIVO] *Schriften für Wirtschaft und Statistik,* I (1928) Tables IX–XIV (in Yiddish); Aryeh Tartakover, *HaHebrah HaYehudit,* I, Jerusalem, 1957, pp. 72–82.

3. For population estimates of Russian Jewry, see B. Dinur, *Dorot u-Reshumot* (Historical Writings, 4) (Jerusalem, 1978), pp. 202–207; Specific attention to the nexus between East European conditions and emigration will be found in: (J. B. Weber and W. Kempster), *Report of the Commissioners of Immigration upon the Causes Which Incite Immigration to the United States,* 2 vols. (Washington, D.C., 1892); United States Immigration Commission, *Reports,* 42 vols. (Washington, D.C., 1907–1911), vol. 4, *Emigration Conditions in Europe;* Jewish Colonization Association, *Receuil de matériaux sur la situation économique des Israélites de Russie,* 2 vols. (Paris, 1906–1908); I. M. Rubinow, "Economic Condition of the Jews in Russia," U.S. Department of Commerce and Labor, Bulletin of the Bureau of Labor, No. 72 (September, 1907), pp. 487–583 (repr. as a book, N.Y., 1975). An important new work, Hans

Rogger, *Jewish Policies and Right-Wing Politics in Imperial Russia* (Berkeley and Los Angeles, 1986), appeared too late to be used here.

4. Raphael Mahler, "Di Yidishe Emigratsye fun Galitsye un iyre Sibes," in E. Tcherikower, ed., *Geshikhte fun der Yidisher Arbeter Bavegung in der Faraynikte Shtatn*, 2 vols., (New York, 1943), I, pp. 113–127 (in English: "The Economic Background of Jewish Emigration from Galicia to the United States," *YIVO Annual of Jewish Social Science* 12 [1952], pp. 255–267).

5. Joseph Kissman, "Die Yidn in Rumenye un di Emigratsye kayn America," in *Geshikhte*. . . , I, pp. 128–147, repr. in his *Shtudyes tsu der Geshikhte fun Rumenische Yidn*. . . . (New York, 1944), pp. 21–53.

6. For examples from Agustov and Kovno, see *HaYom* 2, 4 and 18, 6 and 22 January 1887; cf. H. Ellern, "Uber die Selbstverstümmelung der jüdischen Rekruten Russlands," *Zeitschrift für Demographie und Statistik der Juden* 20, no. 2 (March 1913), pp. 40–43.

7. *HaYom* 2, no. 218, 13 October 1887; cf. a similar report from Eiseshok, *HaYom* 2, no. 6, 8 January 1887. Examples could be multiplied.

8. The history of the emigration traffic has been partially studied. B. Huldermann, *Albert Ballin*, (New York, 1922), pp. 21–69 (German ed., Berlin, 1922, pp. 27–98), has been superseded by Lamar Cecil, *Albert Ballin: Business and Politics in Imperial Germany 1888–1918*, (Princeton, 1967), pp. 7–14, 39–48; Francis E. Hyde, *Cunard and the North Atlantic 1840–1973* (London, 1975), pp. 58–89; Taylor, *Distant Magnet*, pp. 145–166; Maldwyn Allan Jones, *American Immigration* (Chicago, 1960), pp. 183–187; Lloyd P. Gartner, *The Jewish Immigrant in England 1870–1914*, 2d ed. (London, 1973), pp. 30–36, and lit. ad loc.; Bernard Kahn, "Die jüdische Auswanderung," *Ost und West* 5, 7/8, July/August, 1905, columns 473–480, with interesting photographs; United States Immigration Commission, vol. 37; *Steerage Conditions;* Wischnitzer, *To Dwell in Safety*, pp. 37–141 touch on the subject *passim.* The annual *Rapport* of the JCA and the *Geschäftsberichte* produced yearly by the Hilfsverein der deutschen Juden are highly informative from the time these organizations entered the field of emigrant protection in 1904 (see below).

9. *HaYom*, I, no. 165, 24 August 1886.

10. S. Rosenbaum, "A Contribution to the Study of Vital and Other Statistics of the Jews in the United Kingdom," *Journal of the Royal Statistical Society* 68 (September 1905), pp. 526–566. Lloyd P. Gartner, *The Jewish Immigrant* . . . (with full bibliography); id., "Jewish Immigrants in London in the 1880s," *Essays in Jewish Life and Thought in Honor of Salo W. Baron* (New York, 1959), pp. 231–249; id, "Notes on the Statistics of Jewish Immigration to England 1870–1914," *Jewish Social Studies* 21, no. 2 (April 1960), pp. 97–102; V. D. Lipman, *A Century of Social Service," The Jewish Board of Guardians 1859–1959* (London, 1959), contains important statistical material in its appendixes. See also my "East European Jewish Immigrants in England: A Quarter Century's View," to appear in volume 29 of the *Transactions of the Jewish Historical Society of England.*

11. Louis Rosenberg, *Canada's Jews* (Montreal, 1939) is a basic demographic work and is supplemented by B. G. Sack, *A History of the Jews in Canada*, I (to 1897; no more pub.; Montreal, 1945), pp. 178ff. The annual *Rapports* of the JCA contain invaluable information. See Jonathan D. Sarna, "Jewish Immigration to North America: The Canadian Experience (1870–1900)," *Jewish Journal of Sociology* 18 (June 1976), pp. 31–42. On U.S.–Canadian Jewish migration, see Rosenberg, *Canada's Jews,* p. 136, and Lloyd P. Gartner, "North Atlantic Jewry," in Aubrey Newman, ed., *Migration and Settlement* (London, 1971), pp. 128–145, and more generally Marcus L. Hansen and John Bartlett Brebner, *The Mingling of the Canadian and American Peoples* (New Haven, 1940), pp. 219–263.

12. Of a large literature see: Samuel Joseph, *Jewish Immigration to the United States from 1881 to 1910* (New York, 1914, repr. 1969), for detailed statistics; *American Jewish Year Book,*

yearly since 1899–1900; John Higham, *Strangers in the Land: Patterns of American Nativism 1860–1925* (New Brunswick, N.J., 1954), a distinguished book, which also deals with immigration laws; E. Tcherikower, ed., ... *Yidishe Arbeter Bavegung* . . . (see note 9); Charles S. Bernheimer, *The Russian Jew in the United States* (New York, 1905, repr. N.Y., 1970), identical with Edmund J. James, *The Immigrant Jew in America* (New York, 1905); the yearly reports of the Commissioner-General of Immigration; *Reports to the Board of Trade on United States Legislation and Practice as to Alien Immigration.* . . . c. 7125, 1893 (Sessional Papers, 1893–1894, vol. 71), by D. F. Schloss and J. Burnett; *Louis Marshall: Champion of Liberty,* ed. Charles Reznikoff, 2 vols. (Philadelphia, 1957), 1, pp. 109–244; Zosa Szajkowski, "The Attitude of American Jews to East European Jewish Immigration (1881–1893)," *Publications of the American Jewish Historical Society* 40, no. 3 (March 1951), pp. 221–280 (abbr. "Attitude of American Jews"); "How the Mass Migration to America Began," *Jewish Social Studies* 4, no. 4 (October 1942), pp. 291–310 (abbr. "Mass Migration"); "Jewish Emigration Policy in the Period of the Rumanian Exodus, 1899–1903," *Jewish Social Studies* 13, no. 1 (January 1951), pp. 47–70 (abbr. "Rumanian Exodus"). Three excellent works on New York City Jewry also illuminate the European Jewish background: Moses Rischin, *The Promised City: New York's Jews 1870–1914* (Cambridge, Mass., 1962); Arthur Goren, *New York Jews in Quest of Community: The Kehillah Experiment* (New York, 1970); Irving Howe, *World of Our Fathers* (New York, 1976). There is no general study of the Industrial Removal Movement. See Louis J. Swichkow and Lloyd P. Gartner, *The History of the Jews of Milwaukee* (Philadelphia, 1963), pp. 156–159; Max Vorspan and Lloyd P. Gartner, *History of the Jews of Los Angeles* (San Marino, Calif., 1970), pp. 111–112; Lloyd P. Gartner, *History of the Jews of Cleveland* (Cleveland, 1978), pp. 119–123; Robert A. Rockaway, "'Worthy Sir . . .': A Collection of Immigrant Letters from the Industrial Removal Office," *Michael* 3, ed. Lloyd P. Gartner (Tel Aviv, 1975), pp. 152–171. On the Galveston Movement, see Gary D. Best and Bernard Marinbach, *Galveston: Ellis Island of the West* (Albany, N.Y., 1983); Gary D. Best, "Jacob H. Schiff's Galveston Movement: An Experiment in Immigrant Deflection 1907–1914," *American Jewish Archives* 30, no. 1 (March 1977), pp. 43–80. Thomas Kessner, *The Golden Door: Italian and Jewish Immigrant Mobility in New York City, 1880–1915* (New York, 1977), pp. 142–148. For general surveys, see Salo W. Baron, "United States 1880–1914," in his *Steeled by Adversity: Essays and Addresses on American Jewish Life,* ed. Jeannette Meisel Baron (Philadelphia, 1971), pp. 269–414, and Lloyd P. Gartner, "Immigration and the Formation of American Jewry, 1840–1925," in *Jewish Society through the Ages,* ed. H. H. Ben Sasson and S. Ettinger (New York, 1971), pp. 297–312.

13. *Der Yudisher Emigrant* 7, no. 1 (January 1913), p. 4. On returning immigrants, see Jonathan D. Sarna, "The Myth of No Return: Jewish Return Migration to Eastern Europe, 1881–1914," *American Jewish History* 71 (December 1981), pp. 256–268.

14. Swichkow and Gartner, *Jews of Milwaukee,* p. 156; Steven Hertzberg, *Strangers in the Gate City: The Jews of Atlanta 1845–1915* (Philadelphia, 1978), table 14, p. 240.

15. *HaMeliz* 22, no. 155 (25 November/7 December 1886).

16. C. E. Stewart, Consul General at Odessa, to Secretary of State, 12 February 1894. Public Record Office, F.O. 65/1479.

17. *HaMeliz* 22, no. 155, (25 November/7 December 1886).

18. This is described in detail in the yearly *Geschäftsberichte* of the Hilfsverein der deutschen Juden, especially that of 1904, pp. 30–38, and the yearly *Rapport de l'Administration Centrale* . . . of the Jewish Colonization Association. Bernard Kahn, "Der Auswandererfürsorge des Hilfsvereins der deutschen Juden in der Vorkriegszeit," *Festschrift . . . 25 Jahrigen Bestehens* (Berlin, 1926), pp. 35–47. *Der Yudisher Emigrant,* published semimonthly from 1907 to 1914 by the JCA at St. Petersburg, is very valuable.

19. *Der Yudisher Emigrant* 1, 1 (15 October 1907), pp. 15, 18 19.

20. JCA *Rapport . . . 1909* (Paris, 1910), p. 224. The 16,000 emigration queries of 1908 mounted to 33,000 in 1909; ibid., p. 235.

21. The minor place held by emigration is exemplified by the near absence of the subject in the discussions analysed in Jonathan Frankel, *Prophecy and Politics: Socialism, Nationalism, and the Russian Jews, 1862–1917* (Cambridge, 1981).

22. My views on this contentious subject are set forth in "Assimilation and American Jews," *Forum on the Jewish People, Zionism and Israel,* 32 (Fall 1978), pp. 10–20, repr. in Bela Vago, ed., *Jewish Assimilation in Modern Times* (Boulder, Colo., 1981), pp. 171–183.

23. Edward J. Bristow, *Prostitution and Prejudice: The Jewish Fight against White Slavery 1870–1939* (Oxford, 1982), and Lloyd P. Gartner, "Anglo-Jewry and the Jewish International Traffic in Prostitution 1885–1914," *AJS Review* 7–8 (1982–1983), pp. 129–178.

24. The Seminar in Jewish Demography at the Institute for Advanced Study of the Hebrew University, 1980–1981, directed by Professor Roberto Backi, devoted attention to this subject, and participants should be publishing their research in due course. See also William Toll, *The Making of an Ethnic Middle Class: Portland Jewry over Four Generations* (Albany, 1982), pp. 54, 70–71, and Ira Rosenswaike, "The Utilization of Census Mother Tongue Data in American Jewish Population Analysis," *Jewish Social Studies,* 33, nos. 2–3 (April–July 1971), pp. 153–155.

25. This point emerges clearly from the works of M. Rischin, A. Goren, and I. Howe, cited in note 12. See my discussion in "Contemporary Historians of New York Jewry," in *Contemporary Jewry: Studies in Honor of Moshe Davis,* ed. G. Wigoder (Jerusalem, 1984), pp. 109–128.

26. Jeffrey S. Gurock, *When Harlem Was Jewish, 1870–1930* (New York, 1979); Deborah Dash Moore, *At Home in America: Second Generation New York Jews* (New York, 1981). The process is to be seen in smaller communities, e.g. Hertzberg, *Jews of Atlanta,* pp. 98–116; Gartner, *Cleveland,* pp. 210–211, 269–271, 296–297; Toll, *Portland Jewry,* pp. 118–121, 154–156.

2
Jews and Canadian Immigration Policy, 1900–1950
HAROLD TROPER

In January 1882 Alexander Galt, Canada's first High Commissioner in London and no stranger to sharp business promotion, took up a new cause. A few months earlier Czarist-inspired pogroms had swept across the Pale, the heartland of Jewish settlement in eastern Europe, setting off a panicked Jewish flight westward. Sympathetic and hard-pressed Jewish leaders in western Europe geared up to cope with the anticipated Jewish influx. They sought non-Jewish support where they could. Prominent non-Jews in London, including the Archbishop of Canterbury, the Bishop of London, the Earl of Shaftesbury, Charles Darwin, Robert Browning and Matthew Arnold, rallied to protest the Russian atrocities.

They were joined by Alexander Galt, who had something more than humanitarian outrage to fire his passion. Galt wrote the Canadian Prime Minister, John A. Macdonald, that this crisis offered Canada "not a bad opportunity of interesting the Hebrews in our North West." It was not just displaced Russian Hebrews—"a superior type of people" he allowed, "partly farmers but generally trade people"—that Galt hoped to interest in the vast, still underdeveloped and underpopulated Canadian hinterland. Galt saw this act of generosity to these hapless Russian Jews as paying potentially rich dividends in investment capital from wealthy western European Jewish financiers. As Galt confided to Macdonald, welcoming a few Jews into the Canadian northwest, only recently accessible by rail from eastern Canada, would be "of great importance" in cultivating "future influence with leading Jews" in London and Paris, especially the Roth-schilds and Montagues.

Macdonald was not adverse to courting Jewish capital by admitting a few Jews. "A sprinkling of Jews in the North West," the prime minister mused, "would do good. They would at once go in for peddling and politics and be of much use in the new country as cheap jacks and chapman."[1]

Before long a trickle of Jews began to find their way into the Canadian northwest, but the degree to which Galt had much to do with their arrival remains open to debate.[2] It seems doubtful that Galt was able to parlay his concern for the victims of Czarist oppression into sizeable Jewish capital investment. Nevertheless, the flight from oppression was not without Ca-nadian effect. Much of the post-1882 wave of Jewish migration out of eastern Europe eventually found homes in the United States. Canadians, already believing that London's urban problems had been aggravated by the arrival of so many foreigners, especially Jews, looked with concern at the infusion of eastern European Jews into eastern American cities. In Canadian eyes the lower East Side of New York was not a cauldron of nascent Jewish renewal in the New World. It was a validation of Jewish marginality, disruptive competitiveness and social clanishness exacerbating the worst features of urban life. To Canadians, repulsed at what they saw to the south, urban-bound Jewish immigration was not something to be encouraged even by then immigrant-hungry Canada.[3]

For almost twenty years this was not an immediate Canadian concern. Relatively few Jews came to Canada before the turn of the century. Cana-da, if it conjured up any images in the collective Jewish imagination, was likely thought of in the larger context of America; and America, of course, was as much a state of mind as it was a place. Thus, either Canada was part of America in the immigrant consciousness or, perhaps, it played some sort of secondary role in reaching America. For some it might fall into a psychological and geographic grey area—not so much a land of second chance as a land of second choice. While guardians of the Canadian gate looked south with concern at immigrant Jewish hawkers, peddlers and foreign despoilers of the American urban landscape, Jews, if they had any notion of Canada, likely measured its attractiveness by the degree of prox-imity to the real America or by the degree to which Canada already was America. If many Jewish immigrants did not distinguish between the United States and Canada, but thought only of America, it made little difference to the few Canada-bound Jewish settlers that they would under-go slightly different immigration procedures.

In *World of Our Fathers*, Irving Howe describes the departure from home of a band of *fusgeyers*, groups who tramped on foot out of Rou-mania before the turn of the century. They sang the "Song of the

Fusgeyer": "Geyt, yidelelch, in der vayter velt: in Kanada vet ir ferdinen gelt" ("Go little Jews, into the wide world; in Canada you will earn money").[4] The reference to "Kanada" (the only reference to Canada in the massive Howe book) may have more to do with the cadence or rhyme pattern of the song rather than any predisposition by *Fusgeyers* to see Canada as a separate entity. One finds little evidence that these *fusgeyers*, any more than any other Jews, thought of Canada as a primary destination in its own right and very few ended up in Canada or even passed through Canada on their way to their eventual destination, the United States.

If any *fusgeyers* stumbled into Canada, it would have surprised no one if they soon tramped off again for the United States; they'd have been following a well-worn path. Indeed, so pronounced was outmigration to the United States in the years immediately preceding the turn of the century that one wag dismissed Canadian economic prospects as a disheartening trip through the Bible. "It begins," he quipped, "in Lamentations and ends in Exodus."[5]

The turn of the century, however, marked a change in Canada's economic fortunes—a change soon reflected in Canadian immigration policy and a change which would haunt Jewish immigration for the next fifty years. After years of broken dreams and frustrated hopes, Canada found itself swept along by a worldwide surge of economic growth. Long a backwater of economic activity, it suddenly seemed that the world's appetite for Canadian products—wheat, timber, metals—was insatiable. Stretching westward out of the Ontario heartland along the lines of the completed transcontinental Canadian Pacific Railway lay the newly accessible interior forests, mining frontiers and, most of all, the vast agricultural prairies of the northwest, all ripe for development.

A recently elected and development-minded Liberal government, under Wilfrid Laurier, seized the opportunity. It initiated an energetic program of immigrant recruitment designed primarily to fill the agricultural expanse of the Canadian prairies and, to a lesser degree, to assure a pool of cheap labour for the burgeoning mining and lumbering industries. The minister responsible for immigration, Clifford Sifton, explained Canada's primary selection process to the Commons in 1902:

> The test we apply is this: Does the person intending to come to Canada intend to become an agriculturalist? If he does, we encourage him to come and give him every encouragement we can. But we give no encouragement whatever to persons to work for wages as a rule, and give no encouragement to persons desirous of coming out to get clerk situations of any kind, the view being that we should have enough persons to fill situations of that sort.[6]

Hearty immigrants who accepted the isolation of the Canadian prairies were welcomed. Those who were prepared to risk their lives working in mines with few safety standards or could tolerate the crudeness of life in the bush in lumbering camps were also well received. There was no such reception for those who gravitated toward the urban centres. Not only did these immigrants defy the developmental thrust of the government's immigration policy, but many of them, especially Jews, began competing with native artisans. What is more, in the closed Anglo-Canadian world where Canada was seen as a North American outpost of British civility, these Jewish immigrants threatened the very fabric of society. These aliens raised the ugly spectre of urban blight, teaming Petticoat lanes or lower east sides, previously regarded as just punishment for years of British immigration leniency or American immigration mismanagement and corruption. Now it appeared Canada was not immune.

Thus Canadians increasingly weighed the economic advantages of foreign immigration against the disruptive effect likely to be caused by any particular subspecies of foreigners. In this racial sweepstakes, the more any particular group could or would squeeze itself into the narrow social, geographic and economic niche open to it, the greater its desirability. Furthermore, the greater domestic economic need, the further down an ethnic preferential ladder the immigration authorities were prepared to reach to fill that need. In the context of Empire, Canada welcomed British settlers without restriction, also courting white American settlers as "people of independent thought who understand the ways of this continent and its institutions."[7] All others were foreigners, their economic utility carefully calculated against their racial and ethnic desirability. Scandinavians and western Europeans were sought after, encouraged to come, their passages often subsidized. But by the turn of the century there were not enough of these most desirable groups. So for the first time the government approved and paid for systematic large-scale solicitation of agricultural settlers from central and eastern Europe, "stalwart peasants in sheepskin coats."[8]

The government was not alone in recognizing the rich rewards to be reaped from large-scale migration. Land and transportation companies, especially the Canadian Pacific, saw the short-term payoff in terms of long-term national gain. Profits from ticket fares, land sales and per capita immigrant bonus payments government offered to authorized immigration agents unleashed a flood of Canadian immigration promotion in central and eastern Europe. To bring some sense of organization into the chaotic overseas operations the government in 1899 made a secret agreement with a newly formed North Atlantic Trading Company to direct settlers to Canada. Seven years, seventy thousand central and eastern European immigrants and $367,245 later the company, described by government as "not a booking agency . . . but simply an organization comprising many booking offices in almost every portion of the continent," was unceremoniously dropped by the government amid rumours of shady business practices and accusations it was directing less than desirable immigrants to Canada.[9]

The company—and the patchwork of railway, labour agent and British consular officials that replaced it—invariably swept up many Jews, especially from Roumania and the Austro-Hungarian Empire, in their undiscriminating net. These Jews, and others who found their way to Canada by other routes, represented but a spillover of those tens of thousands moving into the United States during these same years; but in Canadian terms the Jews who accepted Canada as their surrogate America had a dramatic effect. In 1891 the Canadian census counted 6,503 Jews; ten years later the number had increased nearly threefold to 16,717. Still more stunning, between 1901 and 1911 the number of Jews had increased to 75,838.[10] Although this growth was dramatic, it was not the simple increase of Jewish numbers that impressed itself on the public mind. Far more significant was the uneasy realization that Jewish immigration, probably more than that of any other group, stood in direct conflict with the social and economic assumptions on which Canadian immigration policy was built. Like the central or eastern European Jew who found his way to London or New York, the Jew in Canada showed neither inclination nor willingness to farm, mine or work the lumbering frontier. For a Canadian public reluctant to accept foreign settlers and seduced into doing so with promises of rich rewards that would flow from these hardworking but isolated foreigners, the Jew was a problem. In 1911, ten years after the government had initiated its program of encouraging agricultural settlement in western Canada, the Jewish population had grown by 400 per cent, but of these less than 6 per cent lived in rural Canada. By the time of the 1921 census only 4 per cent of Jews were listed as living in rural Canada. By contrast, more than 80 per cent of Ukrainian immigrants, almost 75 per cent of Scandinavians and 70 per cent of Dutch and German residents were classed as rural. Indeed, no group in the census had a lower rural residency rate than Jews.[11] To make matters worse, few Jews, even those in the countryside, were farmers. If they accepted the isolation of rural Canada, they were more likely to be small retailers, tradesmen or artisans than agriculturalists. In 1921 fewer than one in four of those few Jews living in rural areas was directly engaged in agriculture, forestry or mining.[12]

It therefore comes as no surprise that in 1931 more than 80 per cent of Canada's Jews lived in Montreal, Toronto or Winnipeg. As in the United States, urban-bound Jews in Canada reflected higher arrival rates in family units or quickly reconstituted family units than did other urban-bound immigrants. Jews, thus, stood in contrast to sojourners, birds of passage, whose immigration charade was knowingly winked at by government

officials. Jews, by and large, were permanent settlers. They did not harbour dreams of returning home with capital earned in North America to
satisfy a personal agenda of family and village from which they came. Once
in America, Jews were home.[13]

Of course, response to Jews in the civic culture was not just a response
to their permanence or to their overwhelming urbanness and fears of their
economic competitiveness. These perceptions of the eastern European
Jew, perceptions that predated their arrival in Canada, merely added to
deep-seated religious and other concerns, which fed anti-immigrant and
anti-Jewish sentiment in both Canada and the United States. But in Canada notions of the Jew as a city dweller conflicted directly with public policy
dedicated to streaming foreigners into rural areas; unlike in the United
States, Jewish economic and social assertiveness in Canada did not complement any deeply engrained national reverence for economic individualism as an ideal.

Nor was the small Anglo-Jewish leadership in Canada unaware of or
unsympathetic to the larger public concern about the influx of central and
eastern European settlers. Like their counterparts in the United States
almost a decade earlier, the small Anglo-Jewish communities of Montreal
and Toronto, strapped for resources and awash in a sea of eastern European Jews, reeled under the economic and status upheaval that threatened.
Partly to ease the financial burden and partly to ease Jewish immigrants
westward out of Montreal, in 1890 Montreal's Young Men's Hebrew Benevolent Society petitioned philanthropist Baron de Hirsch for aid. The
baron, committed to the normalization of Jewish life in the diaspora, in
part through massive agricultural colonization efforts in the New World,
had already invested heavily in Latin American and American projects.
Money was quickly rerouted to Montreal where an infrastructure of Jewish immigration aid programs was gradually established under the umbrella of the Jewish Colonization Association.[14] The JCA was initially
dedicated to a program of Jewish urban removal—of shifting Jewish settlement westward to the prairies to conform with government policy and
ease the burden, social and economic, on the Jewish community. If early
JCA supporters pressed to keep Canada's immigration door open, they did
so in the vain hope that the JCA could direct traffic westward once Jews
entered. In spite of high hopes and expenditures, efforts to encourage
Jewish agro-settlement were, on the whole, a failure. Whatever the
folklore of Jewish agricultural achievement in the Canadian prairies, the
figures are telling: in 1920 fewer than seven hundred Jewish families were
farming a mere 150,000 acres of land in Canada.[15]

The abysmal failure of Jewish colonization efforts, any pretence that
Jews were conforming to the broad outlines of government policy, was
not lost on either the government or the vibrantly growing immigrant,

Yiddish-speaking urban Jewish community. Although the JCA continued in its abortive efforts to plant Jewish agricultural settlements in the soil of western Canada, the Jewish communal reality, especially in Montreal, demanded organization that would support the individual urban Jewish settler. In 1919 the inaugural convention of Canadian Jewry's national umbrella organization, the Canadian Jewish Congress, founded the Jewish Immigrant Aid Society (JIAS) to confront the problems of immigration in the urban context.[16]

However, JIAS was more than a fledgling Jewish social agency designed to assist individual immigrants to Canada; it gave structure to that which government and public increasingly understood as a problem—the failure of eastern European Jews to play the role assigned to foreign immigrants. For their part government officials may have seen the failure of Jewish immigration as partly of the government's own making, a by-product of their shortsighted cooperation in Jewish colonization schemes or their willingness to indulge a faint hope that the magnet of western land settlement would be strong enough to pull even Jews onto the land. In retrospect it seems to have ignored the precedents afforded by London, New York and elsewhere. But whoever was responsible for Jewish admission, the key issue was seen as a pathological Jewish problem. Jews could not and, Canadian officials concluded, in spite of all promises to the contrary, never had had any intention of conforming to the social or economic formula which was the bedrock of Canadian immigration policy and defined the acceptability of the foreigner in Canada. Following World War One, as immigration officials sought to cut back on foreign immigration generally, the Jews caught the eye of officials more than any other group.

In truth, of course, postwar Canadian politicians and immigration officials had more than Jews to contend with. But a general postwar economic downturn, exacerbated by lingering wartime xenophobia, especially in Quebec and western Canada, led the government to introduce a series of orders-in-council that whittled away at regulations under which foreign settlers had previously entered Canada comparatively easily. Undoubtedly, of all European immigrants the most severely affected were Jews. Between 1919 and 1923, orders-in-council restricted the entry of both skilled and unskilled labour, raised monetary requirements for admission, instituted new passport and visa control barriers and moved immigration inspections from port of admission in Canada to port of exit in Europe. This virtually eliminated the ability of Jewish communal organizations to intercede with legal aid for rejected or detained immigrants.

Without changing the Immigration Act, the government in 1923 also made several additional administrative refinements clearly designed to block those avenues still open to Jews. The government narrowed the list of those eligible to enter Canada to first-degree relatives of those already in Canada in such a way as to make family sponsorship very difficult. Yet more devastating, in 1923 the government closed the door to all unsponsored immigrants from central and eastern Europe except bonafide agriculturalists.[17] Only British and American citizens were exempted from these restrictions.

The government then moved to control those described as belonging "to races that cannot be assimilated without social or economic loss to Canada."[18] In a series of rulings government ranked all other would-be settlers by their degree of similar "racial characteristics" to the Anglo-Canadian majority. European countries were divided into three groups: the Preferred Group, the Non-Preferred Group, and a catchall group called the Special Permit Group. The Preferred Group, made up of the countries of northern and western Europe, including Germany, was exempted from nearly all restrictive provisions of the orders-in-council except some visa formalities. The Non-Preferred Group included those from Austria, Hungary, Czechoslovakia, Russia, Yugoslavia, Poland, Roumania and the Baltic states. Emigrants from these countries were permitted into Canada only within the provisions of the regulations, especially the program of agricultural land settlement. Canadian authorities also worked out agreements with the national railway lines authorizing them to act as agents for the government in actively soliciting agriculturalists from non-preferred countries.

The immigration officials, however, were not about to let Jews, except first-degree relatives of those already in Canada, slip in, whatever their country of citizenship. All Jews, irrespective of citizenship or place of birth, including those from Germany (but excepting those born British subjects or in the United States), were lumped into a Special Permit group with those from Italy, Greece, Bulgaria, Syria and Turkey. Because the new Fascist government of Italy had already prohibited outmigration and the number of immigrants from other Special Permit countries was never great, the Special Permit class as it came to be implemented served primarily to restrict the immigration of Jews. In effect, cabinet and immigration officials deliberately revised the immigration regulations in the postwar period so as to make immigration conditions for Jews more difficult than for others holding the same citizenship. In distinguishing Jews from their European fellow citizens, Canada predated the Nuremberg laws by more than ten years.[19]

Immigration regulations had turned the immigration law on its head. Rather than permit immigration of everyone except specifically prohibited groups, the regulations now prohibited everyone, except specifically permitted groups. Except for those few able to squeeze into Canada under existing regulations only one route remained open. For Jews to enter Canada a special permit had to be issued with cabinet approval excepting an individual or group from the regulations. As a result, the immigration of Jews slid precariously from routine administration into the political arena. Wrestling immigration permits out of cabinet for Jews was now a function of political power, political will and patronage. It was a struggle in which Jews would have few victories. "Between the upper and the nether millstone," commented one Toronto rabbi, "the Jew as usual will be crushed."[20]

Thus, for the Jewish community, filing routine applications for individual Jewish immigrants was gradually replaced by organized lobbying at the political level to secure special permits. With the potential for patronage so great and immigration officials resenting any short-circuiting of administrative procedures, the immigration issue festered for years.

Nevertheless, so long as the cabinet or the minister had the power to waive restrictions, there was hope the wall of restriction could be breached. Here or there a member of Parliament might secure an individual permit for a constituent or political friend, often over the objection of immigration officials. But with one important exception, all efforts to wrestle a large block of permits from the cabinet failed again and again. Immigration officials warned a cabinet generally predisposed to restrictionism that Jews as a class had proven themselves unable to fit into the Canadian order and, lest the Cabinet forget the political consequences of any precipitous move, Jewish immigration was unpopular with both English and French voters.

As a result only a few Jews found their way into Canada between 1923 and the onset of the depression in 1930. There was one exception—the 1923 admission of a large group of Russian Jewish refugees stranded in Roumania. In retrospect this proved important not just as an exception, the one and only success the Jewish community was to win in the political arena, but also as the victory which sowed the seeds of later defeats, including those during the tragic years of Hitler's reign and its immediate aftermath.

Research on this episode remains to be done, but the broad outlines of the story are clear. These refugees had escaped the post-1918 upheavals in the Ukraine to find temporary sanctuary in Roumania. With international attention focused on them and rumours that Roumania would force the group to return to Russia if they did not soon find homes elsewhere, an appeal went out to world Jewry to help find these refugees new homes somewhere, anywhere.[21]

A complex series of negotiations began between the Jewish member of Parliament from Montreal, Sam Jacobs, working with Jewish communal and press leaders and the newly appointed Minister of Immigration, James Robb, previously the Liberal whip and leader of the Quebec caucus, and his deputy minister, William J. Black. It would seem that Black was among the last of the optimistic old school of Sifton immigration officials, committed to open immigration as an economic boon. When Black left the Immigration Department shortly after concluding these negotiations he did not leave the immigration field but rather shifted from an evermore restrictionist government public service to begin pro-refugee lobbying for railways, eventually emerging as Director of Colonization for the Canadian National Railway.

At the prodding of Black and acknowledging a political debt to Jacobs, a loyal fellow Quebec Liberal, the new minister quietly agreed to a Jewish package. The package approved by cabinet seemed simple enough. The Jewish community, represented by the JCA, was granted a special quota for the admission of one thousand Russian Jewish refugees from Roumania.[22] In turn the Jewish community, supported by funds from the JCA, agreed that no refugee who arrived would become a public charge, efforts would be made to distribute the immigrants across Canada, with as many as possible to be directed to rural areas, and admissions would be strung out at the rate of one hundred per week.

Almost immediately the Jewish project began to have problems. No sooner did the government grant formal approval than the Jewish negotiators began to protest its final terms. They insisted that the fine print calling for a special quota violated an understanding regarding numbers. It was not, they insisted, one thousand individuals that had been agreed to but one thousand heads of household. If that was so, once families were added the number of Jews admitted might run as high as five thousand. A conciliatory and retiring Black, eager, one suspects, to keep the stream of immigration moving in spite of his department's opposition, readily agreed. On the eve of his departure Black approved a new quota of five thousand individuals.

The new deputy minister, W. E. Egan, however, was fashioned in a more restrictionist mould. He was neither ready to compromise nor look the other way when things went wrong—and they went wrong. First, the transport of immigrants from Roumania and their processing in Canada made it impossible for the rate of arrivals to meet the one hundred per week promised. Only after much pleading did Egan agree to a new rate of three hundred per month. What is more, even loose monitoring of the project by immigration authorities showed, at least in the government's view, that the Jewish community could no more keep its promises than it could, in the end, control the refugees. Not only did the JCA have problems distributing the refugees across the country, it also had problems just keeping them in Canada. Immigration officials were angered when some of those admitted showed their gratitude by immediately attempting to smuggle themselves across the border into the United States. Others who were assigned to small towns in Ontario or to western Canada, perhaps fearing they would be isolated far from the American border, jumped trains in Montreal and disappeared.

By the end of 1923 the Jewish refugee crisis in Roumania began to ease; even as refugees in Roumania were still being processed for Canada it became clear that the entire five thousand quota might never be filled. It needed no more impetus than a partly empty immigration quota to set minds to fiddling for ways to use up rather than lose any part of the quota which might be left.

To the credit of Jewish communal authorities, they at first tried to maintain order; but to their dismay and the vexation of immigration officials, many latched onto the remaining permits as an opportunity, perhaps the only one, to bring friends or, with American Jewry, family into Canada as a back door to the United States.

The five thousand permits were all supposed to be for refugees who had escaped illegally into Roumania. Rather than lose any of the precious permits, however, Canadian and American Jewry attempted to have Jewish refugees in other parts of Europe included in the initial quota. As rumours of bribery and sale of permits circulated, the government refused. A request was then made to allow into Canada independent immigrants or non-refugee relatives of those in Canada but ineligible for admission under the stiff provisions of family ramification regulations. Here, as if to show the entire scheme had been a charade, immigration officials selected a few cases for approval. Immigration officials were unmoved by any and all requests to allow American Jews to sponsor family members for admission to Canada.

By late 1924 the government finally had had enough. With Jewish leaders scrambling to fill almost seventeen hundred unused permits, the government pulled the plug on the scheme.[23]

If the Jews of Canada regretted the loss of the unused permits, they could at least celebrate the larger victory. At a time when immigration restriction was the order of the day that the community had not failed its European brethren remained a point of community pride. But immigration authorities carefully assessed the damage, apportioned blame and determined that they would never again give the Jews such an opportunity. They were as good as their word. Unlike Black, Egan was not anxious to please the Jews any more than he was disposed to other pro-immigration interests. If the minister had been too poorly briefed about Canada's Jewish problem and too free in dispensing patronage to a Jewish Liberal crony, then neither should happen again. If officials could prevent it, never again would the Jewish lobby have such free access to the minister without his civil servants standing guard, cautioning against any deviation from departmental policy.

Little did Canadian Jewry dream that its victory would be so short-lived or so costly. If Jewish leaders saw the problems that had plagued the project as a learning experience, immigration authorities saw them as proof positive that Jews were untrustworthy, would not deliver on their promises, remained intent on using Canada as a way station to the United States, and was not above turning a quick dollar in trafficking in permits. Whatever crude mixture of politics and humanitarian instincts led the cabinet to approve the project would not be allowed to take place again. A rising star in the Immigration Department, F. C. Blair, never forgot the Roumanian incident. Years later he recalled:

> When about two-thirds of them [refugees from Roumania] had arrived it was found that some individuals here, probably more interested in making money out of their distressed fellow-Jews than in carrying out the agreement for the settlement of these refugees, were selling the permits to Jewish people destined to the United States and thus to an extent making Canada a back door to that country.[24]

Blair, who in 1923 had already been in the Immigration Department for twenty years, was then a leading departmental advocate of immigration restriction. In the midst of the Roumanian program, he was promoted to assistant deputy minister. Blair determined never to be duped by Jews again, and he would use his power in the political arena to prevent his or any other minister from putting politics ahead of the Immigration Department's determination to keep Jews and other undesirable immigrants out.

For the next twenty-five years, through depression, war and the post-war period, the immigration of Jews into Canada was kept to a minimum. Only with respect to Oriental immigration was departmental determination to maintain restrictive barriers as great as it was with Jews. After 1933 and the rise of Hitler in Germany, the Jewish need for haven stood second to none. Not for a moment did Canada let down its barriers. This determination of civil service and government to keep Canada *Judenrein* (or as *rein* as possible), a determination supported by most of the Canadian public, was thus not simply an uncaring response to the Nazi refugee crisis.[25] It was a conditioned response—conditioned by years of understanding immigration as a function of development policy, populating the national agricultural hinterland, or affording cheap manpower for labour-intensive sectors of the economy. In this hierarchy of desirability Jews placed at the bottom; they did not fit in.

NOTES

1. A. A. Chiel, *The Jews in Manitoba* (Toronto, 1961), pp. 27–28; B. G. Sack, *History of the Jews in Canada* (Montreal, 1965), pp. 273–275; Norman Macdonald. *Canada: Immigration and Colonization* (Toronto, 1966), pp. 220–224.

2. For opposing assessments of the Galt/Macdonald correspondence, see Harry Gutkin, *Journey into Our Heritage* (Toronto, 1980), pp. 27–32, and Robert Allan Gruneir, "Jewish Immigration into Canada 1896 to 1910: A Survey" (M.A. paper, University of Windsor, 1974), pp. 19–20.

3. The anti-urban and anti-Jewish bias of Canadian immigration policy is discussed in Robert F. Harney and Harold Troper, *Immigrants: A Portrait of the Urban Experience* (Toronto, 1975) and Harney and Troper, "Introduction," *Immigrants in the City, Canadian Ethnic Studies* 9 (1977), pp. 1–5.

4. Irving Howe, *World of Our Fathers* (New York, 1976), p. 33.

5. Robert M. Hamilton, ed., *Canadian Quotations and Phrases* (Toronto, 1952), p. 69.

6. Canada, House of Commons *Debates*, vol. 50, July 26, 1899, p. 8501. For an overview of policy formation during the prewar era, see Harold Troper, *Only Farmers Need Apply* (Toronto, 1972).

7. Charles Alexander Magrath, *Canada's Growth and Some Problems Affecting It* (Ottawa, 1910), p. 85.

8. Clifford Sifton, "The Immigrants Canada Wants," *Maclean's* 1 April 1922, pp. 16, 32–34.

9. Gruneir, "Jewish Immigration into Canada," pp. 28–29.

10. Louis Rosenberg, *Canada's Jews: A Social and Economic Study of Jews in Canada* (Montreal, 1939), p. 10.

11. Ibid., p. 25.

12. Ibid., p. 23.

13. Ibid., p. 30.

14. Simon Belkin, *Through Narrow Gates* (Montreal, 1966), pp. 36–47.

15. Rosenberg, *Canada's Jews,* p. 25.

16. Joseph Kage, *With Faith and Thanksgiving* (Montreal, 1962), pp. 51–55.

17. Order-in-Council, P.C. 183, 31 January 1923; *Canada Gazette,* April–June 1923, p. 4106; P.C. 185, ibid., p. 4107.

18. *Canada Yearbook* (Ottawa, 1922–1923), p. 215.

19. Canada, Senate, *Proceedings of the Standing Committee on Immigration and Labour* (Ottawa, 1946), pp. 171–175. For a complete airing of immigration regulations and procedures, see Canada, *Agriculture and Colonization, Select Standing Committee on Agriculture and Colonization Report 1928* (Ottawa, 1928).

20. Barnett R. Brickner as quoted in Kage, *With Faith and Thanksgiving,* p. 80.

21. Belkin, *Through Narrow Gates,* pp. 132–143.

22. Canada, *Agriculture and Colonization,* p. 61.

23. Kage, *With Faith and Thanksgiving,* pp. 85–86; Belkin, *Through Narrow Gates,* pp. 132–143.

24. Public Archives of Canada, Immigration Papers, Blair to Little, 6 June 1938, vol. 432, file 66445–1.

25. Irving Abella and Harold Troper, *None Is Too Many* (Toronto, 1982).

2

CONTINUITY AND TRADITION

Introduction

Settlement, adaptation, acculturation and innovation have been characteristic of the Jewish immigration experience and have been studied with great energy, acumen and imagination. Yet, as Arthur Goren, Israel's leading historian of America's Jews, persuasively contends, two generations of American Jewish historians have been more interested in the study of discontinuities than in the exploration of continuities, in the transformation of immigrants into new Americans rather than in the adaptation of their Jewish ways to the American scene. The break with tradition, community and folkways rather than their transplantation, maintenance and reconstitution in some form has been the major concern of American historians, argues Goren, and as a result has produced a decided imbalance in our understanding of the process of acculturation.

The papers in Part II, based on the latest original scholarship, represent the best efforts of historians and anthropologists to redress that imbalance. The study of Jewish communal practices, such as communal arbitration and most notably of the most enduring of Jewish institutions, the hevra kadisha, the sacred society for the burial of the dead, of which Goren writes at length, offers insights into the capacity, across the generations, of ancient social and religious practices to meet the challenge of changing American conditions.

For young Jews, coming of age a generation and more after World War Two, the search for Jewish continuities attained a special poignance.

The termination of a millennium of Jewish civilization, not by adaptation or assimilation but by annihilation, was the ultimate in historic disjunction, as shattering and as yet unknowable, in its consequences, in the opinion of some Jewish historians, as the destruction of Jerusalem in A.D. 70. With the extinction of a thousand-year-old European Jewish religious and folk tradition along with most of Europe's Jews, the legatees of that Jewish heritage have found a haven principally in North America and in Israel. There the indomitable remnants persist, not merely as artifacts but as seminal ingredients in contemporary Jewish culture, whether in stories, music, dance, drama, religious ceremonials or other forms of expressive behaviour. In our postmodern era, the folklorist Barbara Kirshenblatt-Gimblett emphasizes the critical role that her discipline has played in identifying, conserving and explicating Jewish folk culture and points to four areas of expression that have proved especially rewarding for scholars: (1) the folklore borne with them by the immigrants from their homes, (2) the folklore and culture produced during the immigrant experience itself, (3) the folklore of ethnicity or the expressive behavior generated amid ever-changing cultural boundaries, (4) and the often inadvertent regeneration of tradition in response to a reflexive need for ethno-psychic continuity.

At the contemporary and popular level, the ethno-cultural revival, quickened in the late sixties and early seventies, became inseparable from the pervasive youth culture. It found spirited expression, especially in music, the most time-honored of the Jewish folk arts, most pronouncedly in the renascence in the 1970s of the East European klezmer tradition of which Giora Feidman, the clarinet virtuoso, is the best-known examplar, and the Ellis Island Old World Folk Band, and the Klezmer Conservatory Band, notable representatives of klezmer ensembles. In his paper on the klezmer tradition, Mark Slobin, the ethno-musicologist, systematically traces instrumental and dance forms to Europe and to America in the era of the great Jewish migration and explains how musicians reinterpreted, adapted and re-created the klezmer repertory in response to changing social conditions.

Finally, a salient expression of North American Jewish continuity curiously has been so self-evident that it has eluded systematic historical investigation. The dynamics of ethnic geography—the perpetuation of Jewish residential patterns beyond the immigrant generation—are analysed for the first time by Deborah Dash Moore. Drawing inspiration from the insights of Louis Wirth, pioneer sociologist of America's Jews, Moore, the leading historian of the postimmigrant Jewish community, relates the internal migration patterns of the last half century to the conditioning of a venerable Jewish past, to the persistence of "geography as a state of mind." In her view the "secondary community," spun off from the New York hub during the era of the great Jewish migration, has become the model for the transplanted postimmigrant ethnic community, eclipsing the prototypical "redemptive community" patterned on the episodic immigrant lower East Side.

3
Traditional Institutions Transplanted

The Hevra Kadisha in Europe and in America

ARTHUR A. GOREN

T he appearance in 1976 of Irving Howe's *The World of Our Fathers* represented in many ways the capstone and synthesis of the labours of a generation of scholars. Significantly, among these scholars were the first American-trained professional historians who chose American Jewish history as their field of specialization. Howe, beholden most of all to the work of Moses Rischin, is, like Rischin, a second-generation New York Jew.[1] In the mid-1930s, both were old enough to witness the still-thriving cultural and social world which the East European Jewish immigrants created in the course of transforming New York into *the* Jewish metropolis. For Howe, growing up in the Bronx, Yiddish was his first language. For Rischin, raised in Brooklyn, it was his third, for Hebrew, learned at age two from his mother, was his first tongue. Yiddish, of course, was the first language for enough of their elders to support four Yiddish dailies. The Jewish labour movement, no less than Yiddish journalism, was also flourishing. David Dubinsky, Sidney Hillman and Max Zaritsky, whose trade union careers had begun a quarter of a century earlier, not only headed powerful unions but also exercised political influence nationally. Before them still lay a decade or more of active leadership. Among the founding fathers of the Jewish radical movements, Abe Cahan, J. B. Salutsky and Baruch Zuckerman were still active, and Yiddish poets and novelists of the calibre of Jacob Glatstein and Isaac Bashevis Singer were approaching their most productive years. No wonder that Rischin and Howe, writing in the 1950s, 1960s and 1970s, brought with them an intimate feeling for the immigrants they studied. Moreover, as native-born Americans, a generation removed from their subject, and shaped at the nation's leading universities, they were especially successful in placing the immigrant experience within the larger context of American cultural and social history.

Rischin and Howe were especially attuned to what they perceived to be the protean radicalism which the Jewish immigrants brought to America. The breakup of East European traditionalist society under the blows of economic dislocation and ruin, pogroms and flight, and communal infirmity and unorthodox ideologies, transformed a passive religious messianism into a secular, activist socialism. The title of one of Rischin's introductory chapters in *The Promised City* puts it succinctly: "Torah, Haskala, and Protest." In America, even while the mass migration was under way, protest was naturalized under the benign conditions of an open, democratic society. Stated implicitly by Rischin and elaborated by Howe, the outstanding trait of American Jewry was its continued allegiance to a radical humanism which was the heritage of the East European migration. No more than passing notice was taken of other components of the immigrants' Jewish inheritance. In the eyes of these second-generation secularists, the religious culture and its traditional institutions were brought from Europe withered or remained stark and listless witnesses of a once vigorous but now irretrievable past. The Orthodox—the older, unbending immigrants—their days numbered, were subsumed within the broader "culture of Yiddishkeit," to use Howe's phrase.[2]

The publication of Howe's book also coincided with the arrival on the scholarly scene of a younger generation of historians who broke new ground, asking the questions of the new social history without neglecting the more conventional issues. At home in America, the younger historians focused on the processes that led to the high levels of acculturation, middle-class status and liberal politics which characterize contemporary American Jewry. Superbly trained as Americanists, these third- and fourth-generation American Jews—Steven Hertzberg, Marc Lee Raphael, Jeffrey Gurock, Deborah Dash Moore and William Toll (I have listed them in the order of the appearance of their most important books)—plowed virgin soil and refined our understanding of the immigrant generation and of those that followed. They focused on patterns of settlement, social structure, mobility, the social dimension of communal institutions and the nature of Jewish ethnicity. Although more interested in explaining Jewish ethnicity than Jewish radicalism, these younger historians posited the same image of the rapid decline of traditional institutions, cultural modes and folkways as had their predecessors.[3]

Few historians of either generation probed deeply into the reasons for the discontinuities and declinations. How are we to explain the beards and side-locks removed with such haste, the crowded Yiddish theatres on the Sabbath, and the low state of traditional Jewish education? Most of us have been satisfied with the broad generalization that the old ways could not withstand the heady effect of freedom: immigrants bent on the pursuit of material success seized the opportunity to integrate into a secular, egalitarian society. Most of us have also accepted the generalization that Orthodox life in Europe had lost its vitality by the time the mass migration began, and in the years that followed, it was shaken to its foundations by the onslaught of secular ideologies. Understandably, such an interpretative pattern allows little place for considering the efforts made by a not inconsiderable number of immigrants to adapt and transform their traditional institutions.[4] Yet even if we retain the interpretative scheme of disintegration, tracing the different rates of erosion for what was, in fact, a miscellany of institutions, dogmas and attitudes which emanated from the East European world of Jewish tradition would surely provide us with valuable insights. A more careful backward look at Europe would enable us to better understand the choices the immigrants and their children made in accommodating to America.

One influential interpretation taken from Jewish labour history will illustrate the thrust of my argument. The "great revolt" of the cloakmakers union in 1910 ended, as we know, in the "protocol of peace." The Jewish unions signed an agreement with their Jewish employers after a long summer of hard bargaining and the mediation of Louis Marshall and Louis Brandeis. A pathbreaking settlement resulted which established a comprehensive arbitration machinery for the continuous adjudication of disputes. The notion of an impartial chairman, grievance procedures and litigation and an elaboration of a "common law of the job" which was the outcome were far ahead of their time. How did all this come about? In seeking an explanation, Will Herberg, the labour historian, suggested one possible reason for this remarkable achievement in collective bargaining: both sides were conditioned by the "age-old tradition of arbitration, of settling their often bitter disputes within the Jewish community without appealing to 'outside' authorities. They shared, too, as a heritage of centuries of self-enclosed minority existence, a marked concern for the good reputation of the Jewish community with the outside world."[5] The counsel for the manufacturers, Julius Henry Cohen, recalling the events years later, made a similar point. In eastern Europe "arbitration was an accepted method of settling disputes. . . . Every Orthodox Jew had training in Jewish law—the Torah. His rabbi was for him always the final arbitrator."[6]

What is revealing about both statements is not their validity but rather that the historians who dealt with arbitration in the garment industry and either accepted, rejected or qualified Herberg's thesis found no need to examine that "age-old" tradition of arbitration and conciliation. Yet it was a tradition central to Jewish communal life in eastern Europe. If it lost much of its effectiveness and scope in the transplantation to America, it was in large measure because secular law undermined its authority. Nevertheless, the tradition of communal arbitration persisted. Immigrant congregations created arbitration procedures to resolve disputes among members, as did the *landsmanshaft* societies. The rabbinical court, or Beth Din, guided by a venerable legal code and judicial procedure, dealt with problems of marriage and divorce and served as an ad hoc conciliation tribunal. In fact, some beginnings were made during the years of the mass migration to adapt the European conciliation apparatus to American conditions and to American law.[7] However, neither the historians who dealt with Jewish labour arbitration, nor those concerned more generally with Jewish communal life in America, seriously examined the possible continuities between Europe and America. Marc Raphael, for example, in his excellent study of the Jews of Columbus, records this intriguing statement by the Orthodox rabbi who served in Columbus during the 1920s. Describing some of his rabbinical functions, Nathan Pelkovitz said: "The rabbi was busy in kashruth. . .in marital affairs, ranging from counselor to president of a Jewish divorce court; in business affairs, since it was still not uncommon for civil disputes about money matters to be taken to the rabbi as arbiter in a *din torah* [court]."[8] A pity we don't know more about the rabbi as arbitrator.

But let me return to my quarrel with the labour historians for they ignored the specific question of how labour disputes were resolved among Jewish workers and employers in eastern Europe. In Bialystock, Vilna and Lodz—which supplied trade union leaders, workers and employers for the garment industry in America—did workers and bosses turn to communal mediators or to their rabbis? Whatever the answer may be, there are conclusions to be drawn for the American experience.

The hevra kadisha, the burial society, has received even less attention from the historians of American Jewish life than has arbitration. Community studies invariably record the acquisition of the first burial ground which often was the earliest indication of an organized community. As Bezalel Sherman expressed it, though a Jew might live among Gentiles, he wanted to be buried among Jews. At that moment in life when death came, even the most wayward sought solace by burying their kin in a Jewish cemetery according to Jewish law and tradition. Not infrequently, the consecration of cemetery ground preceded the establishment of a synagogue. To establish a synagogue, Sherman notes, a quorum of ten males was required but to open a cemetery, only one dead Jew was needed. This order of communal growth was not singular to Jewish settlement in America. In his monumental study of the Jewish community from talmudic times to the end of the eighteenth century, Salo Baron made the point that "many communities sought burial plots even before erecting a house of worship."[9]

As the flow of Jewish immigration to America increased and became diversified, congregations split, new ones were founded and additional cemeteries were established. Not only did the Jew wish to be buried among Jews, but when he had a choice, he preferred *landsleyt*. Because new burial grounds were usually acquired under the auspices of synagogues during most of the eighteenth and nineteenth centuries, our community histories register these developments in treating the growth of the synagogues. They mention, as well, the hevra kadisha which was responsible for attending to the dying, for the ritual preparation of the body for burial (*tahara*), for the internment rites themselves and for various religious services extended to the mourners during the shiva, the seven days of mourning required of the family. Because assuring a Jewish burial was considered the ultimate act of piety and charity, the hevra kadisha buried the poor without cost and gave financial aid to the family in distress. Thus communal histories mention the hevra kadisha in their account of the development of Jewish philanthropy. In all the literature, with one exception that is discussed below, there is no substantive discussion of the hevra kadisha nor its decline and replacement by the undertaker and funeral home.[10] Yet in the communities from which the immigrants came the hevra kadisha was the single most influential society in that network of associational life which formed the traditional kehillah organization. Indeed, in the full Hebrew name by which the burial society was generally known there resonates the prestigious place it occupied in the hierarchy of communal life: hevra kadisha hesed shel emet—the holy brotherhood of true loving kindness.

Although antecedents of the hevra kadisha may be found in the talmudic period, more pertinent to our discussion is the appearance of burial societies in Prague and Frankfurt in the middle of the sixteenth century when they were assigned the exclusive responsibility for attending to the dying and dead. Because Jewish law prohibits deriving private gain from performing so exalted a mitsva, the hevra kadisha assumed a public service role from its inception. The historian Jacob Katz suggests that the growth in the size of the Jewish communities was the determining factor in forming such specialized groups. From the sixteenth to the twentieth century, the hevra kadisha in its inner organization, functions, relationship to the

Jewish community and dominance among kehillah institutions remained remarkably constant.[11]

Its sacred function was not the only source of the hevra kadisha's standing. It exercised considerable power, or, we may say, social control, because of its monopoly of burials and the sombre fact that sooner or later all would require its services. The hevra kadisha determined the fees for its services and assigned the grave plots. Because Jewish law required burial as soon after death as possible, normally within twenty-four hours, the hevra kadisha could pretty much dictate its own terms. It used a sliding scale of fees. Age (an infant's burial being less costly), nonresidency (the dead of a neighbouring village were charged more), location of the burial plot (proximity to the grave of a distinguished person being more expensive) and financial status of the deceased were the determining factors. Isaac Levitats in his discussion of the fees charged by the hevra kadisha makes the following point:

> Woe to the rich who in life habitually failed to discharge their obligations to the community or generally fell out of favor with it! Toward such . . . there was no maximum to the "inheritance tax" it levied against them. All that they should have contributed during their life-time and did not, was now collected from their estate or from their next of kin. The society maintained that it was entitled to be exorbitant in such cases, since the money thus exacted was not for the profit of a private person, but for the benefit of charities shared by the entire community.[12]

The hevra kadisha had recourse to other sanctions in curbing deviant behaviour. The best known of these was the threat of what was called a donkey's burial. Levitats brings us the text of such a decision taken by a hevra kadisha:

> Whereas R. Abraham misbehaved towards God and man, therefore a grave shall be assigned for him at the cemetery to correspond to his deeds, namely, away from decent people. And whereas at present there are alive other rebels, like him, deserving to be buried only outside the cemetery fence, therefore we left space about his grave wherein those like him may be buried.[13]

Discussing the same theme Baron describes a donkey's funeral which took place in a small East European community during the nineteenth century. "An informer's corpse was given ablutions with muddy water by Gentiles, his casket was placed on a garbage wagon on three wheels dragged by an infirm horse, and was accompanied to the cemetery only by gangs of shouting and mud-slinging boys and barking dogs."[14]

Finally, the hevra kadisha's influence also stemmed from the fact that it was the wealthiest society in the Jewish community. Its income came not only from burial charges but from the high initiation fees and dues it charged its members. For these reasons and because of its prestige, the hevra kadisha drew its members from the elite. In some communities the hevra kadisha even maintained its own synagogue. Often the rabbi was an officer of the society, and some societies had their own preachers who also delivered the funeral eulogies. As one might expect, the hevra kadisha's associational life abounded in annual banquets, special services and frequent business meetings. Moreover, it provided its members with a form of burial insurance by charging them minimal burial fees or none at all. During the nineteenth century, the hevra kadisha frequently was one of the few solvent religious institutions. It allocated funds to other hard-pressed philanthropic institutions and rivaled the kahal—the administrative body of the Jewish community—in influence. When the Tsarist government abolished the kahal in 1844, the hevra kadisha became the de facto central religious body in some communities.[15]

The transplantation of the hevra kadisha from Europe to America, its initial adjustment to American conditions, and its later transformation— part of the complex process of the acculturation of American Jewry—raise a host of questions. Some of these questions may be grouped in two categories: first, the society's communal dimension and second, its religious and cultural aspects. What happened to the hevra kadisha as an instrument of social control and as one of the main, if not the main, philanthropic agencies of the community? How are we to understand the rise of the funeral director and the funeral home? To what extent did this phenomenon parallel general American developments and to what extent was there an ethnic component in the Jewish funeral industry? Shall we be satisfied with a simple linear view of the development of the American Jewish way of death which we might summarize as: from communalism to privatism? But if this is the case, how shall we understand the attempts in our time to reconstitute the communal hevra kadisha?[16] Is it a return to traditional ways, a reconstruction of an ancient tradition, a public symbol not without importance or a minor fad? To pose these questions is to plead the complexity and vastness of the subject and the need for a book-length study, rather than to present an agenda for the remainder of this paper.

Before discussing several facets of the East European immigrant experience with the hevra kadisha, it will be helpful to sketch briefly patterns that developed in earlier stages of the American experience. Hyman Grinstein's chapters on mutual aid and funerary customs in the *Rise of the Jewish Community of New York*, the best available treatment of the subject, is highly suggestive.

The first burial society for which we have precise information was established by Congregation Shearith Israel sometime before 1785. In its organization and functions it was a replica of the European hevra kadisha. (The society's name followed Sephardic usage: hevra gemillut hasadim— the brotherhood of righteous doing.) Its members attended the sick, buried the dead, provided a minyan during the prescribed shiva period and allocated mourning funds to compensate the family during the week when it was prohibited from working. The society had its own officers, treasury and an annual celebration. From the minutes of the congregation and from those of other colonial congregations we know that the threat of refusing burial was used to enforce discipline among recalcitrant members and to tax unaffiliated Jews who had avoided contributing to the maintenance of the congregation. The burial society, though autonomous, was clearly subordinate to the congregation, which considered itself the organized community of Jews.[17]

During the nineteenth century, when a diverse immigration produced a multiplicity of congregations, burial societies and cemeteries, the hevra kadisha societies developed in several directions. Some remained integral parts of a congregation while others drifted away from congregational affiliation and either expanded their charitable undertakings or increased the scope of benefits offered to their own members. For most of these societies, conviviality was no less important than charity and sick and death benefits. In describing the formative years of B'nai B'rith, Deborah Moore characterized the newly formed fraternal order as a secular synagogue. Similarly, one might speak of a secular hevra kadisha.[18]

For the most part, however, responsibility for burial and for the cemeteries remained under the aegis of the synagogue during the nineteenth century. The sale of cemetery plots was a source of income for the synagogue, and the hevra kadisha soon evolved into the cemetery committee of the congregation. The *Asmonean* of 8 June 1854 graphically depicted some of these developments, informing its readers that family plots, an American innovation, were for sale at Temple Emanu-El's new Salem Fields cemetery, which "looks like a garden." The name Salem Fields rather than Bet Olam, the name given by Shearith Israel and Bnai Jeshurun to their new cemeteries, the site (Cypress Hills, Long Island) and the garden park arrangement—the well laid-out roads, walks, shrubs and trees—mirrored the new garden-style cemetery that had become the vogue. The *Asmonean* further noted that the income from the sale of plots would defray the cost of the new temple building. As a bonus, apparently, the temple would send its own hearse and charge only five dollars.[19] A year later the *Asmonean* carried what may have been the first advertisement by a Jewish undertaker, one David J. Polaks, who was prepared to attend Jewish funerals, supply coffins and shrouds—"which will be prepared by members of the Jewish faith"—and also carriages and a hearse, "the latter driven by a Jew." Polaks also was prepared to offer additional services. "If required, a respectable person will superintend the *tahara* [the ritual bathing of the dead] and all other funeral arrangements. . . . Charitable societies will be served on the most reasonable terms." Clearly, all the elements which marked the weakening of synagogal control over burial, let alone communal control, are evident in the advertisement. Increasingly, non-synagogal societies entered the religious realm of burying the dead. In a letter to the editor of the *Jewish Messenger* published in 1878, the writer explained that one of the reasons so small a percentage of New York Jews belonged to synagogues was that the mutual benefit societies provided burial plots at less cost. One should add that the synagogues—and we are referring to Reform congregations in the main—attempted to retain some control. The question of allowing non-Jewish spouses to be buried in a Jewish cemetery also arose, and some congregations required that their rabbi receive the approval of the trustees to conduct the funeral of members as well as nonmembers.[20]

The East European immigrants were in a much better position to transplant and maintain their traditional communal institutions than were the German immigrants. Their numbers, density of settlement, common language, Yiddish, and their intensive religious culture enabled the devout and religiously minded among them to re-establish their traditional system in America. The centerpiece of the system was the shul—the congregation peopled by immigrants from the same locale in Europe. These congregations, in the parlance of the day, were known as "anshes," because the Hebrew word *anshe*—the "people of" this or that town—appeared often in the names of the congregations. They were, in a sense, miniature transplanted communities or kehillahs. Besides religious services held daily and on festivals, the anshes maintained a rich associational life with societies for the study of sacred texts, aid for the needy, the visiting of the sick, the providing for interest-free loans and the burial of the dead. The congregation, or in some cases, its hevra kadisha, owned a section of a cemetery. Congregational dues or separate dues entitled the members to a cemetery plot and funeral expenses.[21]

When independent mutual benefit societies, the *landsmanshaftn,* were formed, they mirrored, no less than the immigrant congregation, the associational life of the European kehillah. They were, in a sense, a composite of its functional hevras. However, the death benefits they provided were their most important feature.

In its more authentic form as a synagogal hevra kadisha, or as modified by the mutual aid societies and fraternal orders, the hevra kadisha underwent changes in accommodating to American conditions. The undertaker, or funeral director, a species of middleman made necessary by the complexities of the modern American city, in some measure superseded the traditional burial society. Transportation became a complicated matter. More and more people died in hospitals and their bodies had to be transported first to their homes and then a second time to cemeteries far from the centres of Jewish population. It became necessary to call upon deliverymen to hire coaches for the mourners and a conveyance for the body, some of them coming to specialize in this kind of trade and soliciting the various societies and congregations for business. Apparently, *landsleyt* connections were important. In the 1890s the grandfathers of a number of long established New York funeral directors—for example, Garlick, Gutterman and Schwartz—entered the business in this way.

There were other reasons for the rise of the professional funeral director. Municipal regulations entailed bureaucratic procedures for obtaining the release of the body and a burial permit. Ordering factory-made coffins was another chore. Somewhat later the ritual bathing and dressing of the body was moved from the home to the funeral parlour. All these procedures went beyond the means or the competence of the hevra kadisha's voluntary functionaries, who increasingly performed the religious rites only, in some cases being hired to do so by the funeral director. By 1910, if not earlier, it was possible to bypass synagogue, hevra kadisha and lodge and go directly to a funeral director who would provide all the necessary services, arrange for the purchase of a burial plot and secure the ministrations of a rabbi and cantor for the funeral.[22]

These trends toward the privatization and commercialization of death and the breakdown of all social controls became a matter of public discussion that reached a dramatic climax in 1912, when the notorious Jewish gang leader Big Jack Zelig (William Alberts) was murdered. His confederates arranged one of the most stately and memorable funerals which the Jewish quarter had ever seen. "Only the funeral of Rabbi Jacob Joseph surpassed . . . the funeral of Jack Zelig," wrote one eyewitness. In charge of the funeral was none other than the leading funeral director, Sigmund Schwartz, who enlisted psalm-singing Talmud Torah children to follow the hearse from Broome Street to the Williamsburg Bridge. Thirty-six carriages and twenty-five automobiles took the family and the members of the Sam Paul Association and the Jimmie Kelly and Johnnie Spanish gangs to Washington Cemetery in Brooklyn. At the gravesite, Cantor Goldberg and his choir from the Roumanian synagogue, Shaar Shamayim, chanted the *El mole rachamim* prayer, and Rabbi Adolf Spiegel of the Shaare Zedek congregation delivered the eulogy. To top it off, the "chief of New York's underworld" was interred between the graves of Jacob Gordin, the famous Yiddish playwright, and an "eminent rabbi." "Imagine," the daily *Warheit* asked rhetorically, "the kind of funeral and the kind of burial one such as Zelig would have had in the old country?" The *Forward* spelled it out: "Jews would have given a common criminal, robber, murderer and procurer a 'donkey's funeral' burying him beyond the [cemetery] fence."[23]

A few years later, Shalom Aleichem, writing in New York, lampooned the Jewish funeral in the land of miracles in a satirical sketch which echoed the Zelig funeral. "Do people really die in America?" the Yiddish humorist has his European interlocutor ask. "Of course they die, why shouldn't they die in America? But the way one dies, that is what counts. The important thing is the burial." Shalom Aleichem then proceeds to describe the Jewish immigrant picking out cemetery plots for himself and for his wife and children, bargaining over the price, and finally arranging at the "funeral office" for the first, second, or third-class funeral he will have when the time comes. "A first class funeral," Shalom Aleichem explains, "costs a thousand dollars."

> Such a funeral is generally arranged for the very wealthy. What a funeral! Outside, the sun shines and the weather is magnificent. The coffin is placed on a black bier trimmed with silver. The horses wear black pompons with white feathers. And the clergy—rabbis, cantors, reverends—are all dressed in black with white buttons. Carriages galore follow the coffin and children from the talmud torah schools walk ahead singing out loud: "Righteousness shall go before Him, And shall make his footsteps a way." The singing is heard throughout the city. The second class funeral costs only five hundred dollars. The day is not as bright. The coffin is also placed on a black platform but without the silver trimming. The horses and members of the clergy wear black but without feathers and without white buttons. Third class is a poor man's funeral and costs only one hundred dollars. The weather is cool and overcast. There is no bier, only two horses, and only two members of the clergy.

And the poor, who can't afford a hundred dollars? "The poor man," Shalom Aleichem replies, "is always in deep trouble—nine feet deep. But don't think he is left lying on the street. He gets a funeral without money; it doesn't cost him a penny. No ceremonies, no sign of horses or members of the clergy. Outside is a downpour of rain. Two reverends are on both sides and in the middle is the corpse. The three drag themselves on foot to the cemetery."[24]

The Zelig funeral scandal and Shalom Aleichem's commentary should not obscure the efforts which were made to retain the communal character of the hevra kadisha. One such case was the establishment of the Orthodox Adath Israel of New York. Organized in 1901, the United Hebrew Community as it was known officially in English, reached out to the Jewish public at large by offering funeral benefits for a minimal cost. For three dollars a year members and their families were assured a burial plot, the attendance of the organization's hevra kadisha, transportation to the cemetery and burial in strict accordance with Jewish law. The attractiveness of the low assessment rates transcended *landsmanshaft* loyalties, and, by 1910, Adath Israel had six thousand members, i.e., heads of families, and had established branches in Harlem and Brownsville.[25]

The organization had communal ambitions that went beyond burial benefits. "Most of the societies in New York," a 1912 history of the organization written in Hebrew reads, "are named after the city in the homeland from which their founders came. Only those from that particular city have rights of membership, or at least those who come from the same region. If one comes from another area, or another state—a Lithuanian to a German or Hungarian society—he will not be accepted, how much more so a person from the sect of Polish hasidim mixing with hasidim from Volyn, and certainly a *hasid* will be refused by a society of *mitnagdim*. So, one sect has been estranged from another throughout our history." Adath Israel's purpose was to bring unity to Jewish life.[26]

Within the first ten years of its existence Adath Israel established a sick benefit society, a loan fund and a synagogue. Its 1910 report listed thirty-seven institutions and charities which annually received help from the organization. In 1911 Adath Israel appointed the eminent rabbi, scholar and preacher, Gabriel Ze'ev Margolis, as its spiritual leader. The Adath Israel leadership, with Margolis as its head and with the support of the *Morgen Zhurnal,* the Orthodox Yiddish daily, entered the thicket of communal politics. For the next decade it attempted to federate all Orthodox institutions with the goal of communalizing the supervision of kosher meat and religious education. Although the effort proved abortive, it illustrates the communal thrust latent in the traditional hevra kadisha society.[27]

The establishment in 1907 of the Cemetery Department of the Workmen's Circle represented a response of a different kind. Indeed, it was a major ideological and cultural breakthrough. A brief account of its beginnings, which appeared in the 1938 annual report of the Cemetery Department of the Jewish socialist fraternal order is illuminating:

> Most of the Jewish cemeteries in this country are conducted in strict conformity to the laws and customs of Orthodox Judaism, whereas the pioneers of the Workmen's Circle were nearly all freethinkers. The owners of Jewish cemeteries were averse to the internment of such nonconformists in hallowed ground, lest it hurt their business. And when, with great difficulty, they were prevailed upon to sell a grave, they exacted an exorbitant sum for it. Between these sanctimonious profiteers and the rapacious undertakers, the bereaved family stood helpless.[28]

Undoubtedly there is a measure of truth in the writer's complaints. However, in all likelihood the Orthodox were exercising what they considered to be the ancient prerogative of punishing nonconformers by "exacting an exorbitant sum."

The situation forced the Workmen's Circle to acquire its own cemetery ground as early as 1892. As the organization grew, burial arrangements became institutionalized and a special office was opened and then a cemetery department established. Finally after the 1918 influenza epidemic, a permanent funeral director was appointed.[29]

The Cemetery Department, however, aspired to more than administering the fraternal death benefits efficiently. It searched for ways to replace the Orthodox ritual with a secular one. This ambition found expression in a number of ways. In the 1920s the Cemetery Department enlarged its printed annual report to include a literary supplement in Yiddish and English. The selections, drawn from world literature, were intended to bring solace, raise philosophical questions and pay homage to leading figures from the Jewish and non-Jewish world who had died during the year. A recurring theme in the business reports was the honoured place which the old hevra kadisha had held. Clearly, the Cemetery Department perceived itself as heir to that revered tradition. A brochure entitled *Yizkor* (Remembrance), which it issued contained selections which "modern Jews, freethinkers and socialists" could use at a funeral service or memorial meeting, including the text of a model panegyric which required only the insertion of the name of the person being eulogized. Didactic articles also appeared regularly stressing society's need to commemorate its heroes. The English had Westminster Abbey, readers were told, and the Workmen's Circle had Mount Carmel Cemetery, "the Valhalla, or Pantheon of Jewish literary men and leaders of the labor movement . . . [where] wrapped in eternal sleep, . . . [lie] Sholom Aleichem, Meyer London, Philip Krantz, Vladimir Medem, Morris Rosenfeld"—the list of heroes goes on—"and the victims of the Triangle Shirt fire."[30]

More research is required to trace the evolution of a secular service. At what stage was the traditional vigil between death and burial and the tahara and the religious service at the grave site dispensed with? What secular equivalents were substituted? What was the practice in eastern Europe when antireligious socialists, members of the Bund, died? Could the hevra kadisha be bypassed? We do know that in New York the Bund's anthem, "di shevua," was sung at the internment of prominent radical leaders because their funerals have been reported in the press. One elderly funeral director informed me that the tahara ritual was not performed by the Workmen's Circle Cemetery Department as far back as he can remember. In fact, in the Cemetery Department reports of the Workmen's Circle for the 1930s, cremation, prohibited by halacha, is mentioned as an alternative to conventional burial. In 1938, at the funeral of Charney Vladeck, a leading Jewish labour figure and majority leader of New York's City Council, there were fifty honourary pallbearers; and an elaborate metal coffin, rather than a simple wooden one required by Jewish law, was carried out of the Forward building, where it had lain in state, to the accompaniment of Chopin's funeral march.[31]

Because I have dealt largely with the immigrant generation, discontinuity seems to outweigh the continuities. However, for the immigrants precisely the concern for a proper Jewish funeral continued to be a powerful incentive for organization, perhaps the most powerful. In the broadest sense, a measure of social control remained: non-Jews were not buried in Jewish cemeteries, and in some cemeteries the Orthodox insisted on their separate section. Were we to pursue the subject further we would discover a series of additional developments. In 1932, Jewish undertakers formed the Jewish Funeral Directors of America Association and like their gentile colleagues sought to upgrade their status. State laws aided them by establishing educational, training and licensing requirements. In 1977, a volume entitled *Understanding Bereavement and Grief,* containing the proceedings of two conferences sponsored jointly by the Jewish Funeral Directors of America and Yeshiva University, included papers by an impressive list of psychiatrists, social workers and rabbis, as well as several funeral directors. The skeptic is free to view the conferences and the published proceedings as a ploy for improving the image of the funeral director. But even then, one might also point to continuities. The proceedings were public events, legitimized by an Orthodox Jewish institution, which sought to illuminate and use more effectively the ancient Jewish obligation of bringing the dead to an honourable burial and comforting the mourners.[32]

Finally, several other contemporary developments offer a vantage point from which one can look back upon the institution I have been discussing. In our time, Jewish funeral directors are far more susceptible to the demands of the rabbinate that funerals be conducted more in keeping with traditional practice. Otherwise, they realize, there is little reason to use the services of a Jewish firm. Nor should we overlook local, synagogal attempts to revive the traditional voluntary hevra kadisha, or the existence in San Francisco of Sinai Memorial Chapel, a communal funeral home, whose income goes to the Jewish community. Again, I return to my central theme. A greater sensitivity to the continuities, no less than to the discontinuities in the transplantation of social traditions, offers rewarding insights into the processes of adaptation and acculturation in the modern world.

NOTES

A Senior Lowenstein-Wiener Fellowship enabled me to use the resources of the American Jewish Archives at the Hebrew Union College in Cincinnati, Ohio, and a grant from the Memorial Foundation for Jewish Culture allowed me to pursue my research on the hevra kadisha at the YIVO Institute for Jewish Research in New York.

1. Irving Howe, *World of Our Fathers* (New York, 1976), p. 650. Howe was born in 1920, Rischin in 1925.

2. Moses Rischin, *The Promised City* (Cambridge, Mass., 1962). Compare Rischin's treatment of Orthodoxy, pp. 145–148, with that of Jewish radicalism, pp. 148–168. Lloyd P. Gartner, "New York's Jews," *Jewish Journal of Sociology*, VI (July 1964), pp. 141–145.

3. Steven Hertzberg, *Strangers within the Gate City: The Jews of Atlanta, 1845–1915* (Philadelphia, 1978); Jeffrey S. Gurock, *When Harlem Was Jewish, 1870–1930* (New York, 1979); Marc Lee Raphael, *Jews and Judaism in a Mid-Western Community: Columbus, Ohio, 1840–1975* (Columbus, Ohio, 1979); Deborah Dash Moore, *At Home in America: Second Generation New York Jews* (New York, 1981); William Toll, *The Making of an Ethnic Middle Class: Portland Jewry over Four Generations* (Albany, N.Y., 1982).

4. Community studies generally describe the founding of synagogues and the transition from Orthodoxy to Reform and Conservatism. Studying New York with its more variegated Orthodox life, Gurock and Moore treated institutional changes within the Orthodox community over two generations.

5. Will Herberg, "The Jewish Labor Movement in the United States," *American Jewish Year Book*, 53 (1952), pp. 19–20.

6. Julius Henry Cohen, *They Builded Better Than They Knew* (New York, 1946), p. 186.

7. Arthur A. Goren, *New York Jews and the Quest for Community: The Kehillah Experiment, 1908–1922* (New York, 1970), pp. 187, 196–213; Abraham J. Karp, "An East European Congregation on American Soil: Beth Israel, Rochester, N.Y., 1874–1886," in *A Bicentennial Festschrift for Jacob Rader Marcus*, ed. Bertram W. Korn (Waltham, Mass., 1976), pp. 293–299; Menashe, "Landsmanshaftn farn'n idishn gericht," in *Di yidishe landsmanshaftn fun new york*, ed. Isaac E. Rontch (New York, 1938), pp. 127–130; Israel Goldstein, *Jewish Justice and Conciliation: History of the Jewish Conciliation Board of America, 1930–1968* (New York, 1981), pp. 85–183. Daniel J. Elazar and Stephen R. Goldstein, "The Legal Status of the American Jewish Community," *American Jewish Year Book*, 73 (1972), pp. 12–17, 82–87. Jerold S. Auerbach in his study of dispute settlement in the United States writes perceptively on Jewish conciliation, *Justice without Law? Resolving Disputes without Lawyers* (New York, 1983), pp. 78–89.

8. Raphael, *Columbus*, p. 181.

9. Stuart E. Rosenberg, *The Jewish Community in Rochester, 1843–1925* (New York, 1954), pp. 20–21; Edwin Wolf 2d and Maxwell Whiteman, *The History of the Jews of Philadelphia from Colonial Times to the Age of Jackson* (Philadelphia, 1957), p. 266; Selig Adler, *From Ararat to Suburbia: The History of the Jewish Community of Buffalo* (Philadelphia, 1960), pp. 50–53; Isaac M. Fein, *The Making of an American Jewish Community: The History of Baltimore Jewry from 1773 to 1920* (Philadelphia, 1971), pp. 19–20; Lloyd P. Gartner, *History of the Jews of Cleveland* (Cleveland, Ohio, 1978), pp. 30, 56; Robert E. Levinson, *The Jews in the California Gold Rush* (New York, 1978), pp. 97–99; Raphael, *Columbus*, p. 57; Toll, *Portland Jewry*, pp. 19–20; Bezalel Sherman, *The Jew within American Society: A Study in Ethnic Individuality* (Detroit, 1961), p. 155; Salo W. Baron, *The Jewish Community, Its History and Structure to the American Revolution* (Philadelphia, 1948), vol. 2, p. 146.

10. See, for example, Rosenberg, *Rochester,* pp. 52, 168, 181–182; Hertzberg, *Atlanta,* p. 89; Fein, *Baltimore,* p. 157; Gartner, *Cleveland,* pp. 175–176; Hyman L. Meites, ed., *History of the Jews of Chicago* (Chicago, 1924), pp. 43–44, 57; Raphael, *Columbus,* pp. 64–65, 72–74; Levinson, *California,* pp. 100–107. For the most detailed discussion of the hevra kadisha and related matters, see Hyman B. Grinstein, *The Rise of the Jewish Community of New York, 1654–1860* (Philadelphia, 1947), pp. 104–109, 181–184, 313–332, 348–350; Louis J. Swichkow and Lloyd P. Gartner, *The History of the Jews of Milwaukee* (Philadelphia, 1963), pp. 198–199. Albert I. Gordon, *Jews in Transition* (Minneapolis, 1949), pp. 138–147, quotes Minneapolis's first Jewish funeral director on the beginnings of his business.

11. Jacob Katz, *M'soret u'mashber* (Jerusalem, 1958), pp. 186–188. For an overview of the history of the hevra kadisha, see the entries in the *Encyclopedia Judaica* (VIII, pp. 442–446) and the *Universal Jewish Encyclopedia* (II, pp. 603–604), also Baron, *Jewish Community,* I, pp. 354–355, II, pp. 146–157, and Jacob Shatzky, "Merkvirdige historische factn vegen der amoliger hevra kadisha," *39th yohr cemetery department yohrbuch und baricht* (1946), pp. 28–36; Isaac Levitats, *The Jewish Community in Russia, 1771–1844* (New York, 1943), pp. 107–108, 262–267.

12. Levitats, *Jewish Community,* p. 266.

13. Ibid., p. 267.

14. Baron, *Jewish Community,* II, p. 156.

15. Mordecai Nadav, "Toldot kehilat pinsk: 1506–1880," in *Pinsk,* ed. Zeev Rabinowicz (Tel Aviv, 1972), I, pp. 220, 275; A. S. Hershberg, *Pinkos byalystock* (New York, 1950), pp. 167–174; Joseph Zelkovitch, "A Picture of the Communal Life of a Jewish Town in Poland in the Second Half of the Nineteenth Century," *YIVO Annual of Jewish Social Science,* VI (1951), pp. 253–266; Jacob Shatzky, *Geschichte fun yidn in varsha* (New York, 1947), I, pp. 277–278; II, p. 151.

16. Samuel H. Dresner, *The Jew in American Life* (New York, 1963), pp. 20–49. The chapter is entitled, "The Scandal of the Jewish Funeral." Ira Silverman, "Misrepresentation and Exploitation in the Funeral Industry: A Case for the Revival of Chevra Kadisha," *The National Jewish Monthly* (May 1976), pp. 12–16; Lucy Y. Steinitz, "Reinstituting Hevrai Kadisha," *Response,* x (Winter, 1976–1977), pp. 107–110.

17. Grinstein, *New York,* pp. 104–105, 348.

18. Grinstein, *New York,* pp. 107–114; Deborah Dash Moore, *B'nai B'rith and the Challenge of Ethnic Leadership* (Albany, N.Y., 1981), pp. 1–23.

19. Grinstein, *New York,* pp. 322–323; James J. Farrell, *Inventing the American Way of Death* (Philadelphia, 1980), pp. 99, 110–114; *Asmonean,* x (8 June 1854), p. 63.

20. *Asmonean,* XII (21 September 1855), p. 177; Grinstein, *New York,* pp. 318–320, 377; Morris U. Schappes, *A Documentary History of the Jews in the United States* (New York, 1950), p. 610; Salo W. Baron, *Steeled by Adversity* (Philadelphia, 1971), p. 131.

21. Charles S. Bernheimer, *The Russian Jews in the United States* (Philadelphia, 1905), pp. 150–152; *Jewish Communal Register of New York City, 1917–1918* (New York, 1918), pp. 111–291; E. Verschleiser, "Landsmanshaft constitutions," in *Idishe Landsmanshaftn,* pp. 50–51; Moore, *At Home,* pp. 123–129; Gurock, *Harlem,* pp. 116–136.

22. Interviews with Andrew Jacobs (August 10, 1983), Jacobson (August 10, 1983) and Harold Garlick (August 16, 1983).

23. Story #14, SP 126, Judah L. Magnes Papers, Jerusalem; *Warheit,* 8 October 1912; *Forward,* 8 October 1912.

24. Shalom Aleichem, *Kleine menshelach mit kleine hasoges, Berel Eizik, Ale verk fun shalom aleichem,* vol. 6, pp. 251–254, Vilna-Warsaw, 1925.

25. *Morgen Zhurnal,* 25 February 1910, p. 2; 13 January 1911, p. 2; 27 January 1911, p. 8; 30 December 1912, p. 7.

26. *'Sefer divrey ha'yamim l'hevra adat yisrael; Constitution and By-Laws of the United Hebrew Community of the City of New York, adopted 16 February 1905.*

27. *Morgen Zhurnal,* 31 August 1911; 17 December 1912, p. 4; 29 January 1913, p. 1; *Ninth Annual Report of the United Hebrew Community of New York 1910; Yubile'um zhurnal, adas yisroel of new york, 1926.*

28. Maximilian Hurwitz, "The Cemetery and Funeral Departments," *31st Annual Report of the Cemetery Department of the Arbeiter-Ring, 1938,* p. 97.

29. Ibid., pp. 95–97.

30. *12th yehrlicher report fun dem new yorker cemetery department, Arbeiter Ring, 1919,* pp. 4–14; *34th yehrlicher report fun dem cemetery department, Arbeiter Ring, 1941,* pp. 90–93, 125–126; *35th yehrlicher report fun dem cemetery department, Arbeiter Ring, 1942,* pp. 85–87; Cemetery Depart, *Yizkor,* n.d., YIVO Institute library.

31. *Forvertz,* 2 November 1938, p. 1; 3 November 1938, p. 1.

32. Norman Linzer, ed., *Understanding Bereavement and Grief* (New York, 1977).

4

The Folk Culture of
Jewish Immigrant Communities

Research Paradigms and Directions

BARBARA KIRSHENBLATT-GIMBLETT

T he Conference on Jews in North America has been particularly rich in suggesting areas of convergence and contrast between disciplines. What can the folklorist contribute to the study of Jews in North America? How can the perspective of the folklorist, musicologist or symbolic anthropologist complement the work of the historian?

First, the conference, made possible by the offices of the Multicultural History Society of Ontario, not surprisingly has been primarily oriented to the historical, and, to a lesser degree, to the sociological. In contrast, folklorists stress the ethnographic approaches—that is, qualitative, observational and process-oriented research strategies. As a result, contemporary immigrant communities are of special interest.

Second, the emphasis in much historical and sociological work has been on normative or mainstream Jewish life, however it is defined. For the folklorist, the size or representativeness of the communities being studied is of less concern and the goal is not necessarily to arrive at broad generalizations; a folklorist is as likely to study "exotic" Jewish communities as "mainstream" ones. The emphasis tends to be on small-scale settings and group life at the level of social interactions. Recent work in folklore is closely aligned with developments in symbolic anthropology and sociolinguistics. Increasingly, theoretical concerns are to the fore, many of which are best explored through the close observation of particular cases.

Third, many historical and sociological studies use statistical data essential to the study of migration, settlement and philanthropy, or they examine institutions in their investigation of social organization, or they focus on important individuals and their political activity. Folklorists stress the importance of the symbolic organization of experience through the expressive behaviour of ordinary people in everyday life—parades, memorials, storytelling, humour, food, ritual, song, language and material culture.

Finally, the place of historians and sociologists in the intellectual history of ethnic studies as it relates to Jews is better known than that of folklorists, ethnomusicologists and anthropologists. I will therefore briefly delineate the history of Jewish folklife study in North America for the useful contrasts it provides and for indications of how the various disciplines can complement each other.

Since the 1890s, several paradigms have emerged for the study of Jewish folk culture in North America: the first, salvage ethnography, focuses on the folk culture immigrants brought with them from the old country. This concern with survivals goes back to the beginnings of European folkloristics during the enlightenment and romantic periods. The second paradigm, which has been particularly important in my own work, focuses on the formation of immigrant folklore and culture as a distinctive, if transitional, phenomenon—what I call the folklore created out of and about the immigrant experience. The third paradigm may be loosely termed the folklore of ethnicity.[1] The fourth, which may be designated "the traditionalizing process" focuses on the problematic nature of "heritage."[2] I will deal with each of these in turn.

SALVAGE ETHNOGRAPHY: PRESERVING THE HERITAGE

The following statement, with a few stylistic emendations, could have been written today:

> I am proud of the riches and compass of our Journal [*Journal of American Folklore*], as proving the progress of our science. But there is one thing which I miss, namely: information in regard to Jewish folk-life in America. European journals also offer a similar deficiency, but assuredly not for the same reason . . . . Even now, at the eleventh hour, it is possible to note and record for the purposes of science a folk-life which is in process of rapid decay—I mean that of Jews . . . . Under the pressure of the present tendencies of civilization, this folk-life is rapidly disappearing . . . . [I wish to call] the attention of my co-members of The American Folklore Society to this investigation before it is too late. The next generation of Jews will have become merged in Anglo-American folk-life, now in continual evolution . . . it will have become assimilated to the Yankee, and cease to be more than a variant of Americanism.[3]

These words were written almost a century ago by Friedrich Krauss, a Jewish folklorist working out of Vienna, and active in promoting the study and publication of Jewish folklore in Europe. What would Krauss think if he could see what has transpired in the time since he wrote? Not only has Jewish folklife in North America flourished in a diversity of forms, but scholars are increasingly turning to the subject as a serious field of study.

When Krauss was writing in the 1890s, the field of Jewish folklore was only just beginning to emerge, first in Germany and later in eastern Europe. Furthermore, the Jewish immigrant community in North America was in an early stage of its formation. The relatively small German Jewish communities established in the United States earlier in the nineteenth century fed American popular culture with a stimulus for ethnic stereotypes in humour and popular entertainment, the subject of numerous studies by Rudolf Glanz. In *The Jew in Early American Wit and Graphic Humor,* Glanz gathers together cartoons and jokes from nineteenth-century newspapers and magazines such as *Puck* to make his point. These jokes pivot on images of the Jew as usurous, devious, clever at business, preoccupied with money and lacking in culture and refinement.[4]

For various reasons, German Jews failed to inspire studies of their own folk culture. Jewish folklife had yet to emerge as a field of study in its own right, and once it did, the earliest Jewish folklorists were by and large German Jews: they preferred to study their exotic brothers, the Ostjuden, rather than their own folk culture, which remains to this day a rich, but relatively untapped, research subject.

Sephardic Jews in North America have received even less attention. It was not until 1906 that Sephardic Jews began to immigrate in significant numbers, mainly from Turkey, Greece and Syria. By the early 1970s, Sephardic Jews made up about 3 per cent of the Jewish population of the United States, estimated at about 5,500,000. It is thus not surprising that as late as 1977, Victor Sanua could still write: "Literature on the Sephardic Jews in the United States, apart from journalistic reports, tends to be scarce."[5] Scarcer still is information pertaining to other Jewish communities in North America, for example, those who emigrated from central Asia before and after the new American immigration laws of 1965.[6]

Krauss's statement also signals the prevailing approach to Jewish folklife during the next half decade, namely the salvaging of the last vestiges of traditional culture before it yields in the face of cosmopolitanism and assimilation, whether in Europe or North America. The sense of urgency in the face of change had been propelling European folklorists to study Jewish folklore in Warsaw, the Ukraine and the towns of Poland and Russia. When Y. L. Cahan, a folklorist who pioneered in the collecting of

Yiddish folksongs and folktales in Poland during the 1890s, arrived in New York in 1904, he was delighted to find in the Jewish immigrant community of New York the entire spectrum of eastern European Jewish regional traditions. "Here folklore can be scooped up in handfuls," he is reported to have said. Comparing Europe and America, Cahan explained:

> Expeditions into unknown townlets never worked out [in Poland] because of the prohibitive expenses. Here, however, in America is an undisturbed folklore to the extent that it survives and still lives in the memory of the folk, which awaits its collectors, waits for them to come and gather and research, even in the eleventh hour, before it is too late.[7]

Most of Cahan's folklore collecting was indeed done among Jewish immigrants in New York City. His sense of the eleventh hour, like that of Krauss, was based on a rather strict definition of folklore. The corpus was essentially closed, and as change continued to affect the Jewish community, the corpus could only get smaller, a view that is contested by scholars working today.

By the 1920s, collections of Sephardic folklore made in the United States began to appear. Shortly after M. J. Benardete wrote a master's thesis at Columbia University in 1923 entitled "Los Romances Judeo-Espanoles en Nueva York," Max Luria surveyed dialects of Judezmo using Sephardic Jews in New York City. By the 1930s, George Herzog was making cylinder recordings of Syrian and Iraqui Jewish music in New York City.[8] Sephardic folklore was perfectly suited to survivalist studies which sought in old ballads relics of medieval Spanish poetry.

Though immigration precipitated some interest in studying Jewish folklife, the phrase "in North America" would have to be understood as "old world Jewish folklore as remembered by Jewish immigrants living in the new world." In 1919, the *Journal of American Folklore* published an article entitled "Present-day Survivals of Ancient Jewish Customs." Even in 1928, Leah Rachel Yoffie could write in the same journal:

> The children and grandchildren of Russian, Polish, and Galician Jews in this country, who comprise the Yiddish-speaking group, are fast becoming Americanized. With the gradual completion of the Americanization process, many customs and traditions are dying out . . . . This paper is an attempt to present the popular customs and superstitions which still prevail among Yiddish-speaking Jews of St. Louis, Missouri. The task of gathering the material extended over a period of several years, all of it being collected from the old Russian Jewish immigrants, most of whom have been in this country twenty or thirty years.[9]

Yoffie supplements her collection of texts with detailed comparative notes, showing the antiquity and wide distribution of the charms, rhymes and other items she recorded.

In contrast to folklorists, who focused on the survival of endangered traditions, American anthropologists were directing their attention to the problems of racism. Using the study of physical anthropology to prove that Jews were not a race, Boas and his students measured heads, demonstrated that the presence of immigrants did not lead to the deterioration of native stock, and wrote long reports, all in an effort to influence American immigration policy. This research, which was indebted to the prolific earlier work of Maurice Fishberg, failed to stop the legislation that closed the doors to foreigners in the twenties.[10] However, Boas did set the direction for Melville Herskovits and Melville Jacobs, whose work on Jews was confined exclusively to issues of race. American anthropologists, who were used to studying non-literate, small-scale societies about whom almost nothing had been written, were intimidated by how much preparation would be required to master the languages and cultures of an ancient, literate and diverse civilization. Or in their zealous efforts to combat racism, they claimed that Jews had always borrowed from their neighbours and had, as a result, never produced a culture of their own. Therefore, there was nothing to study, and no basis for the Jew's claims of distinctiveness, an important point in his fight against racism. As a result, it really did fall to folklorists, literary scholars, linguists, folk music specialists and skilled amateurs to study Jewish folklife in America. Anthropologists, the specialists in the study of culture, were not about to do the job.[11]

After the Holocaust and a half-century of Jewish immigrant life, the situation began to change radically. Despite warnings almost a century earlier that Jewish folklife was fast disappearing, folklorists waited until after World War Two to do most of the work we have today.[12] Salvage folklore collecting and ethnography continued, at the same time that new research questions and paradigms found fertile ground in Jewish folklife materials. Whereas before the Holocaust, scholars predicted that Jewish folklife would disappear as its bearers assimilated to American life, the Holocaust destroyed the European settlements and almost all of their Jewish inhabitants.[13] Hereafter the study of Jewish folklife would have to focus on the United States.

In the United States, Ruth Benedict and Margaret Mead, two of Boas's most distinguished students, initiated a pioneering ethnographic project to study eastern European Jewish folklife at a distance, relying exclusively on the memories of immigrants living in New York City during the 1940s. Unlike so many earlier collections of data, which had been inspired by a philological perspective, the Research in Contemporary Cultures Project was shaped by current anthropological theory about the relationship between culture and personality. However flawed it may be, *Life Is with People,* the volume on East European Jews, is based on an extraordinary body of interview materials, which have been preserved as part of Margaret Mead's archives. The focus of *Life Is with People* is on reconstructing culture at an unbridgeable distance.[14]

THE CULTURAL CREATIVITY OF IMMIGRANTS

Salvage ethnography, the need to preserve folklife before it vanishes, though a prevailing perspective for the first half of this century, is but one perspective. Since World War Two, scholars have recognized the capacity of Jewish communities to continue to generate a vital folk culture of their own, shaped by historical experience, regional context—the lox and grits variety of southern Jews comes to mind—ethnic identification and religious orientation.

A particularly vivid example of Jewish folk culture formed by historical experience is the immigrant culture of the mass migration period. The circumstances are special, as millions of Jews, primarily from eastern Europe, migrated during a few years and settled in great density in American and Canadian urban settings, as well as in secondary areas of rural settlement. As I have argued elsewhere, under such conditions a folk culture created out of the immigrant experience has an opportunity to arise.[15] The folklore of the immigrant experience draws on the trauma of upheaval, the shock of culture contact, the ambiguities of transition in a period of rapid change. The result in the case of Toronto and New York City, two settings I have examined, is an efflorescence of Yiddish folksong about life in North America,[16] and multilingual anecdotes about immigrant bunglers and tricksters: there are ludicrous name changes, naive immigrants eat the banana with the peel, cultural misunderstandings lead to comic results. The Borscht Belt humour that plays on the convergences and incongruities of languages and cultures encountered by a Jewish immigrant audience on holiday in the Catskills and other Jewish vacation areas has been much maligned for its vulgarity, yet it offers some of the richest material for study.[17] A scholar such as Alfred Sendrey, for example, so disdained such material that he refused to admit Yiddish theatre music to the list of over ten thousand titles in his comprehensive *Bibliography of Jewish Music*.[18]

In my work among Jewish immigrants who arrived in Toronto during the twenties and thirties from central Poland, I found a distinctive narrative form, identified by my most gifted narrator as "classics" because they depended not on their punch line for their effect but upon the telling. Classics can be told over and over again. In one example, the narrator begins with an elaborate description of the hardships of immigrant life and discourses on the love of Yiddish and the importance of charity. He then relates a personal experience about an old man who always came to his shop asking for donations for widows, orphans, schools and other worthy causes. Finally, the narrator explains that he sent the man to the red-light district of Toronto, and the story imperceptibly shifts to the third person. There, the old man and a prostitute interact, he in Yiddish, and she in English. In the course of their business, each item of his traditional garb, accurately designated by its Yiddish term, is removed by the prostitute. The narrator provides parodic glosses for several items of clothing, explaining that the *gartl* is the belt that separates meat from milk, for example. The punch line, delivered by the old man in Yiddish, is "You should see another year and again give such a nice donation." The features of a classic are its length, easily ten minutes, its substantial prologue which provides information about cultural details essential to an appreciation of the tale, code-switching among up to five varieties of English, Yiddish, Hebrew and other languages, parodic glosses, and other evidences of delight in the ability to play upon the cultural convergences and incongruities so characteristic of the immigrant experience.[19]

Though the period of mass migration is long past, immigration continues to shape North American folklife: the post-Holocaust influx of survivors, especially ultra-Orthodox Hasidism, has contributed to a flowering of religious community life in the east coast area and elsewhere. Since 1965, with the liberalization of American immigration laws, Soviet Jewry has settled in major American and Canadian cities, particularly New York. In the last eight years alone, more than ninety thousand Soviet Jews have arrived, half of them settling in New York City. They have formed regional enclaves: Brighton Beach is known as Little Odessa; the Georgian Jews from the eastern Caucasus have settled in Forest Hills; the Bukharan Jews from Soviet Central Asia now live in Boro Park and Rego Park and Ashkenazic Jews from the western provinces have concentrated in Parkchester and Flatbush.

In the case of Brighton Beach, an ailing neighbourhood has been revitalized by the influx of Soviet families. Today, all the layers of Jewish immigration are represented there: the elderly who came during the first decades of this century; the Holocaust survivors who arrived in the fifties; and the recent Soviet wave. There is a golden opportunity to study intragroup interaction, the emergence of distinctive immigrant institutions— the Soviet Jewish restaurant plays a very special role in this community; the intensification of Jewishness among immigrants from the western republics of the USSR; and the heightened awareness of distinctiveness in the American context. For example, in Tashkent, Bokharan Jews prepared food in much the same manner as their non-Jewish neighbours, whereas in New York, their cuisine sets them apart from other Soviet Jews. Paradoxically, an aspect of Bokharan Jewish culture that, with the exception of kashrut, did not significantly distinguish them from their non-Jewish neighbours, serves here to differentiate them from other Jews. In the North American setting, new contexts are found for old skills—a master kamancha player, Zevulon Avshalomov, teaches American students; Fatima Kuinova, a virtuoso Tadjik singer, now performs at folk festivals; and veterans of the Yiddish stage such as Nechama Sirotin, find appreciative audiences at senior citizen centres and Yiddish clubs.[20]

The immigrant experience continues to generate expressive behavior. Just recently in a beauty salon on Wilson Avenue in Toronto, a Soviet Jewish beautician who has been here four years recounted her immigrant saga. She explained that since Soviet Jews had never been outside the Soviet Union and could not anticipate with any accuracy what they would find, they devised ways to communicate under the watchful eye of the censor; the code was that if those who left were happy with their new circumstances, they would send a photo of themselves standing; if they were unhappy, the photo would show them seated. She received the photo—the emigrants were standing on a table.

The 1950s and 1960s have also seen the arrival of Jews from North Africa and the Middle East. By the early seventies, about twenty thousand Syrian Jews formed a very cohesive religious community in the Ocean Parkway section of Brooklyn. Pockets of Jews from Egypt, Lebanon, Yemen and Israel may be found throughout the metropolitan area. These communities offer opportunities to explore the formation of immigrant culture in situ, in contrast to the studies of the earlier period which have generally been made many decades after the fact.

FROM ASSIMILATION AND MARGINALITY TO ETHNICITY

Oddly enough, immigrant folklore as a subject in its own right arrives late on the scene of American Jewish folklife study. Indeed, for many years this subject was totally overshadowed by the interest in Americanization— that is, in how old world forms are altered or adapted to American life. A classic study of this kind is Beatrice Weinreich's "The Americanization of Passover," in which she describes such innovations as machine-made matzoth, the matzoth made in 1942 in the the shape of a V for victory, the introduction of the third seder (the hotel seder), the increased variety of Passover foods, the association of Passover with freedom ideals and the introduction of new Passover games.[21]

Acculturation studies have generally posited a linear progression from old world culture through acculturation to assimilation, with the eventual disappearance of Jewish folklife, a welcome course of events in some circles and the inspiration to record and preserve what remains in others. A related concept, one that goes hand in hand with minority group theory, is that of the marginal man, that unhealthy creature caught between cultures. The premise here is that divided cultural loyalties lead to psychological pathology. In support of their claim that "ambiguity is the major pervasive element of the current Jewish situation in America," and that this ambiguity derives from the Jew's "position as a perpetual stranger and marginal man," Bernard Rosenberg and Gilbert Shapiro present jokes about conversion, intermarriage, the secularization of religious tradition, self-hatred, status panic and overreactions to imaginary aggressions. For example:

> Three Reform Rabbis are arguing about which of them is the most thoroughly Reform. The first one remarks, "My temple is so Reform that there are ashtrays in every pew. The congregation can smoke while it prays."
>
> "You think that's Reform?" asks the second Rabbi. "In my temple there is a snack bar. The congregation can eat while it prays—especially on Yom Kippur."
>
> "Gentlemen," says the third Rabbi, "as far as I'm concerned, you are practically Orthodox. In my temple, every Rosh Hashonah and Yom Kippur, there are signs on the doors saying, "Closed for the Holidays."[22]

The road from minority group to ethnic group is a long one, and intellectually much more changes in the paradigm than the shift in terminology might suggest. It is only in the last thirty years that scholars have focused on ethnicity as an aspect of Jewish folklife, or at least framed their inquiry in these terms.

Ethnic identity is only one of several identities. It is socially situated and not always relevant to a given interaction. This approach, which views ethnicity as a social construction, stands in contrast with quests for an absolute, immutable and authentic Jewish identity independent of any particular social context. Perhaps the question should be rephrased: not, What is Jewishness? but rather, When does an individual foreground his identity as Jewish, by what means, and to what ends? What is the cultural content of this social differentiation? What is the display of Jewishness counterposed to? Who are the relevant others?[23]

The answers to some of these questions are dramatized emblematically in the dress code of Hasidim, in the inversions of this code on Purim, as well as in their expressive styles. Salient intracultural boundaries differentiate Hasidim of different courts: Lubavitch, Bobov, Munkatch, Satmar, Stolin, Klausenberg, Bratslav and others. These boundaries are made visible in minute distinctions of dress: hats, socks, shoes, jackets, women's headgear and stockings. Groups are also distinguished by regional varieties of Yiddish reflecting the court's place of origin, distinctive musical repertoires, and specific customs. Thus, Lubavitch is famous for its

farbrengen, but adopts a spartan attitude to the decoration of the inside of
the *suke.* In contrast, Bobov is famous for its elaborate *suke* and its Purim
play. Stolin is known for its emphasis on dance as an expression of piety.
Hasidim also distinguish themselves from modern orthodoxy and of
course, from non-observant Jews and from non-Jews. Nor are non-Jews
an undifferentiated category. In the playful costumes worn by children on
Purim, Hasidic Jewish identity is defined by what it is not as well as by
hyperbolic exaggerations of what it is. Children appear as non-humans
(animals, androgynous creatures, objects, clowns), as non-Jews (blacks,
cowboys, Indians, Arabs, "ordinary" kids in blue jeans and T-shirts, seduc-
tive females), and as figures of stature and power (kings, police, soldiers,
Ronald Reagan, old Hasidic men, married Hasidic women). Small details
are revealing, for example, the preoccupation with neckties: they appear in
every size and variety and more than one may be worn at a time. Similarly
sunglasses, especially gigantic ones, are a source of fascination. Both ties
and sunglasses are considered very non-Hasidic, and they appear in ludicrous forms in these Purim costumes.[24]

In this context, the folklore of ethnicity may be defined as expressive
behaviour on and about cultural boundaries. The folklore of ethnicity
grows out of a heightened awareness of cultural diversity and ambiguity,
out of mastery of multiple cultural repertoires and the ability to choose
and switch among them. As I have stated elsewhere:

> A special feature of the folklore of ethnicity is a heightened awareness of
> cultural diversity and ambiguity, a well-developed capacity for reflexivity or
> self-reflection. The presence of cultural alternatives, which is, after all, at the
> heart of the immigrant/ethnic experience, [in Keesing's words] "brings to
> consciousness . . . premises or assumptions hitherto in the main covert or
> implicit." The experience of culture contact throws aspects of each into high
> relief, creating what may be called the *cultural foregrounding* effect, as one
> inevitably compares one's own ways with those of others, noting similarities
> and differences. The issue is not the degree of cultural difference involved,
> objectively speaking, but the social significance attributed to any similarity
> or difference, however small.[25]

Where the boundaries are drawn and what cultural content is used to
render the boundaries visible will vary according to historical as well as
social interactional context. Thus, for Sephardic Jews, confronting Jewish
communities dominated by Ashkenazic culture, the boundary between
Ashkenazic and Sephardic styles is particularly salient.[26] During earlier
periods, the boundary between German and Polish Jews was of special
relevance.

The interest in ethnicity is itself part of the history of American Jewish
life. It represents a shift from a preoccupation with the disappearance of a

distinctive Jewish way of life, with the anxiety of being a marginal person in a society of minority groups that are by definition at a disadvantage in relation to the dominant culture, to a positive identification with Jewishness, whatever form it takes. The shift is from anxiety about one's otherness to a celebration of it. The ethnicity framework not only constitutes a more constructive alternative to an acculturation/assimilation model, it also posits a much more fluid situation.

Rather than identifying a group and looking within its boundaries for its distinctive culture, scholars now recognize that group boundaries are not "given." Rather, they are socially constructed and situated, constantly negotiated; they are multiple and complex. A subject for study is therefore how people use expressive behaviour to invoke special identities and under what conditions, how they use folklore to define social boundaries and to play on them. In the course of this shift, ethnicity has become the dominating concern in Jewish folklife studies of the last two decades.[27]

THE TRADITIONALIZING PROCESS

Preservation, reconstruction, revival, awareness and innovation are all aspects of the "traditionalizing" process, a complex venture that involves the constant making and remaking of heritage. In her study of the elderly Jews at the Israel Levin Senior Citizen's Center in Venice, California, Barbara Myerhoff examines the resurfacing of particular traditions as an aspect of the life cycle, rather than in relation to assimilation; that is, she examines how the elderly recycle their dormant natal culture, which may have been inactive through their middle years, for the special needs they face in their advanced old age. Narration, song, dance, festival—these are not simply examples of cultural survivals and adaptations. There is a life-cycle pattern at work here, one that converges with the disjunctures of secondary migration.[28]

Though Myerhoff's case may seem like an extreme example, it is especially helpful because it emphasizes how active continuity is. Survival has connotations of passivity: we tend to think of cultural elements surviving, rather than of people choosing to activate a musical or narrative tradition. Stated differently, the premise in such work is that persistence is the norm, and that change is what needs to be explained. We may want to distinguish between a reluctance to change and a desire to perpetuate. In either case, continuity must be considered as an active process, as an aspect of traditionalizing.

In Lenore Weissler's study of a Havurah[29] in an east coast city, a group of young, American-born professionals have formed a religious fellowship in which they pursue their core concern with the problematic

nature of tradition—what to incorporate, how to resolve conflicts between particular religious traditions and values they hold as modern
Americans. Their discussions of the problems and their ingenuity in devis-
ing solutions, some more successful and enduring than others, offer rich
evidence for examining continuity as an active process. While the cen-
trality of the Torah and of prayer are accepted, the status of the commen-
taries is questioned, especially relative to the importance of making a
personal connection to the reading of the week. Indeed, the Torah discussion, an important feature of a Havurah service, often focuses on the
difficulty of reconciling a particular passage with values held by the participants. Especially troubling are sections on menstrual impurity and animal
sacrifice, for example. The conduct of the service itself, even to the way in
which the chairs are arranged, expresses the value placed on egalitarianism:
there are equal opportunities for men and women to lead services, there is
no figure of authority to conduct the service as a paid professional, and
rituals for girls are created as counterparts to those that exist for boys. The
baby-naming ceremonies for girls are among the most ingenious.[30]

Innovations may lead to the creation of novel expressive forms to suit
new social and historical circumstances, or they may serve to strengthen
traditional values. Modern Orthodox and Hasidic Jews have been particularly inventive in adapting modern technology to further their abilities to
adhere strictly to Sabbath and holy day prescriptions against work, while
living in modern highrise buildings that require the use of elevators. Sabbath clocks which regulate the electrical lighting of a residence as well as
the motor of the refrigerator are another example.

Traditionalization also takes the form of reconstruction, which is
closely tied to the interest in revival. Both may be seen as aspects of
ethnicity—that is, as efforts to find, create, or reconstruct the right cultural
content for emerging new identities. Forms which have changed radically
or which have disappeared from the scene for decades are now being
revived by Yiddish folksingers, klezmer bands, and Sephardic musical
groups. The results are fascinating, as Slobin demonstrates in his presentation of the doina. The entire process reveals the extent to which tradition
is itself a construction and a process. At least two principles are at work
here: first, the act of reviving is simultaneously an act of constructing a
hypothetical original; and secondly, each generation stands in a special
relation to that which has come before.[31]

These revivals are part of a larger development, namely folk festivals
and public programs devoted to the traditional arts of Jewish communities
in a given area: the shtetl fair in Washington, D.C., the Jewish Arts festival
on Long Island, the Jewish cultural days and weekends on college campuses, the workshops and demonstrations at museums, and the National

Jewish Film Festival that originated in San Francisco. Such events, many of them new contexts for old skills as well as showcases for new talent, are worthy of study in their own right. They should be viewed in relation to other expressive forms such as parades, demonstrations, commemorations and new days of observance in the Jewish calendar (Yom HaShoah, Israel Independence Day).

What would Friedrich Krauss have said could he have been in Brooklyn last Purim? Or at Carnegie Hall when the California Klezmorim played recently? Or at the Odessa restaurant where Soviet Jews celebrate in Brighton Beach? Or if he could have heard Zevulon Avshalomov from the Caucasus play the kamancha, or have seen Firuz from Bokhara dance? He would have been impressed with the evidence that North American folklife is a well-spring of cherished tradition and irrepressible innovation, a diverse and vital array of life styles. The eleventh hour has lasted a century. Research concerns that have informed decades of study—salvage ethnography, the culture of immigration, the folklore of ethnicity, the traditionalizing process—may now be applied to Jewish situations that have not been examined before or that have newly arisen. What folklorists can offer are approaches and tools for examining the expressive behaviour of Jewish communities in North America, the symbolic manifestations of the immigrant experience and ethnic boundaries and the process by which traditions are constructed and meaning is made.

NOTES

1. See Stephen Stern, "Ethnic Folklore and the Folklore of Ethnicity," *Western Folklore* 36, no. 1 (1977), pp. 7–32.

2. See Dell Hymes, "Folklore's Nature and the Sun's Myth," *Journal of American Folklore* 88, no. 350 (1975), pp. 345–369.

3. Friedrich S. Krauss, "Notes and Queries: Jewish Folklife in America," *Journal of American Folklore* 7 (1894), pp. 72–75.

4. (New York: Ktav Publishing House, 1973), pp. 126, 114. See also Rudolf Glanz, *The Jew in the Old American Folklore* (New York, 1961).

5. "Contemporary Studies of Sephardi Jews in the United States," *A Coat of Many Colors: Jewish Subcommunities in the United States,* ed. Abraham D. Lavender (Westport, Conn., 1977), p. 277.

6. See Rebekah Ziona Mendelsohn, "The Bokharan Jewish Community of New York City," master's thesis, Columbia University, 1964; Dina Dahbany Miraglia, "Yemenites in America: The 'Invisible' Jews," *Jewish Folklore and Ethnology Newsletter* 4, nos. 1–2 (1980), pp. 12–13; Uri Sharvit, "The Role of Music in the Yemenite Jewish Ritual: A Study of Ethnic Persistence," Ph.D. dissertation, Columbia University, 1977, and Dina Miraglia, "An Analysis of Ethnic Identity among Yemenite Jews in the Greater New York Area," Ph.D. dissertation, Columbia University, 1983.

7. J. Shatzky, "Yehudah Leyb Cahan (1881–1937): materyaln far a biografye," *Yor-bukh fun amopteyl fun yivo* 1 (1938), p. 21.

8. M. A. Luria, "Judeo-Spanish Dialects in New York City," *Todd Memorial Volumes* (New York), 2 (1930), pp. 7–16. I am indebted to Pamela Dorn for the information about George Herzog. Sephardic ballads and songs continue to be collected in North America: I. J. Levy, "Sephardic Ballads and Songs in the u.s.a.: New Variants and Additions," master's thesis, University of Iowa, 1958; R. R. McCurdy and D. D. Stanley, "Judeo-Spanish Ballads from Atlanta, Georgia," *Southern Folklore Quarterly* 15 (1951), pp. 221–238; D. Romey, "A Study of Spanish Traditions in Isolation as Found in the Romances, Refrains, and Folklore of the Seattle Sephardi Community," master's thesis, University of Washington, Seattle, 1950; and most recently, Pamela Dorn, "Transmission of Ethnic Music and Dance among Greek, Jewish, and Syrian Lebanese Americans in an Urban Setting," b.a. honors thesis, Indiana University, 1977. The Sephardic folktale has also received considerable attention in André E. Elboz, ed., *Folktales of the Canadian Sephardim* (Toronto, 1982).

9. "Popular Beliefs and Customs among the Yiddish-Speaking Jews of St. Louis, Mo.," *Journal of American Folklore* 38 (1925), p. 375.

10. One of the most interesting outgrowths of Boas's work is the dissertation by his student David Efron, *Gesture and Environment: A Tentative Study of Some of the Socio-Temporal and "Linguistic" Aspects of the Gestural Behavior of Eastern Jews and Southern Italians in New York City, Living Under Similar as well as Different Environmental Conditions* (New York, 1941).

11. For a detailed consideration of this subject, see Barbara Kirshenblatt-Gimblett, "From Race to Ethnicity: American Anthropologic Interest in Jews, 1890–1952," *Ashkenaz: Essays in Jewish Folklore and Culture* (Bloomington, Ind., forthcoming).

12. For example, Ruth Rubin, a native of Montreal, pioneered in the recording of Yiddish folksong in Canada and the United States from the 1940s to now.

13. The Holocaust also began to serve as a subject in its own right for such folklorists as Toby Blum-Dobkin, who is interviewing survivors living in New York City in her efforts to reconstruct the expressive culture of Jews in displaced-persons camps immediately after the war, and for historians such as Yaffa Eliach, whose collection of stories from survivors about their experiences, particularly miracle narratives, is entitled *Hasidic Tales of the Holocaust* (New York, 1982).

14. Mark Zborowski and Elizabeth Herzog, *Life Is with People: The Jewish Little Town in Eastern Europe* (New York, 1952). Though their focus was on East European Jews, the team also interviewed Yemenite and Syrian Jews in New York City. The project and its methods are described in Margaret Mead and Rhoda Metraux, *The Study of Culture at a Distance* (Chicago, 1953). For a critique of the project, see Barbara Kirshenblatt-Gimblett, "'In Search of the Primitive': The *shtetl* Model in Jewish Ethnology," *Ashkenaz*.

15. "Culture Shock and Narrative Creativity," *Folklore in the Modern World*, ed. R. M. Dorson (The Hague, 1978), pp. 109–122; "Studying Immigrant and Ethnic Folklore," *The Handbook of American Folklore*, ed. R. M. Dorson (Bloomington, 1983), pp. 39–47. On distinctive Jewish immigrant organizations, see William E. Mitchell, *Mishpokheh: A Study of New York City Jewish Family Clubs* (The Hague, 1978) and Philip Goodman, "The Purim Association of the City of New York," *The Purim Anthology*, ed. Philip Goodman (Philadelphia, 1949), pp. xx–xxx.

16. See E. G. Mlotek, "America in East European Yiddish Folksong," *The Field of Yiddish: Studies in Yiddish Language, Folklore, and Literature*, ed. Uriel Weinreich (New York: Publications of the Linguistic Circle of New York, 1954), pp. 179–195 and Ruth Rubin, "Yiddish Folksongs of Immigration and the Melting Pot," *New York Folklore Quarterly* 17 (1961), pp. 173–182.

17. Compare R. M. Dorson, "Jewish American Dialect Stories on Tape," *Studies in*

Biblical and Jewish Folklore, ed. Raphael Patai, Francis Lee Utley and Dov Noy (Bloomington, 1960), pp. 133–146, and Sam Levenson, "Dialect Comedian Should Vanish," *Commentary* 14 (1952), pp. 168–170.

18. (New York, 1951). In contrast, see Mark Slobin, *Tenement Songs: The Popular Music of the Jewish Immigrants* (Urbana, 1982) and Herbert J. Gans, "The Yinglish Music of Mickey Katz," *American Quarterly* 3 (1953), pp. 213–218.

19. See Barbara Kirshenblatt-Gimblett, "Traditional Storytelling in the Toronto Jewish Community: A Study of Performance and Creativity in an Immigrant Culture," Ph.D. dissertation, Indiana University, 1972.

20. See *Festival of Soviet Jewish Folk Traditions of Central Asia, the Caucasus, and the Western Republics of the USSR* (New York: Federation of Jewish Philanthropies of New York, 1982).

21. *Studies in Biblical and Jewish Folklore,* pp. 329–366. The questionnaires and responses that form the basis for this study may be found at the YIVO institute for Jewish Research in New York.

22. "Marginality and Jewish Humor," *Midstream* 4, no. 2 (1958), p. 74.

23. An important project on Fairfax, a very diverse Jewish neighbourhood in Los Angeles, begun under the direction of Barbara Myerhoff, should offer interesting hypotheses for research elsewhere. Myerhoff adds questions about the relationship between ethnicity and territory, the inner city enclave as fictive homeland, ethnicity as achieved social differentiation and as mediating structure, and the role of elders in creating and transmitting culture in a modern urban setting. See also Leonard Plotnikov and Myrna Silverman, "Jewish Ethnic Signalling: Social Bonding in Contemporary American Society," *Ethnology* 17, no. 4 (1978), pp. 407–423.

24. See Sydelle Brooks Levy, "Shifting Patterns of Ethnic Identification among the Hasidim," *The New Ethnicity: Perspectives from Ethnology,* ed. John Bennett (St. Paul, 1975), pp. xx–xxx. Hasidim in North America have received considerable folkloristic attention as well. Jill Gellerman has videotaped and analysed several hundred hours of Hasidic dance in New York City as the basis for her dissertation in Performance Studies at New York University and has published "The Mayim Pattern as an Indicator of Cultural Attitudes in Three American Hasidic Communities: A Comparative Approach Based on Laban-Analysis," *CORD: Dance Research Journal,* 20 (1976), pp. 111–144. See also Ellen Koskoff, "The Concept of Nigun among Lubavitchers in the United States," Ph.D. dissertation, University of Pittsburgh, 1976; Shifra Epstein, "The Celebration of a Contemporary Purim in the Bobover Hasidic Community," Ph.D. dissertation, University of Texas, 1979; Jerome R. Mintz, *The Legends of the Hasidim: An Introduction to Hasidic Culture and Oral Tradition in the New World* (Chicago, 1968). Better known are the sociological monographs of Solomon Poll, George Kranzler, Israel Rubin and William Shaffir. For bibliographical material, see *Jewish Folklore and Ethnology Newsletter* 4, nos. 1–2 (1981).

25. "Studying Immigrant and Ethnic Folklore," pp. 43–44. See F. M. Keesing, "Recreative Behavior and Culture Change," *Men and Cultures,* ed. Anthony F. Wallace (Philadelphia, 1960), pp. 130–133.

26. See Stephen Stern, "The Sephardic Jewish Community of Los Angeles: A Study in Folklore and Ethnic Identity," Ph.D. dissertation, Indiana University, 1977, and Ruth Fredman, *Cosmopolitans at Home: The Sephardic Jews of Washington, D.C.* (Philadelphia, 1982).

27. Contrast sociologist Milton M. Gordon, *Assimilation in American Life: The Role of Race, Religion, and National Origins* (New York, 1964) with anthropologists Fredrik Barth, ed. *Ethnic Groups and Boundaries: The Social Organization of Cultural Difference* (Boston,

1969); Robert A. Levine and Donald T. Campbell, *Ethnocentrism: Theories of Conflict, Ethnic Attitudes, and Group Behavior* (New York, 1972): and Anya Peterson Royce, *Ethnic Identity: Strategies of Diversity* (Bloomington, 1982).

28. *Number Our Days* (New York, 1978). See also Giselle Hendel-Sebestyen, "The Sephardic Home: Ethnic Homogeneity and Cultural Traditions in a Total Institution," Ph.D. dissertation, Columbia University, 1969, and Jack Kugelmass, "The Miracle of Intervale Avenue: Aging in the South Bronx," *Natural History* 89, no. 2 (1980), pp. 26–35.

29. The Havurah is a religious fellowship established as an alternative to established congregations. Small, intimate, egalitarian and highly participatory, the Havurah offers its members the opportunity to experiment with Jewish tradition and find personal meaning in the liturgy and ritual. Since the 1960s many such groups have formed.

30. "Making Judaism Meaningful: Ambivalence and Tradition in a Havurah Community," Ph.D. dissertation, University of Pennsylvania, 1982. See also, Riv-Ellen Prell-Foldes, "Strategies in Conflict Situations: Ritual and Redress in an Urban Jewish Prayer Community," Ph.D. dissertation, University of Chicago, 1978. For comparable treatments of modern orthodoxy, see Samuel C. Heilman, *Synagogue Life: A Study in Symbolic Interaction* (Chicago, 1976) and id. *The People of the Book: Drama, Fellowship, and Religion* (Chicago, 1983).

31. A theoretical framework for analysing such activities is provided by Richard Schechner, "Restoration of Behavior," *Studies in Visual Communication* 4 (Summer 1981), pp. 2–45. See also Mark Slobin, "The Neo-Klezmer Movement and Euro-American Musical Revivalism," *Journal of American Folklore* 97 (January–March, 1984): pp. 98–104.

5
Fiddler Off the Roof
Klezmer Music as an Ethnic Musical Style
MARK SLOBIN

In 1973 Robert Klymasz delineated the goals and rewards of studying immigrant folklore in North America. He was interested in the transition from Old World peasant folklore to the American ethnics' expressive culture, and noted that "many of the old folkways are abandoned without any massive resistance; others linger on; still others are reexamined, revamped, and reactivated in an effort to depict, validate, and perpetuate the community's sense of ethnic loyalty and identity."[1] Despite Klymasz's urgings, little has been done to follow up on his suggestions. His own work with Ukrainian-Canadians and the work of another Canadian, Barbara Kirshenblatt-Gimblett, on immigrant Jewish folklore stand almost alone in the field.

The aim of this paper, therefore, is to follow up on where Klymasz pioneered, bearing in mind his statement that each group will provide different answers, "since so much depends on the inner specifics of the given folklore complex itself as well as a host of other external variables."[2] I will examine the secular instrumental music of Jewish-Americans, or *klezmer* music as it has come to be known, using the Yiddish term for professional instrumental folk musicians. In a previous study,[3] I looked at popular song during the immigrant period (ca. 1880–1924) from a similar point of view, and some of my conclusions in terms of methodology in that research provide a context for this present study of klezmer music.

First, I found that there was little use in applying terms such as "folk," "popular" or "classical" to the repertoire, nor in distinguishing oral, printed or commercially recorded material for purposes of analysis. This approach is inherent in Klymasz's work, as well as that of an admirable group of researchers of Anglo-American and Afro-American expressive culture, including Archie Green and Norm Cohen.[4] These scholars have amply demonstrated that whether a performance was done at home or on record, for love or for money, or was transmitted in print or by ear, it represents a significant stage of evolution in a group's self-perception.

A second methodological perspective is that each generation starts over in reassessing and re-creating the expressive heritage it receives. Here I take slight issue with Klymasz who, although admitting that "the immigrant folklore complex" is "in a dynamic state of flux,"[5] tends to favour what he calls "a rather conventional route" marked by a sequence of three stages: resistance (to change), breakdown (due to change), and reconstitution (adjustment to change).[6] At least in the case of the Jews, the process is more complex. Although Ukrainian folklore might be viewed as relatively old and stable by the time its carriers arrived in America, Jewish expressive culture was in a state of enormous ferment at the very time of emigration from Europe. The urbanization and proletarianization of the mass of eastern European Jews and their invention of various forms of internal mass media coincided exactly with their departure to America in the 1880s. So what we see on these shores is a continuation of a long-term process of breakdown and reconstitution, not simply a response to the sudden shock of immigration and acculturation.

Once ensconced in America, each generation starts over in reassessing its position vis-à-vis its heritage. Rather than a straight-line process of departure and return, destruction and reconstruction, I prefer to look for long-term patterns of continuity and disjuncture. Of course, as Klymasz notes, this evolution takes place in the context of a dialectic between self-perception and pressure from the mainstream culture.

A third lesson my work on popular song taught me is that it is folly to seek a "pure" ethnic style. From its earliest known beginnings, eastern European Jewish music, like that of the Jews in the Mediterranean world, was highly eclectic. To the extent that I was able to find a strong trend toward continuity within the song tradition, it was, paradoxically, in its eclecticism. This was not a feature just of repertoire, but of social organization and taste, and perhaps marks a distinctive feature of the Jewish material as opposed to Klymasz's data. Early professional songwriters of Jewish New York turned out to be men who had skill in a variety of styles back in Europe. The audience also expected, and got from publishers, a broad range of musical styles, from Roumanian to Russian to classical to those tagged Jewish, the last-named style often itself made up of diverse layers.

Turning now to klezmer music, I will argue that all the trends cited hold true. First, I will consider it as an internal ethnic phenomenon, then as an arena of internal-external contact, stressing the middleman role of the mass media. Klymasz has aptly characterized the media's function as one of "the various generative tools and productive vehicles with which [the group can] reshape and refine the old folklore legacy."[7]

THE INTERNAL WORLD

Within the internal world, I would like to identify three main aspects: continuity within a tradition of expressive culture; disjuncture; and the importance of key individuals in shaping major trends within an ethnic group.

Continuity has many facets; we have already seen that an attitude and practice like eclecticism can remain constant within different geographic and historical circumstances. Another good area to look for continuity is in repertoire. Sometimes genres or specific items may carry across generations despite radical change. One such example is the persistence of the *doina* in Jewish entertainment music. The *doina* is a folk form indigenous to Roumania, and is related to Middle Eastern musical styles. Hence, there is nothing distinctively Jewish about it. Yet it has remained a favourite symbol of the Jewish sound for decades, illustrating the eclecticism cited earlier. The earliest surviving recorded Jewish *doina,* performed about 1910 in Lemberg (Lwow), Poland, was released by Columbia Records in the United States, far from its Roumanian roots. This shows how items of expressive repertoire move along a distinctively Jewish network, regardless of the taste of the surrounding non-Jewish population; the *doina* was just as foreign to the Polish population of Lemberg as it was to the Irish and Italian Americans among whom the Jewish immigrants were living in New York.

The basic sound of the *doina* is unmistakeable: sparse back-up chords against which a soloist improvises a weaving, twisting, plaintive melody. Here the instruments are flute and *tsimbl,* the latter being the Jewish version of the cimbalom, a central and southeastern European folk instrument. Instruments also have great symbolic significance, as we will see later in discussing the role of the *tsimbl* in maintaining culture.

The persistence of the *doina* is nowhere more clearly evident than in its transformation by the celebrated popular singler Aaron Lebedeff into what is one of the most famous of all Jewish songs, "Roumania, Roumania." In this classic of the postimmigrant age (late 1920s and beyond), Lebedeff uses the *doina* in a quintessentially nostalgic way to evoke the spirit of the Old World. The words praise Roumania's wonderful countryside and food, clearly identifying the *doina* with a specific, not an imaginary, landscape, and using the correct musical medium to do so.

Even when klezmer music declined in the 1930s and 1940s because of economic hard times and the strength of the assimilationist drive among American Jews, the *doina* did not die out. A *doina* played by Dave Tarras, an important musical figure, probably recorded in the late 1940s, was reissued in the early 1950s. It was aptly titled "Wedding on Second Avenue," as the klezmer sound is associated with weddings. The Second Avenue reference to the Yiddish theatre, however, indicates that it is a staged sense of wedding, not a domestic one. Klezmer music had drifted away from the cultural role it had traditionally played in rites of passage to being commercial entertainment. Despite all these qualifications, which hint at the disjuncture we will discuss shortly, the Dave Tarras *doina* is totally in the style as defined in nineteenth-century Europe and continued in the vintage recordings.

The *doina* has even survived the sharp decline of the Yiddish-language entertainment that culminated in performers like Lebedeff and the Second Avenue theatre tradition. In today's revival by young musicians of the old klezmer repertoire, a phenomenon which began in the mid-1970s, the *doina* is always accorded a place of honour as a distinctively European, intensely ethnic genre. In a recent *doina* performance, by the Klezmer Conservatory Band of Boston, the clarinetist, a black American, has carefully reconstructed the style of older masters like Dave Tarras. Beyond the sharp disjuncture implied by this social fact, the music of the *doina*, in this 1981 manifestation, is intact as an ethnic tradition.

We have already seen various aspects of disjuncture, even within the continuity so clearly demonstrated by the survival of the *doina*. Let me summarize these and try to group them under handy rubrics.

1. *Disjuncture in material culture.* In the case of musical instruments, there have been sharp breaks with tradition. Some of the basic instruments of European klezmer music have declined sharply in popularity in America. The fiddle was perhaps the archetypal Jewish instrument of eastern Europe, even being included in works of fiction by major writers like Sholom Aleichem or Chekhov as a symbol of Jewish music and Jewishness. Yet by the time of the heyday of klezmer recording, in the 1920s, the fiddle had been superseded by the clarinet. This shift may be due, as are other instrumental changes, to the primitive nature of early recording, which would have favoured the more penetrating sound of the clarinet.

Certainly the virtual disappearance of the *tsimbl,* that faint, if eloquent, hammered dulcimer, can probably be ascribed to acoustic demands. Another casualty was the string bass, which was largely superseded by the tuba in the recording studio. Here we see the influence of one aspect of material culture—the record—on another, the musical instrument. What this means for continuity is significant. When today's revivalist fervour attempts an accurate reconstruction of the Golden Age commercial recordings, they tend to adopt the instrumental biases of that period. Thus, only one meticulous performer (Zev Feldman) has tried to reintroduce the *tsimbl,* and he is no longer active as a performer. The tuba predominates over the string bass, and the clarinet is more often the centrepiece of the new klezmer bands than is the violin. This shaping of a group's expressive traditions by the mass media is, of course, not only a fact of Jewish musical life. All American ethnic groups are involved in this process, which has only recently begun to be studied as a major shaping force, beginning with the Library of Congress conference on ethnic recordings in 1977.[8]

2. *Radical change in the context of expressive repertoires.* For klezmer music, this has been particularly dramatic. Back in eastern Europe, the principal occasion for hearing the klezmer sound was the wedding, where ritual and music were inextricably linked in the folk mind. This meant that musicians depended on private patronage, often appearing at public events of a personal nature. In America the advent of commercial recordings freed the musical repertoire from its context, becoming accessible on demand. An interesting reflection of this process is the issuing of mock wedding records, which became the rage in the late 1920s for a number of ethnic groups. On these landmark discs, authentic wedding folklore is mixed with parody to create a unique genre of ethnic entertainment. In *Di boyberiker khasene* ("The Boyberik Wedding") of 1927, the pronouncements of the *badkhn,* the traditional wedding bard, and the ethnographically accurate interludes of the band, puctuate key moments in the ceremony such as the entrance of the groom's side or the processional march to the *khupe* (wedding canopy).

So by 1927 the reconstruction of the traditional wedding could provide a context for klezmer music, frequently now no longer used for the live event. With commercial recording, patronage moves from private to public, in the form of a collective of record buyers whose will is expressed through the corporate entity of the record company. Throughout the postimmigrant age, klezmer music was also publicly supported by the Yiddish theatre, as well as by the brief but influential Yiddish film industry of the 1930s and 1940s. With the revival of the 1970s, a new medium emerged: the klezmer concert, where the public paid to attend live performances. Concerts were made possible only by the popularity generated by recordings, which was then convertible into concert tours. Here we see how in an in-group, ethnic tradition mimics the basic workings of mainstream America, where record sales supply the energy to support the tours of pop music groups. Of course, the ethnic market is much too limited to support the mainstream's tradition of industry-financed tours to spark the sales of record albums. As always in America, the ethnics must look out for themselves in maintaining their traditions and cannot count on the mainstream machinery to provide for minorities.

3. *The dissociation of cultural packages.* In these situations, items that were bound together at one stage of ethnic life break apart under the stress of change. In the case of klezmer music, the dance tradition is an excellent case in point. In the context of community life, the dance at weddings was part of the rationale for the music, and shaped the repertoire. In the context of the recording or the concert hall, however, dance loses its authority, and the dances themselves are forgotten. At one of today's klezmer concerts, one sees an inarticulate groping for a dance form to accompany the lively, foot-tapping music coming from the stage. To fill the dance gap, everything is thrown in, from Israeli horas to mock-Hasidic steps and even rock movements. No longer is there anyone who knows how to do the *sher,* the *freylakhs,* the *bulgar* and a dozen other dances associated with klezmer music. Such loss represents a serious manifestation of cultural disjuncture.[9]

Finally, in the internal development of an ethnic repertoire, we have seen that key individuals like Abe Schwartz play an important role. Single-handedly, he produced dozens of records at Columbia, and his band became a multiethnic performing group for the company, taking different names on the record labels to suit the music they played. Dave Tarras is another major figure. His style is enormously influential in the current klezmer revival due at least as much to his status as the sole survivor of the Golden Age, as to his great artistry. Much of the impetus for New York's role in the revival movement comes from Zev Feldman and Andy Statman's work with Tarras, which involved convincing him to teach the secrets of his craft as well as to make a triumphal reappearance on the concert stage. Particularly in such sharply delimited ethnic traditions as klezmer music, it is easy to single out a handful of influential personalities who epitomize and even create stages in the quest for self-identity. There is also Lev Liberman, whose band (the Klezmorim) was the first to issue a klezmer revival album, in 1977, and Henry Sapoznik, whose research led to the important folkways reissue album of Golden Age klezmer classics that has become a textbook for new converts to the music.

INTERNAL-EXTERNAL RELATONS

Having briefly surveyed some of the key trends in the internal evolution of a given ethnic repertoire, it is time to look at the internal-external
dialectic, the other main determining factor of American ethnicity. We
have already touched on one of the most important themes: the involvement of the mass media. We have seen that this mainstream industry has
heavily influenced the course of the internal evolution, most vitally by
providing a classic canon of performances permanently fixed on record.
The pop machine has ever allowed for the seepage of styles across ethnic
boundaries into the general American musical world. The example of Abe
Schwartz has already been cited, who turned his indigenous klezmer
eclecticism to good use by recording a wide variety of ethnic musics for a
number of groups outside his own tradition. Here the commercial technology has greatly amplified the voice of a versatile group, the Jews, who
thus reach into other people's domains. Schwartz was not alone in this
respect. Another gifted performer, David Medoff, who has been trilingual
since his youth in the Ukraine, has made dozens of discs in Yiddish,
Russian and Ukrainian in America. It is said that Ukrainian-Canadians
took this New York Jew's recordings of their own liturgical music as
genuine specimens of their sacred tradition.[10]
Another aspect of the seepage of repertoire is the often-cited effect of
klezmer music on jazz. Today's klezmer groups insist on asserting such an
influence to bolster their own identification with the music and to try to
make it more than a parochial exercise in ethnic revivalism. Though I am
unconvinced that jazz owes as much to klezmer music as today's adherents
maintain, it is true that the Jewish sound, a stereotyped package typical of
mainstream American popular culture, made its presence known here and
there in early jazz. An interesting episode in this trend occurred when
Eddie Cantor, a Jewish immigrant who rose to stardom, sang "Leena
from Palestenna" in the early 1920s. This slightly salacious song has a
definite klezmer background, and it is entirely appropriate that Cantor
should perform it in blackface to show his Americanism. The immigrant
here distances himself not only from his origins but also from his material
through the all-American, anonymous emblem of popular culture: the
simulation of the black. The song was then picked up by the Original
Dixieland Jazz Band, the first well-known recorded jazz ensemble. Appro-
priately, it was an all-white, if non-Jewish, group.
The internal-external dialectic does not operate only in the popular
music sphere; it is also quite active in the music usually labelled "folk."
Here again eclecticism rears its head. We have seen how Abe Schwartz

took advantage of the klezmer's knowledge of many European ethnic styles in the early days of recording. This versatility in regard to traditional music has carried over into the current klezmer scene. Most of the activists in the klezmer revival movement switched to Jewish music after many years of performing other people's repertoires. Jazz is one source, Anglo-American traditional music another, and Balkan styles yet a third place that the neo-klezmer has called home before discovering the Jewish sound. To understand this situation, we must identify an intermediate stage of development, for today's klezmer eclecticism is not a direct descendant of Abe Schwartz's modus operandi. Although Schwartz was able to profit from the commercial interests of the major recording companies, the generation born in the 1950s and 1960s found itself not in the mainstream but rather a tributary of American music: the folk revival movement of the 1940s to 1960s.

The folk revival began as a leftist and populist movement among a few urbanites who teamed with rural blacks and Anglo-Americans. It took root after World War Two and spread its branches into American music. One branch led to appreciation of a variety of world folk music styles, particularly those of the Balkans, as part of the internationalism inherent in the movement. Another led toward appreciation of rural American music, ranging from the down-home blues of black America through such folk-based white forms as bluegrass. Yet a third branch grew toward urban and commercial styles with political overtones like those of Bob Dylan and his circle. Young Jewish musicians were deeply involved in all these developments, even producing some artists in the forefront of the movement such as Bob Zimmerman turned Dylan. So it was only natural for a number of these adventurous musicians to rediscover a repertoire of their own ethnic group that was diverse enough in itself to include their interests. Scanning the current crop of klezmer bands, one notices shaping forces at work that can be traced to the folk revival. Some have revived old leftist songs. It is perhaps not surprising that the New York band, Kapelye, has been most interested in this facet of the Jewish-American patrimony. The memory of labour struggles and of the radical Jewish heritage is still strong in New York. Others, such as the Klezmorim of Berkeley or Zev Feldman, have looked to the Balkan connections. Common to many of the young musicians is a strong interest in improvization and instrumentation that comes partly from the American folk tradition. Andy Statman, for example, who learned Dave Tarras's clarinet style, is also a top-ranked bluegrass mandolinist and performs on both instruments when playing klezmer music.

Finally, one more layer of mainstream music can be considered as part of the interaction of internal and external factors: classical music. In the early decades of the twentieth century, klezmer children and grandchildren regularly abandoned ethnic styles for the international classical repertoire. Mischa Elman was the first of the many famous violinists to emerge from a klezmer family. Benny Goodman, claimed by the klezmer revival movement as honorary ancestor, moved into jazz but also delighted in his skill at classical music. Pinchas Zuckerman's father briefly played music in the streets in Poland. At the moment, the strongest link between the klezmer and classical worlds is the Klezmer Conservatory Band of Boston. It was founded by Hankus Netsky, a jazz teacher at the New England Conservatory and member of a klezmer family. He had drawn a group of conservatory students into his band, many of whom are non-Jewish.

The group's classical roots are apparent in some of their arrangements, such as their version of the Yiddish theatre classic "Papirosn," where we hear their approach to stylization, with its meticulously planned entrances of instrumental voices, followed by an impassioned live performance of the song by its author, Herman Yablokoff. Of course, we are not strictly talking about klezmer music here; this was Yablokoff's trademarked Yiddish vaudeville performance, a point which brings us full circle, back to the question of evolution within the group.

The neo-klezmer revival movement is not just a rehashing of old ethnic dance tunes. It is a restatement of self-perception by the current generation of Jewish-American musicians and, by extension, of the enthusiastic audiences that have been causing bands to pop up like mushrooms all over America. Expressive culture remains at the core of a group's sense of identity. The contemporary resurgence of ethnic awareness among American Jews, dubbed "retribalization" by some, allows activists to draw on any and all instruments, styles, repertoires, languages (even Yiddish has returned) and attitudes toward their group's past. The 1980s show every indication of being one of the liveliest decades in the expressive culture of Jewish Americans.

NOTES

This paper represents the *klezmer* movement as it was ca. 1982. True to the dynamic social process argued for here, the movement has proliferated and changed in many interesting ways over the last five years. I have described the same period in two other publications: "*Klezmer* Music: An American Ethnic Genre," *Yearbook for Traditional Music* XVI (1984), pp. 34–41, and "The Neo-*Klezmer* Movement and Euro-American Musical Revivalism," *Journal of American Folklore* 97 (January–March 1984), pp. 98–104.

1. Robert B. Klymasz, "From Immigrant to Ethnic Folklore: A Canadian View of Process and Transition," *Journal of the Folklore Institute* 10 (1973), pp. 131–139.

2. Ibid., p. 135.

3. Mark Slobin, *Tenement Songs: The Popular Music of the Jewish Immigrants* (Urbana, 1982).

4. Green and Cohen are the pacesetters for a whole group of scholars whose works can be found in the *John Edwards Memorial Foundation Quarterly* and in such volumes in the University of Illinois' Music in American Life Series as: Archie Green, *Only a Miner* (1972) and Norm Cohen, *Long Steel Rail* (1981).

5. Klymasz, "Immigrant to Ethnic Folklore," p. 138.

6. Ibid., p. 134.

7. Ibid., p. 139.

8. For a state-of-the-art survey on ethnic recordings, see J. McCulloh, ed., *Ethnic Recordings in America: A Neglected Heritage* (Washington, D.C., 1982).

9. Recently there has been a limited attempt to revive some of the traditional dance forms, e.g., by Lee-Ellen Friedland.

10. For a summary of Medoff's life and work, see Mark Slobin and Richard Spottswood, "David Medoff: A Case Study in Interethnic Popular Culture," *American Music* 3 (Fall, 1985), pp. 261–276.

6

The Construction of Community

Jewish Migration and Ethnicity in the United States

DEBORAH DASH MOORE

I n the United States the construction of community has always been linked to migration, whether within the North American continent or in the form of immigration from overseas. The factors shaping the character of migration, including personal data such as age, sex and family status, as well as such impersonal forces, as famine, political upheaval and persecution, moulded the emerging community in city or town, village or countryside. To speak of community in the United States, especially of ethnic community, means to speak both of time and place, time in the life cycle of the individuals involved and place in the environment structured into meaningful space. By implication, most ethnic communities have been subjected both to the liberating possibilities of people on the move and to the constraints of a contentious milieu (though some have argued for the conservatism unleashed by migration and the openness of the receiving society).

Interpretations of American communities have ranged from "old world traits transplanted" to the famous frontier hypothesis wherein the setting radically changed the settlers.[1] Indeed, one competing vision often followed on the heels of another: John Winthrop's city upon a hill yielding within a generation to the half-way covenant and then to Jonathan Edwards's unfulfilled errand in the wilderness.[2] Jews, too, have their ethnic version of the New England drama of immigration: The transplanting of their redemptive community is epitomized in the immigrant city within a

city, succumbing to the half-way covenant of the gilded ghetto, and finally
falling prey to a disintegrating errand into the suburbs.[3]

Although this jeremiad of declension from true community serves as a
fecund source of cultural creativity for Jews and others, it has often frustrated historians and social scientists trying to describe accurately the
nature of ethnic settlement patterns. The drab reality of census records and
city directories has proven intractable in yielding a portrait that might be
called a community. So historians, in their efforts to put flesh on the
bones of migration networks and settlement patterns, turn to institutions
as the visible incarnations of an ethnic spirit. Yet the location of Ys and
theatres, synagogues and labour lyceums, fails to capture the psycho-social
reality conjured up by the two competing, or succeeding, hypotheses of
community. Nonetheless, this modern methodology paints a complete
picture of spatial relationships even if it lacks those mythic elements that
would answer the question why we are here.

By the beginning of the twentieth century many American Jews understood their New World communities not as mere immigrant slums but
as ghettos, that is, as characteristically Jewish environments connected
through history with earlier patterns of Jewish urban residence and endowed with a particularist Jewish flavour. The concept of the ghetto on
the American scene allowed Jews to perceive a congruence between their
external geography and inner identity. In his journalistic portrait of New
York City's lower East Side Hutchins Hapgood captured this correspondence of social situation and spiritual condition.[4] Ironically, when
Hapgood's "vital ghetto" entered American social thought, it was transformed by the sociologist Louis Wirth. Through his negative characterization of Chicago's Jewish West Side Wirth depicted the ghetto as a deviant
way of life. "In quest of sociological uniformities," as Moses Rischin
astutely points out, Wirth "confounded the ecology of the ghetto with its
spirit" and missed "the fierce drama of values and sensibilities and the
gargantuan assimilative propensities of Hapgood's ghetto." But Wirth
also effected a conceptual transplantation that paralleled the physical removal of Jews from Europe to the United States. By demonstrating the
continuity of Jewish residential patterns from European to American cities, he suggested that immigrant Jews' distinctive geography explained the
persistence of Jewish culture and mentality in the modern city of Chicago.[5] Although the historical data do not sustain Wirth's analysis, his
paradigm correlating geographic areas of settlement with social organization and personality types has not needed to rely on historical accuracy to
convince scholars. Its conceptual boldness and schematic simplicity have
proven powerful. And its persuasiveness as a model has been magnified by

its resonance with other works in the canon of American historiography that explore the notion of geography as a state of mind.[6]

While the historical reality of Jewish immigrant neighbourhoods in America's large cities lies somewhere between the two paradigms of lower-class slum and ghetto, Hapgood's sympathetic formulation came closer to approaching Jewish self-understanding. Immigrant Jews both on the lower East Side and in East Baltimore called themselves "downtown Jews" in juxtaposition, of course, to the wealthy American Jews of German background who were dubbed "uptown Jews." Jews often knew who they were by where they lived. "We were Brownsville—*Brunzvil,* as the old folks said—the dust of the earth to all Jews with money," Alfred Kazin has written about the Brooklyn immigrant quarter of his youth.[7] The use of geographic shorthand distinguished *yidn* from *yahudim,* emphasizing their differences in class and occupation, cultural background, religious behaviour and political values. Geographic terms of reference spoke to a fundamental cleavage within American Jewry caused by the onset of mass immigration in 1881.

But the distinction between uptown and downtown Jews also belied the diversity of immigrant life in the neighbourhood. "The dominating characteristic of the streets on which I grew was Jewishness in all its rich variety," recalls the writer Vivian Gornick. "Down the street were Orthodox Jews, up the street were Zionists, in the middle of the street were shtetl Jews, get-rich-quick Jews, European humanist Jews."[8] Although aware of this multiplicity, most American Jews—and many Israelis—would still probably concur with Louis Wirth's dictum: "If you would know what kind of a Jew a man is, ask him where he lives; for no single factor indicates as much about the character of the Jew as the area in which he lives. It is an index not only to his economic status, his occupation, his religion, but to his politics and his outlook on life and the stage in the assimilative process that he has reached."[9] In the Jewish historical imagination, external geography often bespeaks inner identity.

Wirth's incisive statement points implicitly to migration running beneath American Jewish communities. He knew from experience as an immigrant to the United States that migration carried Jews into the modern world and shaped their encounter with modernity. Unlike European or colonial societies, Jews initiated modernization largely by moving, leaving behind the old society in exchange for a new one. Migration influenced Jewish adaptation to modern life because it did not draw randomly from the Jewish population. Those who chose to migrate selected themselves for the task, which is not to say that they were not made more amenable to this choice by external social, economic and political pressures.

The self-selected migrant moved most often not to a neighbouring town, slightly larger than where he had lived previously, but to a city on the cutting edge of change. Indeed, the newness of a city and its apparently unlimited opportunities attracted the person who decided to migrate.[10]

Immigrant Jews, choosing to leave traditional society, moved into the most rapidly modernizing segments of their world. When the transition is placed in the context of the dislocation engendered by migration, it is clear that the nature of Jewish self-identification would undergo rapid revision. Migration created peer group Jewish societies, lacking the constraints of a parental generation and, temporarily, the needs of children. Migration helped reorient the locus of Jewish identity from tradition, the past and the religious community, to ethnicity, the future and the secular individual. Though not abrogating the past and its values, the communities established by Jewish immigrants reinterpreted tradition, seeking a usable past that foreshadowed the future and legitimated their claim to Jewish authenticity. Jewish immigrants of necessity blended tradition with modernity, reconstructing a fictive past.[11] When World War Two destroyed the remnants of home, the world that had been abandoned, modern Jews were left bereft of the foil of an imagined past they could reject.

In this condition of homelessness, Jews adopted the shtetl as a symbol while they fashioned for themselves several new, modern homes. Like American immigrants from other backgrounds, Jews discovered the source of their identity less in tradition than in the future, less in their parents' bequest than in themselves. With their visions of the new world to come, Jews have been subject to the sense of declension afflicting all American immigrant groups. The future, when it arrives, never fulfills its promise, for the past, against which it is to be measured, has disappeared.[12] Jews scan the horizon for the signs of the new Jew, not recognizing that he has appeared. "Manifest most visibly and most uninhibitedly in Los Angeles," Moses Rischin observes, "was a problematic Jewish life style, post-Judaic, post-secular, and remote even from an earlier subculture of Jewishness."[13]

Americans, too, as the youthful society, share the same dilemmas of modernization produced by immigration. For the small towns, nostagically remembered by those who have moved to the big cities, never approached the *Gemeinschaft* ideal of social science. They began as boom towns, modern in their capitalist spirit, hoping to secure a position of prominence in the scramble for the new world's riches.[14] So, too, Jewish settlement of the turn of the century, the famed immigrant quarters, lacked the elements of intimacy, tradition and intergenerational continuity associated with *Gemeinschaft*. Instead, like the small towns of America, the immigrant neighbourhood mixed the ingredients of social stability and tradition with those products of social change associated with modernity, formulating simultaneously a new tradition and modern society.

The contours of this new tradition emerge from the many Jewish community studies written during the last two decades. One historical perspective, best exemplified by the works of Lloyd Gartner, presents the Jewish community as bounded less by geography than by a network of institutions situated in a single locale.[15] The institutions' development charted the immigrants' progress. As the expressions of community, the institutions changed slowly. As a result these studies depict a relative continuity in collective Jewish behaviour rather than a sense of decline. A second perspective in the writing of Jewish community studies in the United States is embodied in the social survey approach. This method assumes a mode of Jewish identification neither with geography nor with institutions but with a class of social services.[16] Perceived as consumers of services, Jews acted Jewishly by participating in or contributing to selected Jewish events and organizations. Surveys counted the number of times Jews attended synagogues, how much money they contributed to Jewish charities, the organizations to which they belonged and other quantifiable activities. The statisticians then extrapolated a social and psychic reality from these data, often charting behavioural practices across several generations and classes. Implicit in the survey approach is a norm of Jewish behaviour usually drawn from those "Jewish" Jews whose actions approximated traditional ideals.

Although Wirth defined a Jew by where he lived and Gartner defined a Jew by his interaction with communal institutions, Sidney Goldstein and Calvin Goldscheider—apostles of the social survey approach—defined a Jew by individual behaviour seen collectively. Differences between big-city Jews and small-city Jews might appear, but the surveys only rarely measured either the urban dimension or the institutional framework as critical variables. Both were replicable and the crucial factors, which tended to overlap, were class and generation.

With the appearance of Arthur Goren's influential book on the New York Kehillah, the field of Jewish community studies acquired additional dimensions that modified the reigning models. Goren's book focuses on a single comprehensive institution—the organized Jewish community of New York City called the Kehillah—and shows how the categories of previous institutional analyses did not explain sufficiently the scope of Jewish urban life. The Kehillah not only tried to solve the problems of a chaotic Jewish educational system, but also attempted to control the activities of Jewish criminals. It mediated labour disputes between employers and workers, as well as between rabbis and *shohetim* (ritual slaughterers). And it most certainly overcame the boundaries of the lower East

Side ghetto, demonstrating that uptown and downtown Jews shared a common language.[17]

If Goren's work revealed the weaknesses of the institutional perspective in Jewish community studies, recent books on Harlem and Atlanta have suggested inadequacies in Wirth's urban geography. Jeffrey Gurock and Stephen Hertzberg demonstrate that the immigrant quarter was much more variable—including members of other ethnic groups—and permeable—including middle-class Jews—than Wirth had suggested.[18] Furthermore, both indicate that instead of bitter conflict, Jews from Germany and eastern Europe engaged in joint organizational efforts. Yet neither challenge Wirth's central assumption: the external urban situation reflects an internal social reality.

In his recent history of Portland's Jews, William Toll argues against any assumption of norms of Jewish behaviour by describing how Jews adopted an instrumental attitude toward their ethnic organizations.[19] Jews used their organizations to advance simultaneously personal and group ends. Communal structures served as social networks for individuals rather than expressions of collective consciousness designed to perpetuate Jewishness or to further acculturation. Though Toll reinterprets the surveys' indexes of Jewish behaviour, he also advocates a class and life cycle analysis to explain the constant fluctuations in Jewish institutional life and the recurring patterns of occupational and physical mobility charted by the social statisticians.

Although there is much to be learned from these different perspectives of Jewish community studies, the crucial insight regarding the interplay of social, psychological and spatial forms in the Jewish urban experience cannot be abandoned. How Jews arrange and rearrange their urban environment remains an important issue in studying urban communities. We need to resurrect ethnicity, migration and geography as tools of analysis, and to recognize their influence in shaping Jewish urban life. From this perspective, two major types of immigrant Jewish communities developed and each fostered a new tradition of collective identity, despite the staggering physical mobility of immigrant Jews.

Jewish immigrants often only paused for a couple of years in the ghetto before moving on to a different neighbourhood, usually in a slightly better section of the city. In the ten years between 1905 and 1915— the peak years of mass immigration—approximately two-thirds of the Jews living on New York's lower East Side left the area.[20] Even in the small city of Columbus, Ohio, with a Jewish population of several thousand, only one Jew maintained his residence on a popular immigrant street in 1920 after a period of eight years.[21] But the places of those who left were filled by new arrivals until Congress restricted immigration. The newcomers disguised the fluidity of the immigrant community by giving the impression of continuity. Those who remained in the immigrant quarter were a minority, and the reasons for their decision to stay put have to be framed in the context of the majority's choice to move.

The most visible community model and tradition of ethnic identity derived from the influence of primary migration, epitomized in the fragmented, volatile lower East Side. Here the density and sheer volume of people allowed for forms of social organization not possible elsewhere, even in other New York immigrant neighbourhoods. It is understandable then that both contemporaries and historians view the lower East Side as a world apart, a unique Jewish milieu. One former resident nostalgically remembered: "The East Side of my boyhood was a completely Jewish world. The language of our home was Yiddish. The newspapers that came into our home were Yiddish. The store signs were all in Yiddish. The only holidays we observed were Jewish holidays. . . . As Friday night approached, the pushcarts left the street, the stores began to close. . . . Early Saturday morning found the streets deserted; everybody was in *schul*."[22] Such memories describe the historical reality less than they convey the spirit of the temporary resident's sense of the neighbourhood. On the lower East Side the potential existed to create a redemptive community.

At the beginning of the century the lower East Side housed three-quarters of the Jewish population of New York City, and that population, in turn, represented half of all American Jews and one-tenth of the body of world Jewry. This formidable concentration of Jews on a fraction of Manhattan's land, as densely packed as Bombay, India, ignited a cultural explosion that radiated far beyond its boundaries and produced contradictory images of immigrant community that we contend with to this day. The lower East Side claimed fame as the home of the Jewish version of the American myth of the self-made man at the same time as it bred American Jews' only generation of gangsters. It nourished a vibrant secular Yiddish culture as it spawned an Americanized, alienated Jewish youth who spurned that culture and its values. It cradled a religiously traditional community and vehemently antireligious radicals. Within its borders immigrant Jews could afford to be parochial or cosmopolitan, secular or religious, Yiddishist or Hebraist, radical or conservative. The density and size of the lower East Side encouraged these bitter intramural arguments; Jewish immigrants who lived there could afford the luxury of ideological purity more so than Jews in other immigrant quarters.[23]

Moses Rischin and Arthur Goren have studied the fruits to be garnered from the flourishing of an immigrant community that was almost totally Jewish in population. This dense concentration permitted Russians, and Roumanians, and Galicians the chance to claim their own turf even as it forced each immigrant subgroup to come to terms with the other's presence. New York's immigrant Jewish entrepôt could give birth to a dream of democratic community—a modern kehillah—and encourage a collective politics inaccessible to Jews who lived elsewhere. Lower East Side Jews pioneered in developing institutions and cultural styles that reflected the sense of security fostered by large numbers and compact settlement. Only Jewish immigrants who settled in New York could believe that their city *was* America. Those who moved on to Chicago or Milwaukee, Philadelphia or Cleveland, knew that their choice of home represented that one alternative. At the very least, they recognized that one other possibility existed, namely, New York. Secondary migration channelled those Jews who followed its paths on a different course away from the vision of redemptive community. The ethnic communities they established embodied the second new collective tradition of American Jews, a model of urban ethnic cohesion that combined modernity and social stability in a form different from the one favoured by New York Jews and issuing forth a different mentality.

Less diverse, less dense, but more integrative, the immigrant communities shaped largely by secondary migration received the particular stamp of the networks of individuals who built them. In a city like Atlanta or Milwaukee, Litvaks could gain the upper hand without needing to accommodate others because there were so few of them. In Chicago or Cleveland, Zionists could capture the city's major immigrant organizations, giving an ideological identity to the ethnic community. In Baltimore or Philadelphia, an American orthodoxy could take root, and pass on its style and substance. In Cincinnati or San Francisco, the established native Jewish community could set the dominant tone and boundaries of the city's Jewish life.[24] These possibilities existed because of the power of migration to sort out individuals. The unsuccessful ones who failed to fit in usually packed their bags again and either moved elsewhere or returned to New York City.

Some of the forces guiding these secondary migrations differed from those shaping immigration itself, highlighting specific aspects of selectivity. The histories of the Jewish communities created initially through secondary migration support the contention that a change in residence implies a shift in modes of Jewish identification. For example, Hertzberg's study of Jewish immigrants to Atlanta reveals that they did not come randomly, but were drawn to the Gate City by social networks of relatives and *landsleit*. Although three-quarters of all East European Jewish immigrants to the United States before 1910 were Russian, in Atlanta over 90 per cent were Russian, and of these 70 percent came from Lithuania, 30 per cent from Kovno alone. "The unrepresentative character of Jewish immigration to Atlanta was influenced by the multiplier effect of family and regional ties; the early arrivals sent for their relatives and countrymen, thereby perpetuating the proportions of the original groups." Hertzberg continues his analysis: "because of the selective influences of inertia, fear and the [New York] ghetto's sociocultural comforts, most of the few thousand Jews who went south—or at least those who went without outside assistance—were probably more adventurous, independent, and acculturated than the two million who remained in the North." Undoubtedly, the experience of a year's residence on the lower East Side facilitated immigrant Jews' adjustment to Atlanta. Yet the decision to move involved more than just choosing "a salubrious climate, superior housing, and significant commercial advantages." As David Yampolsky, who moved to Atlanta after experiencing the privations and pleasures of the lower East Side observed, "In New York I would have found my soul but without my body, and in Atlanta, a body without a soul."[25] The most successful migrants placed economic opportunity above the psychological security and cultural fulfillment of living in a large Jewish neighbourhood like the lower East Side. Thus the desire for economic independence and individual achievement as well as kinship and social networks guided the secondary migration that led to the establishment of Jewish immigrant communities outside New York and the major port cities.

In fact, even in New York City such selective forces shaped Jewish residential mobility. In his study of Harlem, a large Jewish immigrant neighbourhood established at the beginning of the century, Gurock discovered that it housed few needle-trades workers, an unusual fact because the garment industry was the largest single employer of immigrant Jewish labour in the city. By contrast, building trades workers chose to move to Harlem in substantial numbers because, unlike their garment worker comrades, they found ready work available during the years of Harlem's rapid growth. The predominance of construction workers in Harlem subsequently influenced the character of the area's Jewish socialist organizations, indicating how the selectivity of secondary migrations moulded the immigrant community.[26]

The emerging ideological coloration of an immigrant community also appears to have enticed like-minded Jews to move. The "vigorous political atmosphere" of Milwaukee, especially the role of the Social Democratic Party in the city's life, encouraged Jewish interest in socialist politics although over half of Milwaukee's Jewish immigrants were in business and the average head of household in 1908 earned a larger annual income—a munificent $534 per year—than his east European *landsman* in New York.[27] Similarly, Baltimore acquired a reputation as a "great radical city," and as a pre-eminent Zionist city. The popular Yiddish Zionist orator, Zvi Hirsh Masliansky, described Baltimore in his memoirs as "the American Bialystok."[28] By contrast, Cleveland, with a substantial garment industry and a viable Jewish trade union movement, never became a stronghold of Yiddish socialism. Its Jewish immigrant workers blended unionism with *landsmanshaft* traditionalism. It is difficult to gauge the attractions of such intangibles as ideology, but the evidence shows that once the decision to relocate to another city was taken, the persistence rates for Jewish immigrants in the city of choice, albeit not in any one neighbourhood, were consistently high. The initial effectiveness of the selectivity of Jewish secondary migration continued even when many subsequent immigrants travelled directly from Europe to the American city of their choice.

Other elements of the new communal tradition of American Jews resulted from received circumstances. Outside New York City, Jews usually shared their immigrant quarter with other ethnic groups. Rather than a completely Jewish world, "a kind of grimy Eretz Yisrael without Arabs . . . where no alien group imposed its standards," residential clustering along certain streets near the business district predominated.[29] Jews were too small a part of most cities' populations to do more than set the tone through the establishment of organizations and businesses and by the presence of religious and cultural activities. They could dominate blocks but never whole neighbourhoods. Outside New York City and its tenements, Jewish communities also differed in their degree of residential density and in the character of their housing. In Philadelphia, as in Atlanta, immigrant Jews lived in two-story attached brick buildings above their stores or in dilapidated frame houses nearby. In fact, a contemporary description of Atlanta's Jewish district along Decatur Street, one of the major commercial thoroughfares of the city, could serve equally well for Philadelphia or Baltimore. "The street was lined with two-story, attached brick buildings, stores alternating with saloons and poolhalls, which together with the segregated vice district . . . nearby . . . gave the neighborhood an unsavory reputation." Another observer expressed disdain for "long rows of dingy shops below and dingier dwellings above—markets where everything from eggs, overripe, to women's caresses have their recognized price and alleged value."[30] In the midwest in such cities as Milwaukee and Chicago wooden buildings predominated, although Jewish immigrants in the former enjoyed the pleasures of trees and vacant land around their homes. Yet, as Adler and Connolly write of Buffalo's Jewish district, which had lawns and tree-lined streets where Jews never made up more than half of a block's population, William Street "was a state of mind as well as a physical settlement."[31]

In these immigrant communities the confluence of work and residence transformed the public character of the streets. Indeed, the streets provided the arena for many interactions: men found work at the *hazir* (pig) market—the curbside employment markets—women shopped from push-carts lining the sidewalks, children played their games on the block. In the evenings couples courted on the streets and in the parks, while orators matched skills at street-corner meetings debating political questions. The streets also hosted the immigrant communities' major battles: workers on strike marched and rallied there, fights between immigrant groups took place there, housewives boycotting the high cost of kosher meat rioted there, and families facing eviction protested there. Though Jews expressed an internal solidarity based on kinship networks, religion, culture, language and institutional vitality, not on physical contiguity and concentration, in the United States they often located the source of their cohesion in the spatial relationships of the immigrant community. Thus they imagined a model of a transplanted ethnic community: cohesive, integenerational, voluntary. This second "new tradition" subsequently would guide future generations of Jews in their settlement choices when the achievement of middle-class status made the possibility of establishing residential enclaves feasible.[32]

Of the two new traditions of community and collective identity, the second alternative appears to be the most powerful one. Internal migration within the United States has replaced secondary migration as the force beneath contemporary patterns of Jewish settlement.[33] Only the elderly still adhere to a settlement ideology resembling the one which created the lower East Side community of the immigrant era. By the shores of the Atlantic and Pacific oceans, peer group communities replicate the culture of Yidishkayt with its ideological fervour, unrestrained by the demands of family solidarity and only peripherally concerned with efforts at transplantation. These are redemptive communities, even in the face of the approaching death of their members, and they continue to generate mythic images.[34] But most American Jews have chosen the selective paths of secondary migration, a dispersed, clustered and segregated settlement pattern, and the new tradition of transplanted community. Their ethnic identity remains bound to the place where they live and the years of the life cycle that they lived there. Wirth's insightful dictum still provides the best single guide to understanding an American Jew.

NOTES

1. Oscar Handlin, *The Uprooted* (1951, repr.; Boston, 1973); Maldwyn Allen Jones, *American Immigration* (Chicago, 1960); Marcus Lee Hansen, *The Immigrant in American History* (1940, repr.; New York, 1964); Robert E. Park and Herbert A. Miller, *Old World Traits Transplanted* (Chicago, 1925); Philip Taylor, *The Distant Magnet* (New York, 1971); Frederick Jackson Turner, *Frontier and Section,* ed. Ray Allen Billington (Englewood Cliffs, N.J., 1961).

2. Perry Miller, *Errand into the Wilderness* (Cambridge, Mass., 1958).

3. Marshall Sklare discusses this under a slightly different framework in his essay, "The Jew in American Sociological Thought," *Ethnicity* 1 (July 1974), pp. 151–174.

4. Hutchins Hapgood, *The Spirit of the Ghetto,* ed. Moses Rischin (Cambridge, Mass., 1967).

5. Louis Wirth, *The Ghetto* (1928, repr.; Chicago, 1956); Rischin, "Introduction," *Spirit of the Ghetto,* p. xxix.

6. On geography as a state of mind, see, for example, William R. Taylor, *Cavalier and Yankee* (Garden City, N.Y., 1961) and Henry Nash Smith, *Virgin Land* (Cambridge, Mass., 1950).

7. Alfred Kazin, *A Walker in the City* (New York, 1951), p. 12.

8. Vivian Gornick, "There Is No More Community," *Interchange* (April 1977), p. 14.

9. Louis Wirth, "The Ghetto," *On Cities and Social Life,* ed. Albert J. Reiss, Jr. (Chicago, 1964), p. 94.

10. Paula Hyman, "The Social Foundation of Jewish Modernity," *The Solomon Goldman Lectures,* III (Chicago, 1982), p. 75.

11. Vladimir C. Nahirny and Joshua A. Fishman, "American Immigrant Groups: Ethnic Identification and the Problem of Generations," *Sociological Review* 13 (1965), pp. 311–326.

12. Timothy Smith, "Religion and Ethnicity in America," *American Historical Review* 83, no. 5 (December 1978), pp. 1155–1185.

13. Moses Rischin, "Foreword," *The Jews of Los Angeles 1849–1945: An Annotated Bibliography,* comp. Sara G. Cogan (Berkeley, 1980), p. viii.

14. Lewis Atherton, *Main Street on the Middle Border* (Bloomington, 1954); Richard Wade, *The Urban Frontier* (Chicago, 1959).

15. Lloyd P. Gartner, *History of the Jews of Cleveland* (New York, 1978); Lloyd P. Gartner and Louis J. Swichkow, *The History of the Jews of Milwaukee* (Philadelphia, 1963); Max Vorspan and Lloyd P. Gartner, *History of the Jews of Los Angeles* (Philadelphia, 1970).

16. The best example of this genre is Sidney Goldstein and Calvin Goldscheider, *Jewish Americans* (Englewood Cliffs, N.J., 1968). See also Sophia Robison, ed., *Jewish Population Studies* (New York, 1943); Herbert Gans, "The Origins and Growth of a Jewish Community in the Suburbs: A Study of the Jews of Park Forest," *The Jews,* ed. Marshall Sklare (New York, 1958), pp. 205–248.

17. Arthur Goren, *New York Jews and the Quest for Community* (New York, 1970).

18. Jeffrey Gurock, *When Harlem Was Jewish* (New York, 1979); Steven Hertzberg, *Strangers within the Gate City* (Philadelphia, 1978).

19. William Toll, *The Making of an Ethnic Middle Class* (Albany, 1982).

20. Thomas Kessner, *The Golden Door* (New York, 1977), p. 148.

21. Marc Lee Raphael, *Jews and Judaism in a Midwestern Community* (Columbus, Ohio, 1979), p. 112.

22. Zalman Yoffeh, "The Passing of the East Side," *The Menorah Journal* (December 1929), p. 266.

23. Moses Rischin, *The Promised City* (Cambridge, Mass., 1962); Irving Howe, *World of Our Fathers* (New York, 1976); Ronald Sanders, *The Downtown Jews* (New York, 1969).

24. On Atlanta, see Hertzberg, *Strangers,* p. 79; on Milwaukee, see Gartner and Swichkow, *Jews of Milwaukee,* p. 156; on Chicago, see Rivka Lissak, "Myth and Reality: The Pattern of Relationship between the Hull House Circle and the 'New Immigrants' on Chicago's West Side, 1890–1919," *Journal of American Ethnic History* 2, no. 2 (Spring 1983), pp. 25–30; on Cleveland, see Gartner, *Jews of Cleveland,* p. 248; on Baltimore, see Isaac M. Fein, *The Making of an American Jewish Community* (Philadelphia, 1971), p. 181; on Phila-

delphia, see Robert Tabak, "Rabbi Levinthal and the Orthodox," *Jewish Life in Philadelphia 1830–1940*, ed. Murray Friedman (Philadelphia, 1983); on Cincinnati, see Michael A. Meyer, "A Centennial History," *Hebrew Union College–Jewish Institute of Religion: At One Hundred Years*, ed. Samuel K. Darff (Cincinnati, 1976), pp. 81–82, 108, and Stephen G. Mostov, "Dun and Bradstreet Reports as a Source of Jewish Economic History: Cincinnati, 1840–1875," *American Jewish History* 72, no. 3 (March 1983), pp. 340–341, 344–347; on San Francisco, see Peter Decker, "Jewish Merchants in San Francisco: Social Mobility on the Urban Frontier," *American Jewish History* 68, no. 4 (June 1979), pp. 403–407.

25. Hertzberg, *Strangers*, pp. 78–80.

26. Gurock, *When Harlem was Jewish*, pp. 40, 60–85.

27. Gartner and Swichkow, *Jews of Milwaukee*, pp. 65, 166.

28. Fein, *American Jewish Community*, p. 169.

29. William Poster, "Twas a Dark Night in Brownsville," *Commentary* (May 1950), p. 461.

30. Hertzberg, *Strangers*, p. 112.

31. Selig Adler and Thomas E. Connolly, *From Ararat to Suburbia: The History of the Jewish Community of Buffalo* (Philadelphia, 1966).

32. Charles Jaret, "Recent Patterns of Chicago Jews and Residential Mobility," *Ethnicity* 6, no. 3 (September 1979), pp. 235–248; Carol Agocs, "Ethnic Settlement in a Metropolitan Area: A Typology of Communities," *Ethnicity* 8, no. 2 (June 1981), pp. 127–148.

33. Lloyd Gartner, "The History of North American Jewish Communities: A Field for the Jewish Historian," *Jewish Journal of Sociology* 7, no. 1 (June 1965), p. 27.

34. Barbara Myerhoff, *Number Our Days* (New York, 1978), pp. 93–98.

3

THE FATHERS OF
JEWISH ETHNIC CULTURE

Introduction

The great Jewish migration, itself a product and a source of a vast upheaval that shook Jewish life to its core, inevitably generated the need for its reconceptualization in terms responsive to the conditions of modernity. Louis Wirth, Simon Dubnow, and Horace M. Kallen, Chicago sociologist, East European historian, and Harvard philosopher-disciple of William James, grappled with the problem from entirely different perspectives. In three complementary essays, three intellectual historians analyze the distinctive responses of these major thinkers to the challenge of modernity and ethnicity.

In an age of renewed ethnic pride and sensibility, like our own, older notions of assimilation, once sanctioned by law and public opinion in the United States and to an extent in Canada as well, no longer prove compelling. No proponent of benevolent assimilation therefore would appear more out of step with our times than the noted urban sociologist portrayed by Fred Matthews, for Louis Wirth's views of equality and individual opportunity, still in the ascendant in the early 1960s, more than a decade after his death, were thoroughly in accord with his indifference to ethnic and Jewish concerns. Yet Matthews is persuaded that had Wirth lived on, he too would have regarded the ethnic revival as the necessary response to the crisis of identity and leadership in our contemporary world.

By contrast with Wirth, the great Russian Jewish historian, Simon Dubnow, who singularly combined a passion for Jewish history with an

ideology of Jewish ethnicity, is seen by Robert Seltzer as the East European grandfather, or at the least, as the great uncle, of North American
Jewish ethnicity. Indeed, Dubnow's biographer attempts to show how
apposite the Russian historian's vision has been for contemporary ethnic
thought and implies that Dubnow saw the great migration to America as
the grand prologue to the culminating American epoch in his conception
of a vital and continuous hegemonic diaspora of his historic people. Whatever the limitations of Dubnow's historical theory for the North American
setting, his sensitivity to the velleities of modern ethnicity, argues Seltzer,
continues to give his vision resonance and contemporaneity.

Closest of all to the American experience was Horace M. Kallen,
American Zionism's foremost intellectual. More sensitively and incisively
than any of his contemporaries, Kallen, as William Toll makes clear, attempted to reconcile the polarities of American ethnic consciousness with
the dominant philosophical themes of his age. What Kallen called "Cultural pluralism," more than any other idea of America, directly anticipated
not only the ethnic climate of our time in North America but has proven
terminologically congenial even to religious Jews, perhaps, ventures Toll,
because despite Kallen's secularism and anticlericalism, he made no effort
to define the content of Jewish ethnicity but pragmatically celebrated
pluralism as ceaseless transformation.

7
Louis Wirth and American Ethnic Studies

The Worldview of Enlightened Assimilationism, 1925–1950

FRED MATTHEWS

L ouis Wirth was one of the most influential and active students of
ethnic and "minority" relations among America's social scientists
between the late 1920s and his sudden death in 1952, at the height of
his activity and influence. Yet apparently he is now little read and almost
forgotten, except perhaps among the local tribe of Chicago sociologists
who defend the memory of their once-dominant institution in a much
larger and more varied scholarly world. Wirth's very distance from the
present, in assumptions and approach to ethnicity, make him interesting as
an index of how far American ethnic studies have moved from the paradigm of benevolent evolutionary assimilationism, the concern with integration and equality of opportunity, that dominated the mind of academic
experts on intergroup tension from the 1930s to the 1960s. The worth of
Wirth, for a generation far removed from the problems and priorities of
his prime, may be found in his perfect embodiment of the mentality of a
generation in which intellectuals unselfconsciously talked of "America" as
an entity.

Although fond memories persisted among his old colleagues, it is
difficult to conjure up a clear sense of the personal Wirth. He was devoted,
hard-working, enthusiastic about his tasks. Sometime in the 1930s he
realized his personal power as a negotiator and persuader; from that time
on he spent more and more time speaking, consulting, organizing, arranging that needed research be done, ensuring that results be broadcast to

concerned citizens, and so on. As chairman of a large department, as a frequent moderator of the University of Chicago radio roundtable, he tried to embody the midwestern ideal of the concerned scholar as expert consultant to the responsible public of disinterested citizens. One result of this activity is an absence of deeply considered, thoroughly researched writing on Jewry after the publication of his doctoral dissertation, *The Ghetto,* in 1928. Thereafter, his publications were occasional pieces, designed to orient the general public toward the perceived "problems" of minority groups, intergroup and interpersonal relations. Their very off-handedness and short-term problem orientation make them revealing of the position from which academic social scientists viewed ethnicity and the assumptions that guided their conclusions.

An affectionate brief account written by Wirth's daughter leaves the impression that he was a man whose life so perfectly embodied an understanding of the modern history he taught that it enabled him to avoid the alienation which intellectuals have seen as the consequences to wrenching shifts in culture and environment. He was born into a tight *Gemeinschaft* community, a Jewish family that had lived in the same house in a small Rhenish village for four centuries. Both parents came from relatively prosperous cattle-merchant families, though his maternal grandmother had come from an urban line of merchants and rabbinical scholars. At the age of fourteen, Wirth went with his uncle to Omaha, Nebraska, where he learned fluent English, became a high-school debater and met William Jennings Bryan, who made him sign the pledge. His assimilation into the subculture of the serious-minded regional intelligentsia was rapid. Upon graduation from high school he won a regional scholarship to the University of Chicago. World War One ended any thoughts of returning to Germany.

As an undergraduate Wirth participated in radical protests against American entry into the war, and thought of himself as a Marxist, a loyalty more tolerated at Chicago than at many universities because of the interest of Albion Small, the founder of the sociology department, in the major European theorists. Although explicit Marxism was later replaced by the apolitical neutrality of Chicago sociology, one finds in his later work echoes of concern for the distorting influence of "power groups" on the communication of knowledge that may stem more from Bryanite populism than from Marx.[1]

After graduation Wirth worked in his beloved Chicago, in the division of delinquency of the Bureau of Personal Services of the Jewish Charities. In 1923 he married Mary Bolton, the daughter of a Bryanite and fundamentalist Baptist from a small Kentucky town. Her father had wanted to give her the advantages of America's leading Baptist university, much as Wirth's mother had wanted her son to escape the narrow limits of

Gemunden. In both cases emancipation continued beyond parental expectation, making the couple eminent representatives of the new subculture
of liberated professionals that was growing around university campuses.
As Elizabeth Wirth Marwick put it,

> Wirth's assimilationist inclinations and principles, like those of his wife,
> partly derived from their common reaction against dogmatism and provin-
> cial ethnocentrism. Their two daughters were to be encouraged in ag-
> nosticism with audible atheistic overtones, at the same time that they were
> to acquire a 'generalized minority' ethnic identification.[2]

Even the notion of a "generalized minority" identification reflects the
broad evolutionary assumption of the Chicago sociology that Wirth absorbed and developed, since Chicago theory stressed the mutability, the
constant shifting quality, of ethnicity as of other social institutions.

His wife's salary as a social worker allowed Wirth to return to the
university for a Ph.D. degree. Following the usual pattern encouraged by
Robert Park, the dominant personality of Chicago sociology in the 1920s,
Wirth studied what he knew—the Chicago Jewish community he had
observed at close range during the years as an official of the Charities. *The
Ghetto* established his scholarly credentials, and allowed entrée into the
world of teaching, organization and influence, which seems to have been
most congenial to him. He never wrote another book, and his most famous essay, "Urbanism as a Way of Life" (1938), is largely an assemblage
of ideas drawn from his mentor Park and older theorists of the urban-rural
paradigm, such as Tönnies and Simmel. After a couple of tense years
teaching at Tulane in New Orleans, where an association with birth control clinics offended the administration, and a fellowship to travel in Germany and France studying the sociology of knowledge, Wirth returned to
Chicago in 1931 at the instigation of Park. He remained for twenty-one
years, active in university affairs, in the development of the college curricu-
lum, in organizing sociological research in Chicago and the numerous
conferences and consulting tasks noted earlier.

Wirth was so fully assimilated to the emerging subculture of the secular social expert that his understanding of Jewry and Judaism must be
approached through the worldview of Chicago sociology, its self-image
and its model of social change. The role prescribed for the scholar-expert
by the Chicago school was shared by most American academics of the
generation. The scholar's civic duty was to provide disinterested information and suggested solutions to perceived problems to a general public of
rational citizens whose devotion to the civic good was taken for granted.
Because public officials were assumed to be the legitimate representatives
of this atomic field of citizens, it was natural to inform and work with the

legal authorities. The status of "minority" interest groups was less clear; to identify too closely with one particular minority might involve a loss of broad perspective, and indeed of scholarly status. The distinction between distinterested scholar, working within a rational community according to universal rules of conduct, and the agitator, who "knew" truth through emotional insight unavailable to scholarship, was vital to that generation. This was perhaps partly because academic freedom was still insecure at most universities, but also because of the power of the ideal of citizenship propagated by the Progressive movement, with its faith in reason, knowledge and the natural audience of disinterested citizens. This "public," in practice, tended to crystallize as a group of patrons of sociological research: other academics, the city bureaucracy, the foundations just beginning to sponsor social investigation, and "enlightened" civic groups including businessmen, charities and some ethnic organizations.[3]

The very orientation of the scholar-citizen helped impose an "elitist" or "Olympian" view of ethnicity as of other urban phenomena, as a series of demographic traits that might lead to tension and conflict. The academic expert therefore became an analyst of potential conflict and a manager of human relations. The idea of committed action *with,* as well as *for,* people outside the civic consensus was alien to this model of responsibility, and Chicago sociologists sometimes had to rebuke their eager students for too-complete an empathy with the people they studied.[4]

This recognized role of the scholar dovetailed perfectly with the large interpretive paradigm, the system of assumptions through which Chicago sociology comprehended its specific researches. The evolutionary scheme of movement from closed rural societies to the open, dynamic urban civilization of the twentieth century was already a cliché, or at least a truism, but it did impose conceptual choices. It had relatively little to say about class and class conflict; and although ethnic groups and accommodation to new societies were at the centre of its interest, it conceptualized them in a pattern of sweeping historical change, which would ultimately homogenize them into the urban pattern that defined the modern world. Further, its particular concern to be "scientific" encouraged a distanced, analytical, comparative view of ethnic groups, which did not quite drain all the specifics of their culture but tended to stress both their common taxonomic traits and the large historic processes which they illustrated. Chicago studies of ethnic communities (as of any urban institution) tended to be triumphs of large-scale conceptualization over the particularities of lived experience, and Wirth's one extended study of Jewry can illustrate the point as well as any other of the Chicago monographs.[5]

The scientific Olympianism of the Chicago school appeared immediately in *The Ghetto*'s preface, where the Jewish community became an ideal type of broader social processes, "the physical symbol for that sort of moral isolation which the 'assimilationists' are seeking to break down," and which every organized and self-aware group tries to impose in order to maintain its existence. And it concluded that "the full story of the ghetto" would be "a laboratory specimen for the sociologist that embodies all the concepts and the processes of his professional vocabulary. The institution of the ghetto is not only the record of a historical people; it is a manifestation of human nature and a specific social order." It is fair to note that these attempts at large theoretical significance were and are a common ploy for the scholar seeking scientific status, and don't automatically rule out empathy with the subject. And such empathy is not wholly lacking, though usually accompanied by an ironic tone about the dilemmas of those torn between extrovert and introvert tendencies, the desire alternately to escape the confines of the closed community and then to fend off the hostility of the greater world outside. In discussing the rise of Zionism, Wirth ascribed it to "the recrudescence of anti-Semitism in recent times" and offered a characteristic irony: an independent Jewish state, "it is becoming evident to many, . . . would merely result in making the ghetto international."[6]

The frame of reference that underlay this irony needs more explicit exposition, but one should carry on the theme of Wirth's scientism. In his later, more activist years as a New Deal liberal, Wirth certainly thought that his work would promote greater justice by providing that rational public with data and techniques allowing it to act to reduce group discrimination, to educate the broader citizenry in the fallacy of racist thinking, and so on. But his determination to remain the distanced scholar, aiding in mutual understanding among groups but prisoner of none, did not diminish. In the 1930s he translated and promoted Karl Mannheim's sociology of knowledge (perhaps his most significant academic role), and it is tempting to see this as a groping for a larger perspective within which to reconcile his belief in social justice with the puritanical neutrality of the Chicago school. In the mid-1940s he noted that

> we are, of course, . . . interested in understanding what is, rather than what ought to be. But . . . almost everything we do is tied up with the problem of values. Values determine our intellectual interests, the selection of problems . . . , selection and interpretation of the data . . . to a large extent also our generalizations. . . . Therefore, . . . the sociologist . . . must . . . make explicit the value premises from which he proceeds.[7]

This was a frequent theme in the forties, as many scholars had to face the widening gap between their commitment to social justice and the conservatism of their fellow Americans. It allowed an activist like Wirth to reconcile concern and scholarship rather than repudiating the disinterested, Olympian ideal altogether.

The conflict with Wirth, however, was not between Olympian neutrality and a new commitment to Judaism. Throughout his work early and late there runs the general framework of evolutionary assimilation drawn from the work of Herbert Spencer as well as from contemporary observation, the assumption of a unilinear motion towards one vast modern society, which will be urban, industrial, rational and increasingly integrated.[8] This evolutionary tide would swamp much of value in traditional cultures, and there would likely be resistance, temporary setbacks, conflicts. But the general tendency was inevitable and on the whole benevolent, advantageous for most of the individual human beings who made up the ethnic groups approaching the grinder of the modernizing process.[9] The evolutionism of the Chicago school can be called "enlightened" in part because it was a late manifestation of the eighteenth-century Enlightenment, but also because it was vociferously tolerant. With their stress on the long term and the minimal degree of cultural change needed to get along in the new modern context, with their hostility to biological racism and their stress on the malleability of personality, the Chicago sociologists argued against the exclusionism and forced-assimilation programs of the years during and after World War One. Some, like Robert Park, were notably sympathetic to "minority" cultures and to students from those cultures. But there was often a kind of voyeurism or connoisseurship lurking in their interest, like that of anthropologists hurrying to record vanishing tribal rites. Their duty was to document an inevitable historical process, and in doing so to rake the occasional genius from the rubble of obsolescing customs and neighbourhoods.[10]

This account, written in light of the wide range of attacks on liberal scholarship that have become standard of late, may be too harsh on Wirth's mentor Park, who was skeptical of all institutions and suspicious of all improvements. It was Wirth himself who embodied it, who wrote more often on the modernization process as necessarily ambivalent but overall desirable. His usual explanation for Jewish resistance to assimilation was the hostility of outsiders, rather than any intrinsically valuable elements of Jewish community or tradition. The "return to the ghetto," described in 1928, was due largely to a mix of guilt and loneliness but primarily inspired by the varying degrees of resistance felt in gentile neighbours in areas of later settlement.[11] Writing near the end of World War Two, he predicted: "the eventual resumption of the assimilationist trend among the Jewish minorities in the Western world appears to have favorable prospects once the cult of racism declines." The same essay offered a general statement of the rural/urban theory which would soon be called modernization:

> Since the disintegration of tribal society the human stocks occupying virtually every area of the world have become progressively diversified. Through conquest and migration formerly compact groups have become dispersed and split up among different political entities. Through modern transportation, communication, commerce & technology, the surviving folk cultures are being increasingly drawn into the vortex of world civilization. There still remain . . . some relatively limited islands of homogeneity & stability in a sea of conglomerate & swiftly moving heterogeneity, but on the whole the civilizing process is leveling them. Minority problems are symptomatic of this profound world-wide transition.[12]

Wirth's preference for the dynamic world of the modern city, inspired by his own experience, was reinforced by the conceptual lenses of Chicago sociology. Not only their historical vision but their psychology, their theory of personality made it logical to assume that separatist movements' what Wirth later called pluralistic minority consciousness were temporary eddies in the long river of assimilation. The social psychology of the Chicago school, built on the theories of John Dewey and Charles H. Cooley of Michigan, shared with the retrospectively better known Columbia anthropology of Franz Boas, Ruth Benedict and Margaret Mead a sweeping environmentalism. Personalities developed in interaction with others, in the "primary groups" of family and school and local community, and remained open to new association, new stimuli, which might provoke a reformulation of interests and attitudes throughout life. Chicago sociology was perfectly aware that cultural attitudes and loyalties were part of the personality transmitted through interaction. But its vision of personality (and everything else) as an ongoing process, rather than a fixed structure or a predetermined essence, joined with its Deweyite faith in discussion, in people meeting to work out their contemporary problems in light of an ideal of a better future, to give a relatively minor weighting to "inherited" loyalties, those transmitted by parents, as against the loyalties and interests gained at school through friendship, and in the daily life of the city and the workplace. Like so much liberal scholarship, this sociology was reacting against the racist assumptions of fixed biological inheritance of the previous generation, and so tended to be impatient with doctrines that would limit the freedom of individuals to choose. "Social types," or group character-stereotypes, and even physical types, as Wirth noted in 1928, are products of isolation, like the flora and fauna of the Galapagos, and will be modified as the walls of isolation come down and experience broadens.[13]

There was also a cultural preference mixed in with the environmentalism of Chicago sociology. More was better, more richness and variety of human interaction helped produce a more fully developed human personality. The "closed" community, which tried to limit all but the most superficial ties beyond the pale, seemed not only historically reactionary but psychologically unhealthy, a deliberate stunting of the growth of the young. The twenties and thirties saw the first wide flowering of mental hygiene ideas among the educated; and one of the most popular ideas, since it appealed to native attitudes, was Jung's extraversion/introversion typology of personality. Health was reaching out, expanding; sickness was introversion, narrowness even if it brought depth. This stereotype lies behind Wirth's frequent reference to "the humdrum ghetto existence" and its frustrating, restrictive quality. "In the close life within ghetto walls, almost nothing was left to the devices of the individuals. Life was well organized." The closed society led to inbreeding, higher rates of insanity and mental defect. Wirth's sympathy was for the "braver" spirits who wanted to escape the narrow community.

> It took a larger world to satisfy the craving for new experience, for excitement and adventure on the part of the restless spirits among the ghetto inhabitants. The formal restrictions that bound them served merely as an additional stimulus [to] entrance into the forbidden world.[14]

A more differentiated account, with both affection and veiled irony, can be found in the most concrete personal history offered in *The Ghetto*.

> "Let us go to America" said a Jew from Kiev to his wife, after he had lost his fortune in a pogrom, "let us leave this hellish place where men are beasts, and let us go to America, where there is no ghetto and no pale, where there are no pogroms, and where even Jews are men."
>
> He came, but he landed in the ghetto. It took him some time to find out that it was a ghetto. . . . He had become a citizen, and he had voted at elections; he had a business on Jefferson Street, and he had accumulated a comfortable fortune. He had allowed his beard to grow, and he went to *Shul* as he did in Kiev. His wife kept a Kosher house, and he had brought up his boy to play chess and to discuss the Talmud. It had never occurred to him that there was a ghetto in America and in Chicago.

His discovery of the ghetto came when his oldest son, a law student, urged moving away, because the family could afford it and he could then invite friends home. His shocked father said, "What do other people have that we haven't got?" However,

> that night the old man could not sleep. . . . His mind was wandering. A month later they moved to Central Park Avenue, in Lawndale. The son felt happier, but the father didn't go down to his store . . . on the street car with

quite the same zest mornings as he used to when they lived upstairs over the business. Nor did he feel the same way when he went to the synagogue. . . .

Two years later, when the son had opened a law office, the father sold his store and began to dabble in real estate. . . . He had found that the synagogue on the near West Side was too far away, and had joined a congregation on Douglas Boulevard, three miles farther west. He had trimmed his beard a little, too. He still played chess with his son, but instead of discussing the Talmud they discussed the real estate boom on Crawford Avenue.[15]

This expectation that natural character development was outward and upward underlay Wirth's argument that external prejudice, not internal choice, was the main barrier to assimilation.

It takes an extreme courage to 'face the music' of racial hostility as an individual. More often the tendency is to return to one's own people, to the small but human and sympathetic group of the family and the *Landsmann-schaft*, where one is appreciated and understood. The applause is not so loud, but it is more genuine.

What has held the Jewish community together is, not only the return of the disappointed Jews who have sought to get out, and, failing, have returned to become apostles of nationalism and racial consciousness, but also the fact that the Jewish community is treated as a community by the world at large.[16]

Did the ghetto have no positive qualities? Wirth recognized some but they were typically presented in a context that suggested second-bestness, compensation: the ghetto, in Wirth's social-psychological sense of a cultural and geographical shelter, was "the old familiar primary group, where life, though puny in scale, is rich and deep and warm."

Confined as the province of the ghetto was, there was ample opportunity for the display of capacity for leadership. . . . The ghetto community was minutely specialized and highly integrated. At the same time it afforded a rich, intense and variegated life to its members.

Reverence for the elderly and the dead, the richness of pageantry and celebration, were noted within a larger context of historical change which classified them as compensations and, in the 1920s, as social survivals— "the persistence of old outworn institutions long after their raison d'être has ceased to operate."[17]

While Wirth's unsympathetic treatment of communal life stemmed in part from his own secular-rationalist stance, there was also a conceptual rigidity involved. The Chicago understanding of institutions as primarily mental, as mind-sets which determined the limits of intimacy and sympathy, was arguably a sophisticated one. Yet in practice Wirth not only tended to neglect the positive qualities of communal belonging, but perhaps more important, he hardened his categories into unreal alternatives, a "closed" ghetto, mental or geographic, versus that "open" competitive world where talent and energy determined position. These were not the only alternatives, nor necessarily exclusive of each other. Wirth's reification of this misleading dichotomy was guided by his sociological model, but its persistent use in his book suggests that personal animus made it the more sufficient explanation to him.

More general ideological choices were involved in Wirth's impatient treatment of the ghetto as anachronistic survival, and this is where we must step back and view Wirth's own career and even the Chicago theories he embraced as part of a larger historical movement. The best insight comes from the passage with which Wirth continued his discussion of the limiting but reassuring quality of the ghetto:

> But when he emerges from the ghetto he becomes human, which means he has contacts with the outer world, encounters friction and hostility, as well as familiarity and friendship. But sensitive as he generally is even to the slightest gestures of those of whom he is not yet a part, he has difficulty in acting without restraint and with poise. He shrinks from conflict, and is likely to attribute his failures and rebuffs exclusively to the fact that he is a Jew.[18]

The key phrase is not the ascription of personal sharpness or paranoia to the shock created by movement out of a closed community, which is consistent with the general psychological model in which quality and variety of human contact bolster the personality. It is the notion of *becoming human* by leaving the narrow community with its sharply defined characters and customs, limited by historical constraint, and moving out into the large, dynamic world of modernity and competition, which the sociologists saw crystallized in the city of Chicago. There are various intellectual currents which relate to this notion of growth-as-moving-outward. The popular psychology of extraversion has been noted; another current is the midwestern progressivism associated with John Dewey (a major influence on Chicago sociology and psychology) and the prairie school of achitecture. The emergent society of American democracy would be one of equal individuals able to move freely in ample physical and social space, realizing their humanity not in pride of heritage but in acting spontaneously together to solve the communal problems of the present.[19] Even broader is the notion of a universal human essence, a matrix of fundamental traits, potentialities, shared by all but so far frustrated by the historical accidents of culture, tyranny, special interest, and so on. It is not entirely clear how this view of a human essence fits in with the environmentalism of the Chicago school, but if seen as a general set of potentialities it may not be wholly contradictory. At any rate, this Aristotelian universalism is implicit in Wirth's treatment and occasionally explicit as in the quotation. Here the inheritance from the Enlightenment is clear.

Isaiah Berlin has consistently interpreted modern intellectual history in terms of a fundamental conflict between the universalist faith of the Enlightenment in a single human nature and morality, to be discovered by the application of a single valid scientific method, and the pluralism of the romantic movement which stressed the genius of smaller societies, peoples rooted in their region and culture, as bringing greater creativity and happiness than the deracinating standardization of enlightened science. Sociology itself, although accepting the notions of group cohesion derived from the romantic tradition, accepted the enlightened notion passed through Comte of a rational understanding of society in general which would reveal what was universal and functional and what was particular, accidental and therefore remediable. While not necessarily utopian, it stressed the possibility of amelioration by rational understanding through scientific method.[20] The universalism of the Enlightenment as passed down into sociology paralleled a similar universalism which had deep roots in American nationalist thinking. America, the child of the eighteenth century, was the open space in which liberal institutions would give the varieties of (white) mankind free play to shuck their limited identities and develop their common human potential to the maximum. Given the faith in a single human nature and the assumption that people are moulded more by their current situation and their vision of the future than by their past, American nationalists could see the conflicts caused by "tribalism" in the old world being swept away by the freedom and aspiration of the new. There is also an echo of Christian come-outerism in this belief in the liberating power of the new milieu and the new faith: "For I come to set a man at variance against his father . . . and a man's foes *shall be* they of his own household. He that loveth father or mother more than me is not worthy of me. . . . And he that doth not take his cross and follow after me, is not worthy of me."[21]

Echoes of this universalist nationalism which seems both contradictory and arrogant to foreign intellectuals, can be found in the literature devoted to immigration and ethnicity in the interwar years. Marcus Hansen's *The Immigrant in American History* opened with an epigraph from Whitman, "the Nation of Nations," which has a distinct assimilationist thrust, and the book interpreted Americanization in the terms we have seen in the Chicago school. Because immigrant farmers during the Civil War worried about their children away at the front, they became emotionally involved in the cause their children served. "The past in Europe was overshadowed by the future in America," wrote Hansen. And his explanation of the decline of inherited language displays a Darwinian, Deweyite functionalism even more naive than that of the sociologists: "The mother tongue was inadequate to deal with relationships and tasks unknown in the country of origin. . . . The people were obliged to use the vocabulary of the life they lived." As Moses Rischin has shown, Hansen in lectures did lament the conformist nationalism generated by the Civil War, which reduced the possibility of recreating "the many-sided culture" of Europe. But his published works stressed the other side of the coin, the way in which the homogenizing force of late nineteenth-century nationalism "prevented the crystallization of the minority problems that had helped to destroy Europe." Among the Chicago sociologists, Robert Park in particular was a devoted reader of Emerson and Whitman, about whom he wrote an essay; and his sociological model was "American" in its use of the individual and the competitive market-place as basic units, in contrast to the organicism of most European sociology.[22]

And one can find the optimistic view of America in contemporary writings by native-born intellectuals, including some who would later become harsh critics of American mediocrity and viciousness. Mary McCarthy in 1947 could be found defending her country against the condescension of French intellectuals: America had been "founded on an unworldly assumption, a denial of 'the facts of life.' It is manifestly untrue that all men are created equal." The feelings of pseudo-equality engendered by the founding principle were resented by hierarchical Europeans, who could see no good coming from American mobility. Yet they existed:

> generosity, hospitality, equity, directness . . . a peculiar nakedness, a look of being shorn of everything . . . corresponding to the bright thinness of the American light. . . . The openness of the American situation creates the pity and the terror; status is not protection; life for the European is a career; for the American it is a hazard.[23]

A similar rooting in the tradition of Whitman and Emerson can be found in the major champion of ethnic cultures during Wirth's lifetime, the Slovenian immigrant writer and historian Louis Adamic. While a penetrating critic of native American hypocrisy and a champion of the values of ethnic cultures, Adamic nevertheless enveloped his particular stands in an enthusiastic Whitmanesque nationalism of the kind which characterized the culture of the Depression decade and distinguishes it most sharply from later cultural pluralists. As in Whitman's image of the nation of nations, both elements were real and vivid; their "America" was not just a formal or legal entity containing a mosaic or federation of cultures that had a vitality stemming from their deep roots, as in thorough going pluralists like Horace Kallen or Michael Novak. The creative, enriching power of the formal legal structure and civic ideals was equal to that of ethnic tradition; and the inspiration of American space and mobility, American friendship and hospitality, as positive qualities pointing to a broad brotherhood of mankind was salient in Adamic as in Whitman. Adamic's portraits of intellectual life in Yugoslavia, with its personal warmth and intensity, and its demands for orthodoxy, reflect the same contrast between community and society found in Wirth. Adamic's *My America* is a classic chronicle of the creative plurality and openness of his adopted country's life in the 1930s, and he balanced its powers and charms against those of the old world as Wirth had done in balancing the ghetto and the great society. Certainly there is more affection and concern for detail in the artist Adamic, but his pluralism shares with Wirth and Hansen the faith in the positive power of the American social and physical space that would vanish within two generations.[24]

Louis Wirth himself was less an American nationalist than a believer in the decent, pacific world "society of enlightened and cultured persons" (as Fredrich Heer summed up Voltaire's faith) in which conflict would be ameliorated both by mutual understanding and devotion to universal goals. His faith, as expressed glancingly in several essays of the 1940s, resembles Henry Wallace's—education, prosperity and massively increased communication among peoples would gradually eliminate conflict by emphasizing shared values and undermining the special interests of power groups that benefited from misunderstanding and conflict. The world would be united by a common drive towards prosperity, equality and mutual understanding. And his essays on nationalism in Europe stressed the ugly side of group pride and exclusiveness, so that the ethnic conflicts of the old world took on the shape of interest-group exploitation as seen by a Bryanite Populist. He was careful to distinguish American minorities and minority relations from this picture, but by methods that would seem alarming to a pluralist of our own day: most American minorities, most of the time, wished to integrate into the larger society; and the special nature of minority existence in America was governed in great part by the individualism of formal institutions and beliefs, which in the Enlightenment tradition were deliberately blind to group membership and ethnic traits.[25] In 1945, discussing "assimilative minorities," which he saw as logically and in most cases historically following pluralistic minorities, he offered a characteristically vague conflation of ideology and reality that represents his late view:

> The 'melting pot' philosophy in the United States . . . in so far as it was actually followed tended to develop both among immigrants and natives an atmosphere conducive to the emergence of a crescive American culture to

which both the dominant and minority groups contributed their share. This new culture, which is still in the process of formation, comprises cultural elements derived from all the ethnic groups constituting the American people but integrates them into a new blend.[26]

The generation after Wirth's death in 1952 witnessed a conceptual revolution, which made his views repugnant and perhaps incomprehensible to the new pluralism, which argues that the preservation and revival of ethnic identities and cultures is an essential liberation from an oppressive, artificial assimilation to alien values. One aspect of this new pluralism, an aspect new at least in America, is called "corporate pluralism" by Milton Gordon: the formal, legal recognition of ethnic entities by government, which gives them "formal standing as groups in the national polity."[27] Gordon's antithesis of corporate pluralism with the traditional "liberal pluralism," which rejected forced assimilation but assumed that individuals were equal before the law, stresses the level of legal institutions and government policy. This level, with its associated attitudes, is an important one, as Louis Wirth noted in 1941. In it useful here to note briefly some of the broader changes in the beliefs of educated Americans which made Wirth's liberal assimilationism a museum piece.

The most obvious change has been the disappearance from educated circles of the traditional myth of American openness and opportunity, replaced by the vision of Amerika the fascist monster, a closed society run (in various versions) by a corporate elite, an academic-military bureaucracy, a cadre of opportunistic intellectuals whose amoral rationalism derives from their lack of ethnic roots, or all of the above. The last stereotype, of course, is Wirth's ideal of the secular, enlightened policy scientist as seen through the bitter lenses of recent history.[28]

This pervasive vision, the mirror-image of the Whitmanian view, is orthodox among "under-forty" intellectuals outside the United States, and is quite popular inside as well. Clearly the most immediate cause of the alienation is the domestic strife and foreign interventions of the last generation, captured in part by Walter Nugent's recent list:

> the urban and campus riots . . . the assassinations of the Kennedys and Martin Luther King. The Tet offensive. . . . The Democratic Party tore itself apart. . . . Recessions and two devaluations of the dollar. . . . Watergate . . . the unfamiliar, half-forgotten specter of scarcity began to materialize. . . . Inflation. . . . Iranian revolutionaries hijacked the U.S. embassy. . . . Gas lines . . . interest rates.

Not to mention Three Mile Island! "Americans had real reason to be unhappy, for during no comparably long period, except possibly from 1800 to 1817, had they been so variously buffeted."[29] It is less clear, however, that Nugent is right to assume, with contemporary historiography, that we should "look beyond the level of events to broader patterns of historical structures and conjunctures." There is a respectable sociological tradition, descending through Comte, to argue that "opinion" rules external reality by structuring perceptions of it, and the harrowing events of the last generation have meshed with traditions of thought already established to mould a consciousness that despairs of the present but retains hope for the future.

The critique of America as epitome of modern thinness, standardization and vulgarity is not a new one. Matthew Arnold had found the new world "not interesting," Henry James had lamented the thinness of New England culture, native intellectuals like Van Wyck Brooks and Randolph Bourne had shared the fear of cultural blankness, with Bourne turning to the pluralism of Horace Kallen as an antidote both to boredom and aggression. Kallen himself had argued for the preservation of cultures on this ground. All were echoing the pioneer of pluralist thought, Herder, who had seen little hope for cultural value in transplanted settler societies. Louis Wirth himself had noted this secular defence of Jewish separateness in 1928: Jewishness would form a barrier against "a fatal and monotonous similarity and mediocrity invading all sections of national life."[30]

In this vision the open American plain was not a fertile field for human creativity and achievement, but a blank space, without the institutional and cultural resources that helped inspire creation and mould those vivid if specialized characters Wirth had noted in the ghetto. In 1928 Wirth had noted this argument, and Kallen's, and moved on. But by the late 1950s American intellectuals had revived the romantic critique of suburban sameness, conformity, illiteracy, mindlessness, anti-intellectualism. It is not clear whether this critique drew consciously on the pluralist tradition; more solid influences were persisting hatred of Babbitry and the closer contact between European and American intellectuals, which made the latter familiar with the vision of America as a land of robots and morons offered by Simone de Beauvoir, Robert Jungk, C. Vergil Gheorgiu and others. Despite the retrospective reputation of a "complacent" and apolitical intelligentsia in the fifties, the vigorous critique of American culture developed then would pave the way for explicitly radical indictments like that of Herbert Marcuse in the next decade.[31]

And this shift to a stance of romantic alienation can be found among social scientists as well as intellectuals. Louis Wirth had shared with E. Franklin Frazier the teaching of Robert Park, and by the 1940s they were the two outstanding Chicago students of race and "minorities." In the mid-forties Frazier shared Wirth's relatively optimistic liberal assimilationism. In 1949 he employed the Chicago model of movement towards one "cosmopolitan" world to explain the continuing though arduous pro-

gress of Negro Americans towards "integration," and noted without dis-
approval that "a large proportion of Negroes . . . conform to American
middle class standards of living." With allies in the federal government and
an enlightened world public opinion, Blacks could look forward to continued integration into the single society of educated tolerance. By 1957,
however, when *Black Bourgeoisie* appeared, Frazier had turned to a sharp
attack phrased very much in romantic terms congruent with the cultural-
pluralist position. In attempting to eradicate all vestiges of Black folk
culture in order to become anonymous Americans, "successful" businessmen and intellectuals were in "the process of becoming *nobody*." The
assumption that there was not a "crescive" American culture, that modern
professional and civic life did not furnish values to substitute for those of
inherited tradition, shows how far Frazier had moved from Wirth's liberalism towards romantic pluralism.[32]

By the mid-1960s this eagerness to escape the monotony of mass
society through a rediscovery of roots found close parallels in the anarchist
decentralism of the New Left, which distrusted in almost equal measure
the power of the state and the dehumanizing abstraction of large intellectual systems. Its view of American civic education as a dehumanizing
process of "social control" imposed by elites on potentially creative and
spontaneous communities made the New Left sympathetic to ethnic
cultures (though the reverse was not necessarily the case), cultures which
were part of the real democracy of the small community. The New Left
vision has had a lasting impact on American scholarship, leading to the
reinterpretation of the past through the paradigm of Hobbesian populism,
which sees an exploitative elite imposing its will on the natural virtue of
local communities united by ties of class, ethnicity and neighbourliness.[33]

This account may have stressed the "radical" context of the new ethnicity to the neglect of its "conservative" content and intentions. True,
rooted ethnic groups were often hostile to what seemed the infantile
acting-out of 1960s anarchism, and some of the appeal of renewed ethnic
bonds in America as in Europe was as a defence against the loosening
morality of the larger society. A recent survey of America through British
eyes notes the numerical decline of the liberal social gospel churches and
the flourishing of "strict religion" as in part a search for protective discipline for children; and we may note the renewal of ethnic roots as a related
search for protection against fashionable relevance. But both readings of
the return to roots, as radical or as conservative, stress its hostility to the
"self-made" individualism of the American intellectual tradition. The political spectrum is an intellectual artifice, and the ties of kinship between
right and left against the liberal centre have been noted often.[34]

The historian of revivalism, William G. McLoughlin, argues that the
New Left and countercultural movements of the sixties are not passing

fads but form a relatively coherent spiritual reorientation, a "fourth Great Awakening" to offer Americans a reworked system of values and sense of identity. We have noted the strong cast of Christian come-outerism in traditional American nationalism; McLoughlin suggests that a revived, reoriented religious sensibility will join with an ecological concern to think of communities as fragile, interrelated systems to form a new basis for human identity and interaction that will relieve the burden of an "American" identity associated with exploitative liberalism:

> At some point in the future . . . a consensus will emerge . . . [that] will most likely include a new sense of the mystical unity of all mankind and of the vital power of harmony between man and nature. The godhead will be defined in less dualistic terms, and its power will be understood less in terms of an absolutist, sin-hating, death-dealing 'Almighty Father in Heaven' and more in terms of a life-supporting nurturing, empathetic, easy-going parental . . . image. The nourishing spirit of mother earth, not the wrath of an angry father above, will dominate religious thought. . . . Sacrifice of self will replace self-aggrandizement as a definition of virtue; helping others will replace competitiveness as a value. . . . some form of Judeo-Christian socialism will be the new political ideology.[35]

While McLoughlin's vision may now seem further off, he assumes that the transformation must await the decline of the last liberal-individualist generations formed in the 1940s and 1950s. It would indeed constitute a great awakening if people were to become selfless and universally caring; but if one understands McLoughlin to be speaking of an ideological change which may or may not later change human conduct, then his vision is less absurd. The revival of ethnicity, the search for roots and for communal warmth, can then been seen in terms that Louis Wirth would have understood, and perhaps sympathize with: It is a vital element in a response to the present crises of American life and the heavy burden of American identity in a world which sees the old American drive to control the environment as the serpent in an otherwise balanced Eden. The obsolescence of Wirth's enlightened assimilationism is one aspect of the passing of the liberal vision of America and of humanity.

NOTES

1. The reference to "power groups" is in "Ideas and Ideals as Sources of Power," Lyman Bryson, ed., *Conflicts of Power in Modern Culture* (New York, 1947), pp. 499–509, repr. in Louis Wirth, *On Cities and Social Life*, ed. Albert J. Riess, Jr. (Chicago, 1964), pp. 146–156. The brief biography is Elizabeth Wirth Marvick, "Louis Wirth: A Biographical Memoir," ibid., pp. 333–340.

2. Ibid., p. 337.

3. See Fred H. Matthews, *Quest for an American Sociology: Robert E. Park and the Chicago School* (Montreal, 1977), chap. 4, esp. pp. 110–115.

4. Ibid., esp. pp. 115–117. This "elitism" was not only a trait of Chicago sociology; one can find it among political intellectuals as well. When Saul Alinsky, who studied sociology at Chicago but rejected its professional ideology, published *Reveille for Radicals* in 1946, he was attacked in both the *Nation* and *New Republic* for assuming that positive results would come if intellectuals organized communities but subordinated their own insight to the felt grievances of the masses. See Horace R. Cayton, "Awake to What?," *New Republic* 114 (21 January 1946); Ralph Bates, "Rhetoric for Radicals," *Nation* 162 (20 April 1946), pp. 481–482.

5. Louis Wirth, *The Ghetto* (Chicago, 1928), was concerned with "general significance," with typicality, not with "individuality." Wirth's most extensive overview of what by 1940 had come to be called "minority relations" was "The Problem of Minority Groups," first published as a chapter in Ralph Linton, ed., *The Science of Man in the World Crisis* (New York, 1945), pp. 347–372 and often reprinted and cited later. See Wirth, *On Cities and Social Life*, pp. 244–269. This essay combines the problem-orientation which Wirth shared with the social sciences in the 1930s and 1940s with the broad taxonomic and evolutionary paradigm of Chicago sociology.

6. Wirth, *Ghetto*, pp. vii, 287, 106 in that order.

7. Wirth's autobiographical statement, in Howard W. Odum, *American Sociology* (New York, 1951), p. 228.

8. Although the evolutionism of Chicago sociology was discarded as an interpretive model by the late 1950s, it has more recent echoes in the popular theories of modernization used by economists and political scientists concerned with the Third World, and has appeared in various guises in the work of social historians. An ambitious schematic account is Robert F. Berkhofer, Jr., "The Organizational Interpretation of American History: A New Synthesis," in Jack Salzman, ed., *Prospects: An Annual of American Cultural Studies*, vol. 4 (New York, 1979), pp. 611–629. And the very influential work of Samuel P. Hays, collected in *American Political History as Social Analysis* (Knoxville, 1980), has a model of the conflict between modernizing elites and democratic masses which presents the same broad theory within a different emotional context.

9. The term "assimilation" was perhaps the classic example of a word that came to stand for a variety of distinct changes in human perception and behaviour; and the Chicago sociologists often used it as though it were a single process with a clear conclusion. In Robert Park's work, at least, there was a sophisticated conception of it as something involving appearances, stereotypes, "masks," rather than fundamental attitudes. See Matthews, *Quest for an American Sociology*, pp. 167–174. Milton Gordon had contributed greatly to the clarification of the concept through elaboration and subcategorizing, but the process may have to be pushed further. See Gordon, *Assimilation in American Life* (New York, 1964).

10. See Matthews, *Quest for an American Sociology*, esp. pp. 157–167.

11. Wirth, *Ghetto*, chap. 13, pp. 263–281. Also "Problem of Minority Groups," Wirth, *On Cities and Social Life*, esp. pp. 256–257.

12. Two quotations from "Problem of Minority Groups," Wirth, *On Cities and Social Life*, pp. 260, 264–266.

13. Wirth, *Ghetto*, pp. 71–74. Another example can be found in one of the major achievements of Chicago sociology, the *Local Community Fact Book of Chicago*. Wirth's preface to the 1949 edition (ed. L. W. and Eleanor Bernert, Chicago, 1949, 1965, esp. p. vii) gives a keen sense of the relatively modest role played by ethnicity among the various economic, cultural and geographic influences on the formation of neighbourhood communities. These were areas and associations constantly in process, and the loyalties thrown up by the recent past of the neighbourhood seemed as salient to Chicago sociology as the ancestral identity which a local majority might interweave with the neighbourhood past.

The same emphasis on "minority" studies as an overview of an ongoing process, in which all elements are open to change and reformulation, can be found in the useful overview and collection of projects by Chicago graduate students, Ernest W. Burgess and Donald J. Bogue, ed., *Contributions to Urban Sociology* (Chicago, 1964). See esp. pp. 4–11, 389, 404–405, 485, 490–491. This seeping processual and assimilative worldview raises the question whether Wirth *can* be called a "father of Jewish immigration and ethnic studies." It depends on whether one insists on an interpretive paradigm not too dissimilar to that of the present.

14. Wirth, *Ghetto*, pp. 61, 68, 77, 38 in that order.

15. Ibid., pp. 241–242. The first paragraph was attributed to a manuscript "immigrant autobiography." Like most Chicago monographs, *The Ghetto* relied heavily on the existing published literature, plus demographic data gathered from census reports, with an occasional spicing by "personal documents" like the one quoted here. Some of these were gathered by graduate students, some written by those students with direct experience. For a critique of the loose methods of Chicago sociology, see John Madge, *The Origins of Scientific Sociology* (New York, 1962), pp. 88–125. For all their interest in scientific conceptualization, Wirth and his colleagues remained impressionistic essayists when viewed by the next generation with its passion for scientific verification.

16. Wirth, *Ghetto* pp. 269, 270. The second quotation refers not to prejudice in the sense of hostility, but to the influence of outside expectations: the external public assumed, for example, that Jewish agencies would aid Jewish immigrants.

17. Ibid., pp. 290, 38, 62, 67. A trenchant criticism of Wirth's stereotypical treatment of the ghetto, comparing it with the vivid, differentiated, appreciative account by Hutchins Hapgood a generation earlier, is in Moses Rischin's introduction to the John Harvard republication of Hapgood's *Spirit of the Ghetto* (Cambridge, Mass., 1967), especially pp. xxix–xxx. As noted below, the theoretical contours of the evolutionary process provided basic lenses through which Chicago sociology interpreted experience.

18. Ibid., p. 267. Also p. 290: "On the one hand there is the strange and fascinating world of man; on the other, the restricted sectarianism of a little group into which he happened to be born, of neither of which he is fully a member."

19. A valuable overview of "Chicago schools" of thought in the social sciences is Darnell Rucker, *The Chicago Pragmatists* (Minneapolis, 1969). A broader effort to relate these academic schools of thought to architecture and to the temper of the Middle West, written by a Chicago sociologist, is Hugh D. Duncan, *Culture and Democracy: The Struggle for Form in Society and Architecture in Chicago and the Middle West during the Life and Times of Louis H. Sullivan* (Totowa, N.J., 1965). A new study, highly critical of the philosophical assumptions of Chicago sociology, is J. David Lewis and Richard L. Smith, *American Sociology and Pragmatism: Mead, Chicago Sociology, and Symbolic Interaction* (Chicago, 1980). The attack-in-depth made by these authors on Chicago's theories suggests a parallel between philosophical sociology and ethnic studies, a common turn away from process, change and interaction to a concern with permanent structures.

20. Isaiah Berlin, "The Counter-Enlightenment," in *Against the Current: Essays in the History of Ideas* (New York, 1980), p. 1. Berlin's richest discussion of pluralism as a rejection of the Western ideal of a single set of values is "Herder and the Enlightenment," in *Vico and Herder: Two Studies in the History of Ideas* (New York, 1976), pp. 145–216, an essay essential for understanding the origins of cultural pluralism. See also Fred H. Matthews, "The Revolt against Americanism: Cultural Pluralism and Cultural Relativism as an Ideology of Liberation," *Canadian Review of American Studies* 1 (Spring 1970), pp. 4–31.

21. A pioneer study was Hans Kohn, *American Nationalism: An Interpretative Essay* (New York, 1957). See, for example, pp. 150, 171 of the Collier edition. Christian come-outerism: *Matthew* 10, 35–38.

22. Marcus L. Hansen, *The Immigrant in American History* (Cambridge, Mass., 1940), pp. 141, 145; Matthews, *Quest for an American Sociology,* pp. 15–17. Moses Rischin's seminal essay, "Marcus Lee Hansen: America's First Transethnic Historian," in Richard L. Bushman

et al., eds., *Uprooted Americans: Essays in Honor of Oscar Handlin* (Boston, 1979), pp. 319–347, charts the tensions of Hansen's view of assimilation.

23. Mary McCarthy, "America the Beautiful," *On the Contrary* (London, 1980), pp. 6–19.

24. See Louis Adamic, *My America 1928–1938* (New York, 1938), passim, esp. pp. 126–127, 136–137, Adamic, *Laughing in the Jungle* (New York, 1932), p. 34, where the closed/open metaphor familiar in Wirth was also used. These comments are drawn from Fred Matthews, "Louis Adamic in the Development of American Pluralist Thought," a paper presented to the conference on "Louis Adamic: His Life, Work and Legacy" held at the University of Minnesota Immigration History Research Center, May 1981.

25. On the characterization of Voltaire: Friedrich Heer, *The Intellectual History of Europe,* vol. II, trans. Jonathan Steinberg (Garden City, N.Y., 1968), pp. 206–207. Wirth, "Types of Nationalism," *American Journal of Sociology* 61 (May 1936), pp. 723–737, repr. *On Cities and Social Life,* pp. 106–21: "the difference between Europe and America is principally that in Europe the minorities lie together in large numbers, and are not recent immigrants who have been anxious to, and at least partially successful in, shedding their cultural heritage" (p. 119). "One is inclined to believe that a nationality is not complete until it has some minority within its territory whom it can oppress" (p. 121). On the blindness of American tradition to group traits: Wirth, "The Present Position of Minorities in the United States," *Studies in Political Science and Sociology* (Philadelphia, 1941), pp. 137–156, repr. in Elizabeth Wirth Marvick and Albert J. Riess, Jr., eds., *Community Life and Social Policy* (Chicago, 1956), pp. 218–236, esp. p. 218. On Wirth's broader faith: "Ideas and Ideals as Sources of Power," cited above, note 1; and the earlier "Localism, Regionalism and Centralization," National Resources Committee, Progress Report (Washington, 15 June 1936) *American Journal of Sociology* 62 (January 1937), pp. 493–509, repr. *On Cities and Social Life,* pp. 189–206, esp. pp. 190, 195.

26. "The Problem of Minority Groups," *On Cities and Social Life* pp. 244–269.

27. Milton M. Gordon, "Models of Pluralism: The New American Dilemma," *Annals of the American Academy of Political and Social Science* 454 (March 1981), pp. 178–188.

28. Norman Mailer's *Armies of the Night* (New York, 1968) is the most vivid and probably the most sophisticated statement of this familiar view. The novels of Kurt Vonnegut, Jr., Joseph Heller and E. L. Doctorow offer similar visions of hell. The most vivid and probably influential tract of the new ethnic revival, Michael Novak's *The Rise of the Unmeltable Ethnics: Politics and Culture in the Seventies* (New York, 1972), makes clear the close relation of the renewed interest in ethnicity with the recoil from the burden of American identity. An interesting, but controversial, comparison could be made between Novak's view of WASP—Americans, the older anti-Semitic stereotypes of Jews, and indeed Canadian stereotypes of Americans. All seem to share a polarity of rooted, natural virtue versus artificial, alienated vice that has sources in the romantic movement. Isaiah Berlin's essay on Herder (see note 20) is suggestive here.

29. Walter T. K. Nugent, *Structures of American Social History* (Bloomington, 1981), p. 2.

30. Wirth, *Ghetto,* p. 127, citing Joseph Jacobs, "Introduction" to the English version of Arthur Ruppin, *The Jews of Today* (New York, 1913), pp. xvii–xviii. There is no extensive history of romantic social criticism in America, though James Hoopes' superb life-and-times, *Van Wyck Brooks: In Search of American Culture* (Amherst, 1977) is rich in insight. See also Matthews, "Revolt against Americanism" (note 19).

31. Probably the best way to trace this discussion is by reading *Partisan Review* during the 1950s. Also see Philip Olson, ed., *America as a Mass Society: Changing Community and Identity* (New York, 1963). The European critics, whose influence can be traced in the liberal

journals, are: Simone de Beauvoir, *America Day by Day,* trans. Patrick Dudley (London, 1952); C. Virgil Gheorghiu, *The Twenty-Fifth Hour,* trans. Rita Eldon (New York, 1950); Robert Jungk, *Tommorow is Already Here,* trans. Marguerite Waldman (New York, 1954). Herbert Marcuse's *One-Dimensional Man* (Boston, 1964), drew on this body of criticism but placed it in a new context which revealed the kinship between Marx and the classical philosophers. Lionel Trilling's *Beyond Culture* (New York, 1965) stressed the growth of an "adversary culture" in which these critical ideas were conventional wisdom.

32. E. Franklin Frazier, *The Negro in the United States,* rev. ed. (New York, 1957), esp. pp. 704–706, 688–695; Frazier, *Black Bourgeoisie* (New York, 1957), p. 26. I am indebted to the essay by Dale R. Vlasek, "E. Franklin Frazier and the Problem of Assimilation," in Hamilton Cravens, ed., *Ideas in America's Culture: From Republic to Mass Society* (Ames, 1982), pp. 141–156.

For the general intellectual climate of New Deal and Fair Deal liberal "integrationism" in which Frazier was thinking, see the important essay by Philip Gleason, "Americans All: World War II and the Shaping of American Identity," *Review of Politics* 43 (October 1981), pp. 483–518. I am indebted to this and other works of Professor Gleason. A difficult question is the degree of distinction between Wirth's assimilationism and the integrationism of the 1940s and 1950s. While they are much closer to each other than either is to the new pluralism of the 1960s, the integrationist position would usually grant persistent power and value to ethnicity without insisting on the romantic position that traditional cultures were superior to modern civilization, essential to psychic health and so on.

Anthony D. Smith's important book, *The Ethnic Revival in the Modern World* (Cambridge, 1981), notes in chapter 6 the importance of the intelligentsia and its "crisis of faith" in helping to shape the resurgence of ethnic nationalism.

33. A study of contemporary historiography along these lines is Fred Matthews, "Networks and Paradigms," a paper presented to the Organization of American Historians Conference, Philadelphia, April 1982. See the collected essays of Samuel P. Hays, *American Political History as Social Analysis* (Knoxville, 1980), for a rigorous scholarly presentation of the paradigm which underlies much of the recent work here described as "New Left." The name might be unfair to Hays himself, whose work is more Hobbesian than Populist, though there are intimations of sympathy with the "democratic" populace being brought to attention by elitist modernizers.

One can find echoes of this shift in intellectual paradigms in various areas. Joseph L. Blau, in *Judaism in America: From Curiosity to Third Faith* (Chicago, 1976) observes that "much of the apparent 'orthodoxy' of contra-acculturated American Jewish youth involves a distrust of the sincerity of American society and a deliberate testing of American pretensions" by confronting the allegedly tolerant society with "a visible badge of difference."

34. Edmund Fawcett and Tony Thomas, *The American Condition* (New York, 1982), chap. 14, esp. pp. 409–415. The authors stress "strictness" of doctrine and form, rather than conservatism on particular issues, together with friendliness, as crucial to the success of these churches.

35. William G. McLoughlin, *Revivals, Awakenings and Reform: An Essay on Religion and Social Change in America, 1607–1977* (Chicago, 1978), pp. 214–215. A less apocalyptic prediction of a revision in national self-conception based on "mediating structures" like ethnicity and local community, which would replace the liberal polity of individuals and central state, is Michael Novak, "Mediating Institutions: The Communitarian Individual in America," *The Public Interest* 68 (Summer 1982), pp. 3–20. If nothing else, these various predictions may suggest the political breadth of the flight from liberal individualism.

8

Simon Dubnow and the Nationalist Interpretation of Jewish History

ROBERT M. SELTZER

In the spectrum of Jewish cultural and political ideologies at the beginning of the twentieth century, Simon Dubnow stood in splendid
self-isolation. Having rejected orthodoxy, Reform Judaism, and assimilation, Zionism and socialism, he advocated a concept of secular diaspora nationalism that was, he felt, based on theses that had been solidly
established through his study of Jewish history. Although Dubnow made
substantial scholarly contributions to our knowledge of the East European
Jewish past, his reputation among the Jewish public rests above all on his
ten-volume *World History of the Jewish People*.[1] The *World History* is the first
synthesis of the whole of the Jewish past where literature and religious
beliefs are treated as secondary to Jewish society and institutions. In this
paper I will deal with the relationship between Dubnow as a nationalist
ideologue and as a popular historian, to assess both the appeal and the
limitations of his achievement.

A dual career as historian and nationalist ideologue is hardly unusual
in the Europe of the nineteenth and early twentieth centuries. Yet several
factors, personal and historical, prevented Dubnow from becoming the
Jewish equivalent, *mutatis mutandis,* of the Czech Frantisek Palacky, the
Irish Arthur Griffith, the Yugoslav Slobodan Jovanovic, or of Paul Mili-
ukov or Thomas Masaryk.[2] Dubnow had a weak drive for power, a stub-
born proclivity remarkable even among late Victorians not to compromise
in ethical matters (*principialnost,* it has been called), a decided academic

temperament that resented the time that practical politics took from his studies. Moreover, the destruction of the independent Jewish communal institutions in Russia by the Communist regime only a little more than a decade after he achieved prominence, eliminated the natural arena for Dubnow's public career as a statesman.

But Dubnow was not a man of his time. He was a *philosophe* who lived a century late, a *maskil* after the fading away of the Haskalah. He was an amateur who made himself into a professional, a self-taught scholar without any university training. Once he discovered history, he soon managed to support himself and his family through the sale of his historical writings—which few historians can do at present. For Dubnow history was not a career but a mission. Although the two dimensions of Dubnow's thought, history and ideology, attracted somewhat different sets of disciples, for him they were manifestations of the same positive, evolutionary truth and the same life goal and meaning.

Dubnow's commitments to Jewish history and nationalism were complementary strategies toward re-establishing an ongoing tie to the world of his childhood, kin, and peers.[3] Born in 1860 in the Belorussian market town of Mstislavl, he was given a traditional religious education until bar mitzvah. In adolescence he found his way to modern secularism by way of the literature of the Hebrew enlightenment and the government elementary school for Jews in his home town. Unable to complete a Russian secondary education and gain admission to a university, he educated himself. Through reading he absorbed the positivism and utilitarianism of the Russian radical critics of the sixties but rejected their revolutionary politics. His youthful intellectual heroes were Dimitri Pisarev and Auguste Comte, followed by John Stuart Mill and Herbert Spencer, and later Ernest Renan and Leo Tolstoy. Around 1880 he began to write for the Russian Jewish press, mainly literary criticism and essays calling for Jewish cultural reforms. A few years later he gravitated to historical themes, especially in a long series of articles on the rise of Hasidism. In 1890 a move to Odessa brought him in contact with an influential and creative group of Jewish writers and intellectuals, above all with the Hebrew essayist and *hovev Tsiyon* (Lover of Zion) Ahad Ha-Am. Soon after the move came Dubnow's pioneering essay advocating the establishment of a Russian Jewish historical society for the collection and publication of primary sources on the East European Jewish past. In the mid-nineties he issued his first textbook in Jewish history for modernized Jewish schools. After the formation of the World Zionist Organization and the Jewish Workers' Bund of Russia, Poland and Lithuania in 1897, he began to publish a series of "Letters on Old and New Judaism," which became his principal ideological work. The height of active political involvement was his participation in the Society for the Attainment of Full Civil Rights for the Jewish People in Russia immediately after the Russian revolution of 1905 and the creation of the small Folkspartei, for which Dubnow wrote the platform.

In 1906 Dubnow settled in St. Petersburg where he engaged in various undertakings, including teaching Jewish history at the courses in Oriental Studies established by Baron David Günzberg. He was also editor of the quarterly journal *Evreiskaia Starina,* which became the leading scholarly journal for East European Jewish history. The February Revolution of 1917 seemed to herald the fulfillment of Dubnow's political dream of constitutional government for a multinational Russian state. Profoundly antipathetic to the Bolshevik regime that seized power in October of that year, Dubnow received permission to leave the Soviet Union in 1922. While residing in Berlin in the late 1920s he supervised the publication of the German edition of his *World History of the Jewish People* and the first volumes of the Hebrew edition. After Hitler came to power, Dubnow settled in Riga where, among other activities, he undertook the publication of his autobiography.[4] He was killed on 8 December 1941 by a Latvian policeman during the Nazi liquidation of the Riga ghetto.

"Immigration, settlement and ethnic identity" are certainly central themes in Dubnow's historiography. Unlike the other "fathers of Jewish ethnic studies" we are considering, for Dubnow the relevant context of Jewish migration is a specifically Jewish one—the total, continuous history of the Jewish people as a living national organism. The modern migration of Jews is another instance of a pattern appearing in ancient times, when Jews emigrating from the land of Israel were forced to adapt their institutions and way of life to new and challenging conditions. The success of Jewish resettlement indicates for Dubnow the prototypical evolution of the Jewish people from "tribal nation" to "territorial nation" to nonterritorial, global, "spiritual" nation—spiritual in the sense of a nation whose unifying bond is subjective. This subjective, spiritual bond includes common awareness, a sense of common kinship, and a sharing of common historical destiny.[5] In his *World History* Dubnow breaks with his earlier model, the great German Jewish historian Heinrich Graetz, and does not present Jewish history as Jewish thinking and martyrdom. Rather, for the mature Dubnow the story is essentially a political one. (We should note the appropriateness of this shift in emphasis from Graetz's day, when Jewish political commitments were usually defended in universalistic terms, to Dubnow's time, when many East European Jewish intellectuals had been won over to the stance that there were urgent Jewish political priorities.)

The politicization of Jewish history can be seen clearly in the overall structure of Dubnow's *World History*. The first two volumes deal with the ancient period, up to the destruction of the Temple in A.D. 70. There the backbone of the division of the work into books and chapters is the dynasties and states, Israelite, Judean, Hellenistic, Hasmonean and Roman, that ruled the Jewish homeland. The continuation of the story during the centuries in which the Jews became a completely diaspora people ascribes primary significance to the institutions that Dubnow considered surrogates of a Jewish state: patriarchate and Sanhedrin in Palestine, exilarchate and geonate in Babylonia, the office of *nagid* in many later Islamic lands, the *aljamas* in Spain, the *kahals* of northern Europe. These were the crucial societal mechanisms that ensured Jewish survival by maintaining schools, courts of law, *tsedakah* and burial societies, synagogues and *yeshivot*, synods, *vaadim* and *shtadlanim*, all of which enabled Jews to perpetuate their culture, maintain social cohesion and defend their vital interests. Thus Dubnow restored a political existence to a (in the nineteenth-century terminology) supposedly "non-historical" people. For purposes of ideology, he extrapolated from the success of these Jewish political and cultural institutions the idea that the diaspora could continue to function as a self-sufficient setting for the Jewish people. Against the Zionist insistence that physical or spiritual survival entailed a return to the Jewish homeland, Dubnow placed his hope in modern guarantees for ethnic groups in multinational states—guarantees of the kind incorporated in the minority rights treaties of the Congress of Versailles.

But the Jewish diaspora is too vast a stage for a historical narrative, and requires some narrowing down. Fortunately for the historian, some regional Jewries almost always tended to dominate the others. Therefore, Dubnow's periodization of Jewish history was determined by a sequence of what he called hegemonies, whereby one or two branches of the diaspora, or the communal and intellectual leadership thereof, exerted a powerful influence on the smaller centres. Volume Three of the *World History*, covering the period from A.D. 70 to the eleventh century in the Middle East, is divided into the hegemony of the Jewish leadership of the land of Israel under pagan Rome, the dual hegemony of Palestine and Bablyonia under Christian Rome and Byzantium and under Sassanian Persia, and the Babylonian hegemony under the Califate. Volume Four covers the shift of Jewry from east to west, the overarching theme being the settlement and organization of Jewish life in Europe up to the Crusades, a main turning point from Europe as a hospitable to a more dangerous environment for Jews. Volume Five covers the dual French-Spanish hegemony until the thirteenth century and the dual Spanish-German hegemony that followed until the end of the fifteenth century. Volume Six takes as its subjects the dispersion of the Sephardim and the hegemony of the Ashkenazic centre in the sixteenth and first half of the seventeenth century. Volume Seven deals with the Polish hegemony to the end of the eighteenth century. Although Dubnow felt that a different type of periodization was required for the modern period (which I will describe below), the nineteenth- and early twentieth-century migration to America is presented as the establishment of another potential diaspora hegemony.[6] The modern Yishuv in Palestine was yet another such hegemony in the making (rather than being the inauguration of a new era in Judaism, as in Zionist ideology).[7] There have been several efforts in the history of Jewish thought to endow the Jewish dispersion with an inherently positive significance—to negate the concept of exile as punishment or misfortune—and Dubnow's is certainly one of the most ambitious.[8] For some nineteenth-century Jewish thinkers the diaspora was the setting where Judaism could make its destined contribution to human salvation; for Dubnow diaspora was the essence of Jewish nationhood and the irrefutable demonstration of its intrinsic adaptability and perseverance.

I remarked that the modern period in Jewish history had for Dubnow a structure different from the ancient and medieval. In it he discerns two dialectic processes, an internal and an external one. The first moves between the poles of emancipation and reaction. There are three such cycles (this is his conception in the late 1930s). The first emancipatory period, under French auspices between 1789 and 1815, was followed by the first period of reaction under Metternich et al. between 1815 and 1848. A second emancipation, mainly in central Europe but including the Great Reforms in Russia, took place between 1848 and 1881, and was followed by a second period of reaction, as evidenced in the rise of modern anti-Semitism and the pogroms, May Laws and subsequent anti-Jewish government measures in Tsarist Russia. A third emancipation followed in the wake of World War One—Dubnow is here referring to the formal emancipation of Russia's Jews in April 1917 and the conferring of legal rights on the Jews in the successor states in East Central Europe. The coming to power of the Nazis in Germany constitutes for Dubnow a third period of reaction. The internal dialectic, parallel to this transformation of Jewish civil rights, involves a veritable revolution within Jewish culture. The thesis (to use Dubnow's quasi-Hegelian terminology) was the traditional Jewish way of life and the old religious leadership; the antithesis was the Enlightenment that broke the back of theocracy in Judaism, liberating the mind but threatening to dissolve the group by facilitating assimilation. The synthesis was a new Judaism that combined the psychological rootedness, cultural integrity and sociological stability of the old autonomy, with the intellectual freedom afforded by modern secularity and the legitimacy to be rendered ethnic minorities by progressive regimes. This new liberal synthesis would guarantee for collectivities the right of self-determination that the older liberalism had won for the individual. Dubnow, of course, considered that his ideology of autonomism was the most cogent, sensible and well-grounded version of the various forms of Jewish nationalism circulating in the Jewish street during the first decades of the twentieth century.[9]

Within the chronological framework of periods and hegemonies summarized above, Dubnow presented his historical material, material sometimes drawn from his own research but usually taken from pre-World War One monographs and secondary studies. The close connection of his historiography and his ideology—an unaggressive, moderate and tolerant ideology—gave his work a coherent focus and avoided a mere throwing together of discrete episodes, biographies and topics.[10] But the ideology distorted the Jewish past by overemphasizing continuity at the expense of change, solidarity at the expense of internal tensions, the global over the local, the national will over the religious mentality.

A historian of the entirety of Jewish history cannot be expert in the economic, social, cultural and political dynamics of every area in which Jews settled. But noticeably lacking in Dubnow is adequate attention to the specific conditions explaining why a Jewry was able to take root and flourish at certain places and certain times and not others. Lacking is the analysis of how the Jewish economic profile and demography were shaped by local conditions, how the social environment enabled Jews to adapt traditional institutions or create new ones with relative ease, how the image of the Jew and Judaism responded to the presuppositions and goals of the gentile elites. To be sure, comparative generalizations on the Jewish fate in various lands are needed, but Dubnow's explanatory scheme is far too broad to be historically useful, because it was designed to cover every branch of the Jewish diaspora for upwards of two thousand years.

The key to national longevity, according to Dubnow, was the nation's ability to maintain a high morale even in the face of defeat and disaster. A symptom of the strength of this national will was a collective refusal to assimilate to foreign conquerors or host societies. Amost all small peoples have disappeared in the course of time, but not the Jews. Individual Jews have fused with more numerous and powerful nations among whom they lived, but the persistence of the Jewish remnant indicates an especially vital will to group survival at the core of Judaism. The Jewish people continued to live because it willed continuously to live—a circular analysis which appeals to a vitalistic force as metaphysical as the religious explanations that Dubnow firmly eschewed.

For Dubnow, religion is a manifestation of the will to survive, rather than a rationale for survival in and of itself.[11] The downgrading of religion as a causal force, treating it as a kind of protective coloration for Jewish survivalism, facilitates redefining the Jews as no less and not much more than an acceptable nation in the modern secular sense. But, as we know, the Jews are not an ethnic group, as are not the Roman Catholic Church, the nation of Islam, the Mormons. Judaism does contain ethnic features. Indeed, there have been various forms of Judaism with different ethnic features. There have also been Judaisms whose ethnic component was minimal. There are central elements in Judaism, apart from custom and folklore, which have a character far more demanding, the violation of which brought far greater guilt, the observance of which was thought to bring far greater reward, than ethnic custom and folklore. The form of historic Jewishness that may have been the most ethnic was the Jewishness of the East European immigration generation in the New World, whose religious behaviour was relaxed whereas its Yiddish culture and social interconnectedness remained in place and was perhaps even strengthened by immigration.

    In Dubnowism, the will to survive functioned as a substitute for religion as the ultimate motivation for Jewish survival, because in this way Dubnow could accomplish for his philosophy of Jewish history what his ideology of Jewish autonomy sought to do on the political level. The latter was a blueprint for a Jewish community in which secular Jews are granted equal rights to participate, without any constrictions on their freedom to reject any Jewish religious doctrine or practice. His historiography offers a panorama of the Jewish past with which a secular Jew can fully identify, without experiencing any discomfort or strangeness. Dubnow constructed this history for his generation of East European Jews who had deep emotional ties to Yiddishkeit, but whose notions of the scientific order of nature, of human destiny, of aesthetic beauty and of progressive polity were taken from contemporary European civilization circa 1890.

    An indication of this in the *World History* is Dubnow's tendency to interpret conflicts between movements and groups in Jewry as manifestations of a centripetal tendency to the national versus a centrifugal tendency to the universal. Rather than treating past confrontations first and foremost on their own terms, Dubnow often projects onto them the tensions felt by the Jewish intelligentsia of his time and place—especially the tension between giving priority to the special agenda of the Jews and serving causes seemingly more cosmopolitan. (See, for example, Dubnow's conception of the underlying issues dividing the Pharisees and Sadducees. The contrast between the national and the universal in relation to rationalistic Jewish philosophy appears in his discussions of Maimonides and Spinoza.)

    The duality which Dubnow tried to bring into balance was that characteristically Jewish problem, in the recent diaspora at least, of living simultaneously in two worlds, a Jewish and a modern one. His solution, on a more existential level than ideology or historiography, is perhaps indicative of something at work in contemporary ethnicity. I suggest that contemporary ethnicity is an affirmation of a heritage not as an all-encompassing way of life, but as a mode of participation in the larger arena. It is a far more self-conscious stance than the habit of premodern men and women who follow in the footsteps of their parents.

Modern ethnicity is a solution to who one is—a solution combining self-acceptance and deliberate appropriation of an inheritance. This appropriation is voluntary and selective, varying from individual to individual and from stage to stage in his or her life. In its political mode, modern ethnicity may involve a struggle to secure those social means to perpetuate a tradition, or it may be a means of claiming a share in the distribution of existing political power, or it may be a tactic in the fight for separate national sovereignty. Ethnicity as a modern stance chooses participation in a larger universalized version of civilization whose essential features are derived from the West, together with a vigorous self-assertion, sometimes with an exploitative willingness to make use of powerful emotions of belongingness to mobilize a following, certainly with a militant refusal to disappear into one of the other attractive cultures. In a mild-mannered, liberal, humanitarian version, this was Dubnow's stance. And his creativity in this sphere may be of much greater interest to Jewish history than any of his specific reconstructions of the past.

NOTES

1. The German edition, *Die Weltgeschichte des Jüdischen Volkes*, translated by Dr. A. Steinberg, was published in Berlin by the Jüdischer Verlag between 1925 and 1929. The Russian edition was published in Riga between 1936 and 1939. The Hebrew translation, *Divrei yemei am olam*, a felicitous rendition of the German title, was translated by Barukh Krupnik and published in Tel Aviv by Dvir between 1929 and 1939; it has been frequently reprinted and a newly edited version was issued in 1958. A Spanish translation appeared in Buenos Aires between 1928 and 1952. A Yiddish edition also appeared in Buenos Aires between 1948 and 1952. An English translation by Moshe Spiegel (unfortunately very awkward and sloppy) was published by Thomas Yoseloff Co. between 1967 and 1973.

2. On these and other figures see Walter Laqueur and George L. Mosse, eds., *Historians in Politics* (London, 1974).

3. For a more extended treatment of Dubnow's growing up, see Robert M. Seltzer, "Coming Home: The Personal Basis of Simon Dubnow's Ideology," in the *AJS Review* 1 (1976), pp. 283–301.

4. Dubnow's autobiography, *Kniga Zhizni (Book of Life)*, appeared in three volumes: Vol. I (to 1903), Riga, 1934; Vol. ll (1903–1922), Riga, 1935; Vol. III (1922–1933), Riga, 1940; Repr. in New York, 1957.

5. For example, "Letters on Old and New Judaism," pp. 83–88, in Koppel S. Pinson, ed., *Nationalism and History* (Philadelphia, 1958). See also Robert M. Seltzer, "From

Graetz to Dubnow: The Impact of the East European Milieu on the Writing of Jewish History," in David Berger, ed., *The Legacy of Jewish Migration: 1881 and Its Impact* (New York, 1983), pp. 49–60; and Robert M. Seltzer, "Ahad Ha-Am and Dubnow: Friends and Adversaries," in Jacques Kornberg, ed., *At the Crossroads: Essays on Ahad Ha-Am* (Albany, 1983), pp. 60–72.

6. For example, Dubnow's reflections on having observed firsthand the leaving for America of Russian Jews in 1904, *Kniga Znizni* II, p. 16: "These wanderers, creators of Jewish America, will later be blessed when they more than once will save their mother, the European diaspora, from death."

7. Indicative of his change in attitude toward the Yishuv is the contrast between his 1907 comment about political Zionism as a "web of fantasies" and his addendum in 1936 where he acknowledges that the Zionist achievement has been quite substantial and that for him "times have changed." "Letters on Old and New Judaism," English version, p. 164.

8. Interpreting the duties of the people of Israel in the diaspora in a positive sense (although not denying the mystical condition of *galut*) is found in some versions of the Lurianic Qabbalah; interpreting the dispersion of the Jewish people as the setting for the actualization of mission to convey ethical monotheism to the world is found in some versions of nineteenth-century Reform Judaism.

9. Section 59 of Volume Ten is entitled "Equality in States with National Minorities."

10. See Ben-Zion Dinaburg (Dinur), "Simon Dubnow on his Seventy-fifth Birthday" (in Hebrew), *Zion* 2 (January 1936), pp. 95–128 and the studies of Dubnow in Simon Rawidowicz, ed., *Sefer Shimon Dubnow (Simon Dubnow, in Memoriam: Essays and Letters)* (London, 1954) and Aaron Steinberg, ed., *Simon Dubnow: The Man and His Work (A Memorial Volume on the Occasion of the Centenary of His Birth)* (Paris, 1963). Both these memorial volumes contain material on Dubnow's historiography and the effect of his writings in the 1920s and later.

11. See especially the article by Raphael Mahler in Rawidowicz, ed. *Sefer Shimon Dubnow*, pp. 89–135, and Mahler's shorter article in Steinberg, ed., *Simon Dubnow: The Man and His Work*, pp. 57–72. Yehezkel Kaufmann's criticism of Ahad Ha-Am's concept of a national will to survive applies equally to Dubnow. (Kaufmann, *Golah ve-nekhar*, 2nd ed. [Tel Aviv, 1954], Vol. II, 348–385; also Vol. I, 433–455.)

9
Ethnicity and Freedom in the
Philosophy of Horace M. Kallen

WILLIAM TOLL

In an era when most professional philosophers scorned political analysis,[1] Horace Kallen stands out because of his desire to assess the individual within social contexts.[2] The great polarities debated by the proponents and critics of the modern spirit—the One versus the Many, supernatural authority versus scientific uncertainties, nationalism versus internationalism—are all explored in Kallen's writings. As a pragmatist like his friend John Dewey, Kallen tested ideas by their consequences; but unlike Dewey, he made specific cultural references rather than the generalized "individual" the basis on which a social philosophy must rest.[3] "Cultural pluralism," the theory of group and ethnic relations for which Kallen is best known, became a major metaphor for at least one wing of what David Hollinger has termed the cosmopolitan, left-of-centre intelligentsia of the 1920s through the 1950s. But it also played a major role in modernizing American Jewish thought. As a response to the psychological problems of identity and loyalty and to the challenge of political radicalism, Kallen offered a flexible concept of ethnicity for intellectuals who did not feel that traditions must be provincial or that socialism alone could cure society's ills.[4]

Some critics have cited Kallen's failure to discuss social stratification, especially class conflict, as well as his unwillingness to consider how ethnocentrism might constrict a humane social vision. Philip Gleason has also cited Kallen's "romantic racialism" and argued that cultural pluralism "has always been more a vision than a vigorous theory."[5] As a liberal, Kallen did cavalierly argue that social class as a category and "inevitable conflict" as a historicist vision merely abrogated individual responsibility. In addition, early in his career he did romanticize ethnicity as an organic quality. But as he adopted more sophisticated views of the psyche, he saw ethnicity as a set of subconscious resources on which the personality might draw to meet shifting social demands. As American Jewry developed a secular consciousness, such a view of ethnicity provided the ideological leeway for it fully to accept citizenship in a new land. Indeed, Kallen played a dual role in American intellectual history. In his teaching at the New School for Social Research in New York from its founding in 1919, and in his voluminous writings, he showed pragmatic liberals an integral relationship between ethnic loyalty and humane pluralism. Within the smaller domain of American Jewry, he provided the Conservative rabbinate (the heirs of the "historical school") with the metaphor that allowed them to adapt religious loyalty to a secular society.[6] Because Kallen more than any other writer reconciled the polarities of American immigrant consciousness with the dominant philosophical themes of his age, this paper will focus on the origins and permutations of his thought and will turn only tangentially to its consequences.

As a young man Kallen exhibited the anxieties of identity and loyalty typical of immigrant intellectuals who were caught between the provincialism of their ancestors and the lures of a cosmopolitan world. His father, Jacob David Kallen, was born in Latvia, but had resettled in Silesia where he became an Orthodox rabbi. In search of opportunity, he went off to peddle in America. He returned several times, but when deported from Silesia in 1888, he brought his growing family to Boston. Horace, his eldest son, was then six years old. Rabbi Kallen honoured ritual as the cement of community, and forbade Horace to attend the secular public school until the truant officer intervened.[7] Though Kallen never felt close to his father, he did develop respect for the culture which had produced such an intensely loyal personality. As he wrote to his gentile friend, the English classicist and Zionist sympathizer, Alfred Zimmern, shortly after his father's death in December 1917, "His death has made some kind of change in me. . . . His generation is the last that elected to live under a self-imposed discipline and that created its own environment wherever it went. . . . Just in so far as he conceded nothing, he died a victor. I rather suspect that people like I are living on the interest of that self-restraint and consistency of purpose for ideal things which characterized my father's generation."[8]

Like Morris R. Cohen, Jacob Loewenberg and other Harvard contemporaries from immigrant families, Kallen sought tolerant mentors to replace his withdrawn and dispossessed father.[9] In one of them, the American literary historian, Barrett Wendell, Kallen found not only a friend, but a view of American history that allowed him to establish his intellectual roots in the country of his adoption. As a central theme, Wendell emphasized the Old Testament origins of the Puritan social vision, so that Jewry for Kallen was transformed from the archaic ritual of his father to prophetic injunctions for social justice and Jobian courage to face nature's irrationality.[10] But psychologically, Wendell merely shifted the balance between traditional authority and individual freedom which Kallen had seen in his father; he did not condone a radical break with one's past. His Lowell lectures of 1905, which Kallen later stated had greatly influenced him, interpreted the American Revolution as the only one in history fought to preserve a constitutional order. "In the general temper of America," he wrote, "the deepest characteristic is idealism kept within the bounds of order." Wendell further assured his listeners that immigrant youth of Irish, Italian and Jewish origins who had appeared in his classes had uniformly displayed this respect for order.[11] While Kallen displayed more enthusiasm for Jeffersonian freedoms than for Hamiltonian authority, he never relinquished an Aristotelian sense of balance.

Once open to the historical influence of an Hebraic tradition on American culture, Kallen was more receptive to personalities in contemporary Jewry who also emphasized democratic fellowship and unprejudiced inquiry. To revitalize Jewish traditions among college students, in 1906 Kallen helped found the Harvard Menorah Society, the first of its kind in the United States, which was to sponsor Jewish cultural events. At a summer camp he met Solomon Schechter, the president of the reorganized Jewish Theological Seminary in New York.[12] Schechter, a recent arrival from Cambridge University in England, welcomed the American separation of church and state because it did not require that Jews renounce their religious faith in exchange for full citizenship rights. It also allowed for a "Catholic spirit" in Israel by enjoining the federal government from supporting any religious body. Within the Seminary, Schechter advocated personal piety through prayer, ritual and the study of Torah and Talmud, but he also welcomed "scientific" scholarship to validate the folk basis of religious communities. In contrast to Reform rabbis, he staunchly supported Zionism, which he saw as a secular bulwark against the aimless individualism that lured college youth.[13] Schechter's receptivity to internal debate in the context of historical continuity brought Jewish culture to life for Kallen after his father's pedantry had dessicated its philosophical spirit.

Kallen also experienced the prejudice that conflicting ethnic loyalties engendered, as well as the refuge that people might find in ethnic cohesiveness. In his first teaching position at Princeton between 1903 and 1905, he was told that had the university known he was Jewish he would never have been hired. His former Harvard professors Barrett Wendell and Edward Everett Hale counselled him to learn what he could about the social types at Princeton and to persevere, "like a good soldier in an unhealthy climate."[14] Returning to Harvard for graduate study, Kallen met Alain Locke, then an undergraduate in philosophy, who in 1907 was to become America's first black Rhodes scholar. While Locke apparently encountered no overt racial discrimination at Harvard, the undercurrents of social exclusion persisted. When he and Kallen were both on fellowship at Oxford in 1907–1908, and Locke was excluded from social events because of the presence of southern whites, Kallen wrote with indignation to Wendell. He received a shocking response that suggested how prejudice affected even the most sophisticated people. "My own sentiments concerning negroes," Wendell wrote, "are such that I always decline to meet the best of them . . . at table. Professionally, I do my best to treat negroes with absolute courtesy. It would be disasterous [sic] to them . . . to expose them in private life to such sentiments of repugnance as mine."[15] In the face of social ostracism at Oxford, Kallen and Locke discussed at length cultural pluralism as a philosophy on which the dignity of a pariah group might be based. When each man returned to America, he found his warmest support among journalists and cultural nationalists of his own ethnic group.[16]

The conflicts generated as diverse peoples with insular ethnic loyalties were redistributed through an expanding industrial economy provided Kallen with a theme for explaining the tensions in urban America. The philosophical basis for resolving group tensions and for relieving individual disorientation Kallen found in the work of William James. Indeed, James became Kallen's mentor, because clearly the two were bent on parallel courses, in rebellion against deterministic traditions and committed above all to the moral efficacy of the free individual. The era in which James matured was dazzled by the research of Charles Darwin, who as James understood him, argued that life evolved through unconscious "natural selection," as hereditary traits rather than rational choice determined survival. Believing passionately that morality could have meaning only if the will was free, James turned to Kant's hopeful view of human judgment. Kant had argued that the mind had been created apart from nature by a benevolent God. It had been endowed with unique faculties, the most important of which was reason, which could derive laws and principles from the observation of nature. To experience the ideals which lay behind phenomena, however, the mind must rely on "intuition" or faith. As a post-Darwinian, James was able to collapse the Kantian categories of mind and nature by arguing that the mind lay *in* nature and had gradually evolved to a point of self-consciousness.[17] *A priori* truths or essences were logically unnecessary, even though celestial mechanics did imply a natural order. Rather, men should be satisfied to validate partial explanations for natural phenomena and should accept a plurality of truths as a concommitant to a plurality of consciousnesses. The human effort, then, lay in verification, and as propositions were subjected to more rigorous analysis, perhaps a final sense of order could be perceived. As James told Kallen, "Truth is constituted by verification actual or possible, and beliefs, however reached, have to be verified before they count as true. The question whether we have a right to believe anything before verification concerns not the constitution of truth but the policy of belief. It is usually poor policy to believe what isn't verified."[18]

Kallen was captivated by a philosophy that postulated free choice and made truth so thoroughly variable, yet required the individual to create a community for verification. James's colleague and intellectual rival, Josiah Royce, in popular lectures on "Loyalty," also believed that free will could satisfy emotional needs only when absorbed in a cause.[19] Royce more than James also appreciated the ethnic diversity of the American people and granted each group its distinctive values so long as each respected the emotional bonds of others. Mordecai Kaplan, in fact, suggested that American Zionists read Royce to understand the psychology that underlay their own crusade.[20] But Royce also postulated an Absolute Unity beyond individual experience against which all social loyalties were to be seen as partial and tentative. To Kallen, Royce's view of truth as dependent on a teleological whole rather than as part of a persistent process of partial verification seemed an unnecessary regression to the supernatural. As his friend Jerome Frank later analysed the lure of Royce, "James, you, and humble me, who revolt against the totalitarian yearning for unity, are . . . men engaged in fighting against an unusually strong desire in themselves for systems."[21]

The crucial struggle Kallen waged to free the individual from parochial systems lay with the idea of religion. Joining the Jamesian effort to reconcile the apparent irrationality of nature with an evolutionary view of mental processes, Kallen defined religion as an experience with a creative natural force rather than as an institutional creed. James saw religion as an effort by the mind-in-crisis to focus on objects that symbolized an orderliness beyond human experience. "The gods we stand by are the gods we need and use," he had written in *The Varieties of Religious Experience*.[22] Emphasizing that the mind functioned on many levels including the subconscious, all of which needed fulfilment, James chastised scientists who saw rational explanation as sufficient to human understanding. Religion for James became an individualized search. As Joseph Wood Krutch later noted, James and Henri Bergson led the battle against scientific materialism by seeking "loop-holes for the spirit."[23]

Kallen, however, had initially experienced religion as social ritual rather than a personal transformation and he could not separate it from a communal setting. Like James he was willing to accept the existence of the irrational, or as he once clinically wrote, "electrical fields" to which people in preconscious states might be particularly susceptible.[24] As a graduate student in the Harvard psychological laboratory he had induced such states through drugs like nitrous oxide and through yoga to experience various forms of consciousness. The subconscious he saw as the source of creative energy which, when properly symbolized in the conscious mind, might resolve the psyche's emotional tensions. Such religious experiences became acts of faith in whatever was discontinuous, contingent, beyond rational explanation.[25] But Kallen argued that religious institutions transformed inspiration into ideological creed and mindless ritual which stifled subsequent yearnings for inspiration.[26] Beginning with preconscious contact with a possible "supernatural," religion ended by subjecting emotional needs to bureaucratic manipulation.

The distrust of religion was reinforced by the work of Freud, whom Kallen seems to have read intensively during World War One. As his Harvard friend Edwin Holt noted as early as 1915, Freud's emphasis on "the wish" as a unit of cognition demonstrated how each mind shaped rather than merely absorbed stimuli, and how an understanding of human agency required a complex analysis of suppressed motives.[27] Kallen accepted Freud's general description of mental processes, which provided a sophisticated schema for channeling the energy that James and Bergson had described. By then asserting pragmatism's faith in the scientific method with which Freud aggressively concurred,[28] Kallen could criticize the psychological consequences of religious behaviour.[29] As he bluntly wrote in 1918, perhaps under the influence of his father's recent death, "the essential difference between religion and philosophy is this, that religion keeps you weak and insists on your being dependent, while philosophy makes you strong and independent."[30]

But unlike Freud, Kallen did not fear human nature itself, and he distinguished carefully between religion as a primitive form of human response and faith as a mental process without which no hypothesis could be tested.[31] Nor did he divide society into the few who were capable of rational thought and the many who needed religion as an "illusion" through which their hysteria could be channelled. Though Kallen and Freud had both passed their childhoods in the ghettoized world of central

Europe, the latter worked with disturbed psyches in a Vienna dominated periodically by cynical anti-Semitic politics,[32] while Kallen had observed ordinary people whose occasional irrationality had been induced under laboratory conditions. Both he and James had faith that America's varied groups could satisfy their emotional needs within the bounds of a democratic polity.[33] But to release and revitalize those subconscious cultural bonds which familial tensions like Kallen's own had distorted, social forms other than churches would be needed.

The spiritual grounding for a specifically Jewish revival Kallen found in the book of Job, which he presented as a uniquely modern account of human integrity from which all people could profit. The story, he believed, had originally been a folk tale illustrating the vanity of human nature in the face of an omnipotent creator. As a literary work, however, it had been introduced into ancient Israel as a subversive act by an author of prophetic imagination.[34] Kallen presented it as a Greek tragedy to dramatize how the human will must stubbornly assert itself against arbitrary authority. For Kallen, God became the force of nature apart from human judgment of good and evil, and the dogged prophets, he called, the "atheists of their day."[35] He then restored the text of Job to a facsimile of its original, which, he believed, could express the modern, Jamesian revolt against Darwin far better than the official version which had been redacted by the priestly class. Only the advent of modern science had begun to rectify the stark Jobian vision, he wrote.[36]

Man's sophisticated intelligence in the face of nature's creative energy convinced Kallen that American Jewry might reject the isolation of the ghetto while resisting the arid rationalism of Reform rabbis. "Ghetto" for Kallen was a state of mind usually reinforced by a locale, and he reserved the term as an epithet for all efforts to isolate Jews from the most progressive sources of reform. The ascension of a Louis D. Brandeis in the American Zionist movement, for example, Kallen heralded as a break from ghetto ideologies and the advent of a leader whom a secularized American Jewish youth could follow.[37] In the 1930s he characterized Jewish neighbourhoods in the Bronx as ghettoes because these new outlying Jewish community centres seemed uninterested in incorporating Jewish themes into their youth programs.[38] By copying gentile social activities, they cut themselves off from the crusades for social justice centered on the lower East Side. Most of all, he feared that Jewish settlements in Palestine would become isolated "utopias" or "oriental ghettoes" rather than segments of a cosmopolitan society and federated world Jewry.[39] On a visit in 1927, he commented repeatedly on the insularity of local Zionist leaders. They seemed, he said, to exhibit Ahad Ha-Am's worst fears[40] about rigid bureaucrats who would defend the interests of local projects against the wider need for a cultural revival and toleration of other Jewish movements.

Like so many intellectuals who favoured an historical and evolutionary view of Jewry, Kallen abhorred Reform Judaism because it seemed to abstract ideas like the Unity of God and the Brotherhood of Man from their distinctive roots in Jewish history. For people like Kallen, who had to believe that the struggles of their fathers must have had a purpose, Reform rabbis like Kaufmann Kohler of Hebrew Union College seemed to suggest that Jews as a distinctive people had outlived their usefulness. In place of revitalizing traditions, Reform substituted a preoccupation with the Gentile; it launched a "mission of Israel" to preach "ethical monotheism." Such a "mission," however, Kallen, along with secular Zionists like Brandeis and the radical rabbi Mordecai Kaplan, saw as a rationalization for the betrayal of the multiethnic America which they envisioned. To counteract Kohler, Kallen noted that in the ancient world monotheism had not been a belief unique to the Jews. Furthermore, Christianity had spread the doctrine throughout Europe and the Americas. He concluded that a "mission" to preach monotheism would be historically arrogant, intellectually pointless, and socially self-serving.[41] As the Zionist movement grew in America after 1914, Kallen was among those urging Brandeis to challenge Reform leaders directly in order to convert the laity and to leave the rabbis without a following.[42]

A specific philosophy for American Jewry, however, would have to provide a cohesive ideology, not simply examples of Jobian courage or harangues against Reform. What might be the basis for cohesion without religion, however, remained vague. Walter Lippmann stated the issue bluntly in a letter in 1916 to the editor of the Menorah Journal. "If you get rid of the theology and the biological mysticism, and treat the literature as secular, and refuse to regard the Jews as a . . . chosen people, just what elements of a living culture are left?"[43] For Kallen from 1913 through 1921, the most useful movement for revitalizing Jewish consciousness seemed to be Zionism. He admitted in the 1950s that before World War One he had been unfamiliar with most European Zionist ideologies, except for the Herzlian demand for a legally guaranteed homeland and Ahad Ha-Am's concern for a reintegrated, secular Jewish personality.[44] Nevertheless, he developed a uniquely American vision of a Zionist renaissance which would not only rebuild Palestine as a refuge for European Jewry, but would enable American Jews to understand that *all* modern peoples could have multiple loyalties to a provincial past and a cosmopolitan future. "Cultural pluralism" soon became Kallen's general metaphor to legitimate the divided loyalties of the individual, the multiple lines of attachment for groups, and the benefits to American society that had many cultural standards upon which to draw.[45]

Kallen's Zionism rested on a comprehensive analysis of modern history and reflected his concern that American Jewry must first of all understand itself. The major change in Europe and America in the nineteenth century, he concluded with Charles Beard, had been the growth of an industrial system which had generated a rootless proletariat. Only the admittance of that proletariat to full social and political parity would relieve the enormous tensions in all industrial societies.[46] In America the Progressives, a group that included many Jews, such as Abraham Lincoln Filene and Louis Brandeis, had recognized the rootlessness and suffering of workers, but had suggested merely restructuring governmental forms or providing some social insurance programs rather than seeing in the ethnic group the basis for social rehabilitation. Only a handful of intellectuals like Randolph Bourne or social workers like Jane Addams appreciated the vision of America as a multicultural society.[47] In 1909 Rabbi Judah Magnes had defended the right of ethnic groups to maintain themselves, but as Sarah Schmidt has shown, Kallen convinced Brandeis and others that the American constitution, in protecting the civil rights of an individual, included his right to affiliate with a minority cultural group.[48] When Kallen suggested to Brandeis that the Zionists cooperate with American spokesmen for East European nationalities seeking independence, some conservative Zionists accused him of trying to create "an Austrian Empire of the United States."[49] But Kallen saw his effort as an attempt to turn subconscious loyalties to a defence of what American society had become.

As a Zionist in the Mid-West, where he taught philosophy at the University of Wisconsin from 1912 to 1918, he organized Menorah Societies from Columbus, Ohio, to New Orleans, and as far west as Berkeley, California.[50] At the same time, he entered with great zeal into the new American Jewish Congress movement. Initially, Kallen saw the congress as a device to federate American Jewry behind Zionism, but he soon came to see that federation was the crucial means for creating a new sense of secular Jewish identity. The congress as a political tactic promised to wrest control of American Jewry from the German elite headed by Jacob Schiff. But more important, as a cultural process it was designed to teach a new political style to the American-born children of the East European immigrants.[51] When Brandeis reluctantly cancelled it in mid-1917 because it threatened to publicize the divisions among Jews on American entry into World War One, Kallen was bitterly disappointed. He feared that the delay in subjecting ethnic leadership to democratic scrutiny would continue to breed resentment among Jews. It would also reinforce the conspiratorial image of the Jews which the war had propagated.[52]

Kallen combined the congress movement on the political front with an intense interest in democratizing the economic perspective of American Jewry. Contacts with Jewish students from Palestine who were studying agricultural economics at Berkeley from 1915 through 1918 led him to read broadly in the literature of the cooperative movement.[53] As much as any member of the Brandeis faction, he had contacts who persuaded him to believe that in postwar Palestine agricultural planning and the construction of economic infrastructure were far more important than any political advocacy of the sort envisioned by Jabotinsky or even Weizmann.[54]

Consumer cooperation as a structure for rational planning and ethnicity as a subconscious basis for loyalty would seem to rest on different assessments of how and why social cohesiveness might arise. In his early writings on ethnic loyalty, Kallen reflected the Jamesian psychology which attributed social cohesiveness to "instincts." In 1920 he wrote, "social life is organic because the human body is an organism and the institutions of society are the collective elaboration of instincts."[55] As social scientists abandoned the view that acquired characteristics could be inherited or that social groups cohered through "instincts,"[56] Kallen attributed cohesiveness to "culture," that is, to learned though internalized affections.[57] He insisted that social loyalties followed individual preference and not class interests. The followers of "isms" and ideologies, Kallen told Dewey, had ignored "the personality—the seat of values—because they lack faith in themselves."[58] Advocates of "rugged individualism" as well as their socialist antagonists, by defining humanity as "producers" and by lauding the virtues of labour, had incorrectly tied the individual to his necessities, to his biological drives.[59] Societies, he argued, should be organized through separate congresses of consumer and producer cooperatives with individuals joining both to represent their alternating interests; government, in turn, would have as a major function moderating between the consumer and producer interests.[60]

Kallen never argued that ethnic groups incorporate directly into cooperatives, as for example, W. E. B. DuBois did for blacks in the 1930s,[61] because he never reconciled the subconscious sources of ethnic loyalty with the cosmopolitan tastes of the individual consumer. But by the time he published his major study, *The Decline and Rise of the Consumer,* in 1936, he had adopted the view that ethnic grouping must be through a voluntary effort. For Kallen, cohesion to revitalize a sense of historical identity and cooperation to implement the expression of individual tastes had become the defining prerogatives of the free individual. As he wrote Van Meter Ames, "As I see it, life . . . can be nothing except consummatory and aesthetic."[62]

The view that the personality shared a suppressed ethnic memory which might emerge in irrational yet creative drives set Kallen apart from most liberals like John Dewey, who generally ignored the concept of cultural pluralism.[63] In response to Kallen's first essays on the psychology of ethnicity in 1915, Dewey wondered whether such cultural sentiments were not romantic and exaggerated. He told Kallen that he hardly thought of his own English heritage, which was admittedly generations in the past.[64] In his books on individualism and social reconstruction in the 1930s, Dewey spoke to the hypothetical worker who shared with his fellows primarily alienation from mass production. Indeed, he argued that deracination and subjection to assembly-line uniformity were for many European critics the defining characteristics of the American worker.[65] Kallen, in his concurrent writings on individualism, defined it as consciousness based on different subconscious motives that built different needs into each personality. Although people might believe that they made free choices, they also extended into the future demands bred into their personalities in the past.[66] The Jobian dilemma, as it were, had become introverted and subjected to the wily mechanisms of the subconscious, as the individual, by asserting the interests of his ethnic group, endowed it with the courage to persist. Indeed, Kallen refused to sign the Humanist Manifesto of 1933 because it emphasized what individuals held in common rather than those differences which gave each person a sense of his own worth.[67] Precisely these differences generated the vitality in human communities, and they assured that policies predicated on eradicating the past in the name of a utopian ideology would destroy the personality and create social chaos. It should not be surprising, therefore, that Kallen had no correspondence with a rationalist like Morris R. Cohen despite their identical social heritage and formal education.[68]

By seeing that the subconscious as well as institutions conveyed traditions, Kallen came close to the views of Jewish religious thinkers like Mordecai Kaplan, Will Herberg and Jacob Agus, who saw Judaism as an evolving civilization providing ethical and spiritual guidance to meet the anxieties unique to modern Jews.[69] Rabbi Robert Gordis could have been paraphrasing Kallen when he wrote in 1962, "We are beginning to understand that the freedom of the individual is an illusion unless he also possesses freedom of spiritual self-determination, the right to maintain the voluntary group associations which are the hallmark of human functioning."[70] Indeed, because Kallen and the rabbis accepted the premises of Schechter's "Catholic Israel," they appeared together in many symposia on Jewish education during the 1950s and early 1960s, occasionally under the sponsorship of the American Association for Jewish Education, Dropsie College or the Reconstructionist movement.

But even with Kaplan, the rabbi least likely to speculate on the nature of the Divine Presence or the necessity for messianism in resolving anxieties, Kallen drew the line at the need to posit a unified "supernatural."[71]

Indeed, the division between Kallen and the theologians paralleled that between his mentor James and Kaplan's philosophical guide, Josiah Royce. In an era which borrowed Kallen's language about pluralism but transferred it to a religious community, he continued to insist that secular toleration based on ethnic self-consciousness alone could fulfill the American democratic tradition. Secularism had become for him a "faith" because it constituted the ideal toward which he was working.[72] Yet as a liberal yearning for a stable social order, he legitimated American Jewry's multiple loyalties only by leaving the content of Jewish ethnicity an enigma. Unlike his contemporary, the literary scholar Ludwig Lewisohn, he never used the theme of Jewish uniqueness to coax a romantic religiosity back into the Jewish middle class. Compared with the abstract programs of Mordecai Kaplan for reunifying American and world Jewry, Will Herberg's *Angst* over the eclipse of messianism, and Robert Gordis's plea for renewed piety,[73] Kallen applauded the process by which a community of Jewry was to be constantly reformed.[74] The wide acceptance of his pluralist terminology suggests how contemporary Jewry, while regrouping within religious institutions, has followed his anticlerical rebellion.

NOTES

Financial support for the research and preparation of this paper has been provided by a Rapoport Fellowship at the American Jewish Archives, Cincinnati, Ohio, and by a grant from the Samuel Rosenthal Foundation, Cleveland, Ohio.

1. Bruce Kuklick, *The Rise of American Philosophy, Cambridge, Massachusetts, 1860–1930* (New Haven and London, 1977), p. 246.

2. Milton Konvitz, "Horace Mayer Kallen (1882–1974): Philosopher of the Hebraic-American Idea," *America Jewish Yearbook, 1974–75* (Philadelphia, 1974), pp. 75–77.

3. John Dewey to Horace Kallen, 31 March 1915, Horace M. Kallen Papers, American Jewish Archives. (All references to letters will be to the Kallen Papers at AJA, unless otherwise noted.)

4. David Hollinger, "Ethnic Diversity, Cosmopolitanism and the Emergence of the American Liberal Intelligentsia," *American Quarterly* (1975), 140, 142–143. Moses Rischin, "The Jews and Pluralism: Toward an American Freedom Symphony," in Gladys Rosen, ed., *Jewish Life in America* (New York, 1978), p. 62, seems unnecessarily general when he sees cultural pluralism as a theory of "modernization" to secularize tradition for American Jews. Important strata of Jewish intellectuals chose other social philosophies from liberalism to Marxism to achieve the same end. How various intellectuals responded to their subconscious sense of cultural continuity can be seen in Allon Gal, *Brandeis of Boston* (Cambridge, Mass., 1980), pp. 42–44, 145–146, 150–152, 169; H. N. Hirsch, *The Engima of Felix Frankfurter* (New York, 1981), pp. 10, 22–23, 98; David Hollinger, *Morris R. Cohen and the Scientific Ideal* (Cambridge, Mass., 1975), pp. 10–11, 55, 208–212.

5. Milton Gordon, *Assimilation in American Life* (New York, 1964), pp. 148–149; Orlando Patterson, *Ethnic Chauvinism: The Reactionary Impulse* (New York, 1977), pp. 165–171. Even Hollinger, "Ethnic Diversity," p. 142, ignores Kallen's view of the individual. John Higham, "Ethnic Pluralism in Modern American Thought," in *Send These to Me: Jews and*

Other Immigrants in Urban America (New York, 1975), p. 208, reiterates Kallen's disregard of the relationship between ethnicity and class stratification, but emphasizes also the normative intent of "cultural pluralism." Philip Gleason, "American Identity and Americanization," in William Petersen, et al., *Concepts of Ethnicity* (Cambridge, Mass., 1982), p. 97.

6. See particularly, Will Herberg, *Protestant-Catholic-Jew: An Essay in American Sociology* (New York, 1960 ed.), pp. 1–3, 28–41; Robert Gordis, *The Root and the Branch: Judaism and the Free Society* (Chicago, 1962), p. 105; Mordecai M. Kaplan, *The Future of the American Jew* (New York, 1948), pp. 70–71.

7. Horace M. Kallen, "Interview with Milton Konvitz and Dorothy Oko," 31 August and 3 September 1964, Kallen Papers.

8. Horace Kallen to Alfred Zimmern, 11 January 1918, and Kallen to Wendell Bush, 8 December 1917.

9. Hollinger, *Morris R. Cohen,* pp. 10–11; Jacob Loewenberg, *Thrice-Born: Selected Memories of an Immigrant* (New York, 1968), pp. 8, 14–15.

10. Barrett Wendall, *A Literary History of America* (New York, 1917), pp. 42, 45–46.

11. Barrett Wendell, *Liberty, Union and Democracy: The National Ideals of America* (New York, 1907), pp. 8–11, 85–86, 174 (quotation); Horace Kallen to Nathan Glazer, 2 November 1956, Kallen Papers; Kallen to Mark A. DeWolfe Howe, 11 November 1924, Mark A. DeWolfe Howe Papers, Houghton Library, Harvard University.

12. Kallen, interview with Konvitz and Oko, notes that Schechter made the Hebraic tradition "come alive" for him, after his own father had killed it.

13. Solomon Schechter, *Seminary Addresses and Other Papers* (Cincinnati, 1915), pp. viii, 50, 62, 93 (Zionism).

14. Barrett Wendell to Horace Kallen, 3 November 1903, Edward E. Hale to Kallen, 25 February 1904; Ludwig Lewisohn, *Up Stream, an American Chronicle* (New York, 1922), p. 120.

15. Barrett Wendell to Horace Kallen, 3 November 1907; Lowenberg, *Thrice-Born,* p. 83; Horace Kallen, "Alain Locke and Cultural Pluralism," in *What I Believe and Why, Maybe: Essays for the Modern World,* ed. Alfred J. Marrow (New York, 1971), pp. 131–134.

16. John E. Bruce to Alain Locke, 15 December 1911, Alain Locke Papers, Howard University. Alfred A. Moss, Jr., *The American Negro Academy: Voice of the Talented Tenth* (Baton Rouge, 1981), p. 121.

17. Kuklick, *Rise of American Philosophy,* pp. 162–164; William James, *Pragmatism and Other Essays* (New York, n.d., Washington Square Press ed.), pp. 65, notes that the achievement of nineteenth-century philosophy was to replace the notion of an "essence" or "substance" constituting reality with a poetic or all-knowing mind, but that Pragmatism sidesteps the whole issue. For James's contemporary, George Santayana, sidestepping that issue was impossible, even fanciful. See Santayana, *Character and Opinion in the United States* (New York, 1934), p. 160.

18. William James to Horace Kallen, 1 August 1907.

19. Josiah Royce, *The Philosophy of Loyalty* (New York, 1908), pp. 16–19, 23, 27 (where the origins of loyalty as a moral choice are derived from Kant), 275, 278.

20. Mordecai Kaplan to Herman Rubenowitz, 17 September 1914, Mordecai Kaplan Papers. AJA.

21. Jerome Frank to Horace Kallen, 19 July 1931, Jerome Frank Papers, Sterling Library, Yale University. Kallen's fundamental devotion to individual freedom is noted in Rischin, "Jews and Pluralism," p. 71.

22. William James, *The Varieties of Religious Experience* (New York, 1958, Mentor ed.), p. 259.

23. Joseph Wood Krutch, *The Modern Temper* (New York, 1929), p. 132.

24. Horace Kallen, *Why Religion* (New York, 1927), pp. 41, 302, 312.

25. Ibid., pp. 63–64, 75.

26. Ibid., pp. 110, 213.

27. Edwin B. Holt, *The Freudian Wish and Its Place in Ethics* (New York, 1915), pp. 28, 47–49, 60; Edwin Holt to Horace M. Kallen, 20 April 1915.

28. Sigmund Freud, *The Future of an Illusion* (New York, 1927), p. 90; Horace Kallen, *Why Religion*, p. 110; Kallen, *What I Believe*, p. 110; Horace M. Kallen, *William James and Henri Bergson: A Study in Contrasting Theories of Life* (Chicago, 1914), pp. 144–146, 195–197.

29. For pragmatism's relationship to science as method see David Hollinger, "The Problem of Pragmatism in American History," *Journal of American History* 67 (June 1980) pp. 92–94.

30. Horace Kallen to Lucille Cazier, 31 January 1918.

31. Kallen, *Why Religion*, pp. 46, 282; Kallen, *Secularism Is the Will of God* (New York, 1954), pp. 11–14.

32. Carl E. Schorske, *Fin-de-Siècle Vienna: Politics and Culture* (New York, 1980) pp. 118–128; John M. Cuddihy, *The Ordeal of Civility: Freud, Marx, Levi-Strauss, and the Jewish Struggle with Modernity* (New York, 1974), pp. 10, 13, 17, 31–32.

33. Hollinger, "Problem of Pragmatism," p. 99. "The advancement of human purpose [for pragmatists] in the world through inquiry was not to be limited to professional scientists or even to philosophers. It was a mission and a fulfillment open to virtually anyone."

34. Horace M. Kallen, *The Book of Job as a Greek Tragedy* (New York, 1959 ed.), pp. 7, 10–12, 22–27. Note that Hollinger, *Morris R. Cohen*, p. 234, says Cohen as rationalist accepted the standard view that Job submitted to God's will because nature contained an ultimately benevolent, rational order.

35. Horace M. Kallen to Julian Mack, 19 January 1915, Kallen to Eric Bentley, 7 April 1959, Kallen Papers; Kallen to Abraham Cronbach, 16 January 1928, Abraham Cronbach Papers, AJA; Kallen to Jerome Frank, 19 September 1949, Frank Papers.

36. Kallen, *The Book of Job*, pp. 76–78.

37. Horace M. Kallen to Henrietta Szold, 28 October 1914.

38. Horace Kallen to Stephen Wise, 26 July 1933, Stephen Wise papers, American Jewish Historical Society; Horace M. Kallen, *Judaism at Bay: Essays toward the Adjustment of Judaism to Modernity* (New York, 1932), pp. 195, 231; Kallen, "Of Them Which Say They Are Jews," and Other Essays on the Jewish Struggle for Survival* (New York, 1954), 52–54.

39. Horace Kallen to Louis D. Brandeis, 20 December 1913, Kallen papers, YIVO.

40. Horace M. Kallen, *Frontiers of Hope* (New York, 1929), p. 109.

41. Kallen, *Judaism at Bay*, p. 28. See also Mordecai Kaplan to Henry Hurwitz, 17 March 1916, Kallen Papers; Horace Kallen to Judge Julian Mack, 19 January 1915.

42. Louis D. Brandeis to Horace Kallen, 25 January 1915.

43. Walter Lippmann to Henry Hurwitz, 24 December 1916, Kallen papers.

44. Horace Kallen to Moses Rischin, 4 December 1953.

45. Horace Kallen to Ruth Ludwig, 14 August 1915; Horace M. Kallen, "Democracy versus the Melting Pot, Part Two," *The Nation* (25 February 1915), pp. 217–220, provides his earliest and classic argument for the view that the individual has a residual group consciousness and that democracy must guarantee that the individual, in achieving "self-fulfillment," can satisfy his cultural needs. The normative and romantic intent of cultural pluralism is noted in Higham. "Ethnic Pluralism," pp. 205, 207.

46. Kallen, "Democracy versus the Melting Pot, Part One," *The Nation* (18 February 1915), p. 193.

47. Ibid., p. 193; Randolph Bourne, *War and the Intellectuals: Collected Essays, 1915–1919*, ed. Carl Resek (New York, 1964), includes both "Trans-National America," *Atlantic Monthly* (1916) and "The Jews and Trans-National America" (*Menorah Journal*, 1916). Bourne and Kallen split over pacifism, which Kallen opposed when America entered World War One. See Bourne to Kallen, 8 May 1917.

48. Sarah L. Schmidt, "Horace M. Kallen and the Americanization of Zionism" (dissertation, University of Maryland, 1973), pp. 117–123, 126, 133; *Dissenter in Zion, from the Writings of Judah Magnes*, ed. Arthur Goren (Cambridge, Mass., 1982), pp. 19–20.

49. Kallen, "Democracy versus the Melting Pot, Part II," p. 220; Kallen to Louis D. Brandeis, 25 May 1916, Jacob DeHaas to Kallen, 22 February 1917.

50. Horace Kallen to Stephen Wise, 11 March 1915, Stephen Wise papers, AJHS.

51. Horace Kallen to Stephen Wise, 9 November 1915, Wise papers; Melvin Urofsky, *American Zionism from Herzl to the Holocaust* (New York, 1976), pp. 165–181.

52. Horace Kallen to Henry Hurwitz, 10 October 1917, Menorah Association papers, AJA; Henrietta Szold to Horace Kallen, 19 October 1917.

53. David Shapiro to Horace Kallen, 22 November 1915; Kallen to Shapiro, 27 November 1915; Shapiro to Kallen, 5 January 1917.

54. Louis D. Brandeis to Horace Kallen, 1 May 1919, Stephen Wise papers; Horace Kallen to Jacob DeHaas, 28 April 1919; DeHaas to Kallen, 7 May 1919; James P. Warburg to Kallen, 23 November 1920; Kallen to Emanuel Mohl, 17 January 1920; *Trial and Error: The Autobiography of Chaim Weizmann* (New York, 1949), pp. 262, 267.

55. Horace Kallen to Rachel Brooks, 14 August 1920.

56. Hamilton Cravens, *The Triumph of Evolution: American Scientists and the Heredity-Environment Controversy, 1900–1940* (Philadelphia, 1978), pp. 148, 172, 210–211.

57. Horace M. Kallen, "The Struggle for Jewish Unity," (1933), pamphlet, Kallen papers.

58. Horace Kallen to John Dewey, 16 February 1932.

59. Kallen, *Individualism*, pp. 90, 132–134, 170, 229–234; Horace M. Kallen, *The Decline and Rise of the Consumer: A Philosophy of Consumer Cooperation* (New York, 1936), pp. ix, xii–xiii, 61, 390.

60. Kallen, *Decline and Rise of the Consumer*, 12pp. 341, 428, 441–444; Horace M. Kallen, *A Free Society* (New York, 1934), pp. 91–94.

61. W. E. B. DuBois, *Dusk of Dawn: An Essay toward an Autobiography of a Race Concept* (New York, 1968 ed.), pp. 207–216, argues that blacks, like all peoples, are consumers and should initiate a commonwealth fulfilling consumer needs.

62. Horace Kallen to Van Meter Ames, 5 April 1937.

63. Horace Kallen to Jacob Billikopf, 30 December 1947, Jacob Billikopf papers, AJA; Ludwig Lewisohn, *The American Jew: Character and Destiny* (New York, 1950), pp. 46–47, also emphasizes the subconscious recesses of ethnic consciousness.

64. John Dewey to Horace Kallen, 31 March 1915.

65. John Dewey, *Individualism, Old and New* (New York, 1929), pp. 22–23.

66. Ibid., pp. 4, 96; Kallen, *A Free Society*, p. 80, argues that the past can only be modified, because it has been bred into each personality. See the reiteration of this view in Michael Novak, "Pluralism in Humanistic Perspective," in Petersen, *Concepts of Ethnicity*, pp. 42, 51.

67. Horace Kallen to Paul Kurtz, 27 July 1973.

68. Kallen, "Interview with Konvitz," mentions his debates with Morris R. Cohen, who saw himself as an eighteenth-century cosmopolitan with no specific cultural component. Cohen, of course, did assist the immigration of refugees from Nazi Germany in the 1930s.

See Franz Boas to Nelson Glueck, 2 May 1934, Franz Boas papers, American Philosophical Society, Philadelphia, Pennsylvania.

69. Kallen, perhaps because of the early influence of Solomon Schechter and his sympathy for Mordecai Kaplan, strongly endorsed the Jewish Theological Seminary, in Kallen to Henry Hurwitz, 25 October 1933, Louis Marshall papers, AJA.

70. Gordis, *Root and Branch*, p. 16.

71. Jacob Agus to Horace Kallen, 5 January 1962; Kallen to Agus, 13 January 1962; Kallen to Milton Konvitz, 30 April 1951; Kallen papers, VIVO.

72. Horace Kallen to T. S. Eliot, 5 May 1955; Kallen, *Secularism Is the Will of God*, p. 12.

73. Mordecai Kaplan, *Judaism in Transition* (New York, 1936), pp. 80–87; id., *The Future of the American Jew* (New York, 1948), p. 395; id., *The Religion of Ethical Nationhood: Judaism's Contribution to World Peace* (London, 1970), pp. 132, 177; Will Herberg, *Judaism and Modern Man: An Interpretation of Jewish Religion* (New York, 1951), pp. 15–16, 116–118, 261–268; Arthur A. Cohen, *The Natural and the Supernatural Jew: An Historical and Theological Introduction* (New York, 1962), pp. 6–7, 191, 201, 209–218 (criticism of Mordecai Kaplan); Gordis, *Root and Branch*, pp. 91, 158–164; Lewisohn, *American Jew*, pp. 84, 93–94, 108, 165.

74. Once a tolerant polity left the individual free to explore his subconscious loyalties, Kallen then enjoined him to persist.

4

JEWS, COMMUNITY AND WORLD JEWRY

Introduction

Proverbial to the soundness of spirit of the Jews of North America has been their critical sense of community—their relations one to another, to their diverse neighbors and to the Jews of the diaspora. Part IV is devoted to selectively portraying the greater Jewish communal response in a century which saw the Jews of North America become, in association with the Jews of Israel, the prime guardians of Jewish civilization.

In the twentieth century, Jewish philanthropy and Zionism, taken together, have continually constituted the mainstays of Jewish solidarity in the face of a hostile world. For the Jews of Canada, however, Zionism, from its inception, provided a common denominator for national organization that it did not for the historically divided Jews of the United States. After briefly comparing the Canadian with the American, British and South African Jewish experiences, Gerald Tulchinsky, a historian of Canadian Jewry, focuses on the early activities of Clarence de Sola, a Sephardic patrician, singularly responsible, in Tulchinsky's opinion, for endowing Canadian Jewry and Canadian Zionism with a cohesive identity and an enduring élan.[1] Yet, ironically, an astute student of Canadian diplomatic history, David J. Bercuson, demonstrates that during World War Two the Canadian Zionist Organization and its allies were powerless to influence Canadian Palestine policy.

With the outbreak of World War One, the most paramount and longstanding of all Jewish social traditions, the tradition of Tsedakah, acquired a new magnitude and mission. Suddenly, and for the first time, American Jewry was driven to accept major responsibility for the world's less fortunate Jews. With the collapse of Europe and the virtual end of mass immigration, the prime obligations for Jewish philanthropy during and after the war were transferred permanently to the United States. A careful historian of Jewish philanthropy, Marc Raphael, delineates how the organizational and fund-raising skills adopted during World War One became central and permanent features of a sophisticated new American Jewish philanthropy reaching to our own day.

The fundamental problem of sustaining Jewish identity and community outside the great metropolitan centers in North America, particularly in thinly populated regions, has proven to be a continual Jewish dilemma. To explore the problems of communities devoid of a varied and supportive Jewish institutional and human network, the anthropologist, Gerald Gold, an ingenious student of French Canada, juxtaposes the American and the Canadian small-town Jewish experience in two regions where a French-speaking minority has constituted the largest single ethnic group. In comparing the experiences of Jews from central and western Europe who first settled in Opelousas in southwestern Louisiana in the mid-nineteenth century with the experiences of Russian Jews who came to live in Timmins in northern Ontario in the early twentieth century, Gold seems to imply that whatever their differences in religious culture, history and social and economic position, small-town Jews in North America have been unable to maintain a viable group life for long. To be free to be Jewish in some fashion requires a medley of Jewish institutions, a density of numbers, and a range of individual choices that simply do not exist in small cities and towns away from great metropolitan areas unless they are revitalized by new economic developments, Gold argues. As a result, the children of small-town Jews either depart for the great metropolitan centers where more favorable options and conditions prevail, or simply fade away and die out. The decline and often virtual extinction of pioneer Jewish communities in the Maritime Provinces, in western Canada, and in the American South and West, testify to the prevailing trend.[2]

If the fear of the loss of Jewish identity has never been far from the surface among Jews, the progressive intensification of anti-Semitism in the late nineteenth and particularly in the early twentieth century proved to be fraught with catastrophe beyond belief. In Europe, World War One, signalling as it did the breakdown of nineteenth-century civilization, carried with it grim forebodings for the future as western democracies showed themselves inadequate to the problems of the peace and unready to recognize the demoniacal appeal of Hitler, Nazism and the new total-itarianism to Europe's beaten, fearful and rootless millions. For Europe's Jews, there was, in addition, a diabolical new anti-Semitism, in addition to the older variant, that would culminate in the horrors of the Holocaust. In North America, acquiescence in the Nazi madness abroad sparked an increasingly virulent organized anti-Semitism at home that thrived on the xenophobia of a depression-ridden era. In his detailed chronicle of the ugly incidents, anti-Jewish restrictions and pathological anti-Semitic rhet-oric and ideology that marked the period, particularly in Quebec, Irving Abella registers the widespread tensions that afflicted Jews, south as well as north of the border, as World War Two approached.

After World War Two, a whole new climate of culture in North America opened the way to an unprecedented era in interethnic relations. Under such vastly changed Canadian and world conditions, a uniquely gifted Jewish interpreter of Franco-Jewish relations was to discern in their common minority experiences the lineaments of an underlying mutuality. Pierre Anctil is the first to write of Abraham Klein, one of Canada's most distinguished poets, as the harbinger of a new tradition of Canadian com-munity, linking Francophones and Jews.[3] Klein's linguistic, no less than his cultural virtuosity in English, French, Hebrew and Yiddish, nurtured by his lifelong residence in Montreal, enabled him to give multicultural voice, as has no other poet in North America, to a condition distinctive to his native province yet suggestive for an understanding of the cultural currents that have surged in and about North America's "jargoning" ethnics, which are only beginning to be identified and explicated by histo-rians and other historically minded scholars.

NOTES

1. See David J. Bercuson, *Canada and the Birth of Israel: A Study in Canadian Foreign Policy* (Toronto, 1985).

2. See Abraham Arnold, "The Mystique of Western Jewry," in M. Weinfeld, W. Shaffir and I. Cotler, eds., *The Canadian Jewish Mosaic* (Toronto, 1981), pp. 259ff. and other essays in this valuable book. Also see Peter I. Rose with the assistance of Liv Olson Pertzoff, *Strangers in Their Midst: Small Town Jews and Their Neighbors* (Merrick, N.Y., 1977), esp. chap. 8, "City Lights: The Children of the Small Town Jews," pp. 160–194.

3. Also see Gerald Tulchinsky, "The Third Solitude: A. M. Klein's Jewish Montreal, 1910–1950," *Journal of Canadian Studies* 19 (Summer 1984), pp. 96–112; Miriam Waddington, ed., *The Collected Poems of A. M. Klein* (Toronto, 1974), pp. 296ff.; and Usher Caplan, *Like One That Dreams: A Portrait of A. M. Klein* (Toronto, 1982).

IO

Clarence de Sola and Early Zionism in Canada, 1898–1920

GERALD TULCHINSKY

tanding before the delegates to the second Zionist Congress in late
August of 1898, Theodor Herzl issued a call to his sympathizers
everywhere to persuade their Jewish communities to support
Zionism.[1] Over the next few years, his appeal was answered by the remarkable spread of the Zionist movement throughout the Jewish world,
including the growing Jewish community of Canada. Indeed, even before
Herzl's summons to action, several Canadian Zionist groups were already
in existence. As early as 1887, a branch of Chovevei Zion (Lovers of Zion)
was formed in Montreal by Alexander Harkavy, who, a year or two later,
returned to New York, where he achieved great eminence as a Yiddish
lexicographer.[2] Another Montreal Zionist group, formed five years later,
was known as Shavei Zion (Return to Zion); in 1894 some of its members—under the sponsorship of the Paris Rothschilds—actually attempted to settle in Palestine in an agricultural colony at Hauran, in the
northeastern corner of what is now Jordan.[3] After a harrowing year of
unremitting toil, problems with officials and repeated plundering by
Druse neighbours, the Montrealers returned to Canada much sadder and
considerably poorer than when they had left. But the new political
Zionism which Theodor Herzl had set in motion with the publication of
his *Der Judenstaat* (*The Jewish State*) and the convening of the first and
second Zionist congresses in 1897 and 1898 revived the hopes of some of
these early Canadian adherents to the ideal of Jewish national revival in the

land of Israel. In 1898 Zionist groups were organized in Montreal, Toronto and Winnipeg, as well as in Kingston, Hamilton, Ottawa and Quebec.[4] Within a year of Herzl's summons to action, then, Canadian Zionists had begun to organize themselves on an impressive scale; in November of 1899, a national federation of these groups was established, and over five hundred memberships (known as "shekels," the ancient Hebrew coin) and nearly twice as many shares of the Jewish Colonial Trust (which was intended to be the financial instrument of the Zionist movement) were sold to hundreds of Jews across Canada. A few months later, Clarence de Sola of Montreal, the president of the Federation of Zionist Societies of Canada, triumphantly cabled to Herzl, "Canada Takes 1,000 Shares of the Jewish Colonial Trust." Not content with these successes, de Sola, who enjoyed the support of a small but devoted and growing group of followers across Canada, set about spreading the Zionist message to as many Jews as could be reached from the Atlantic to the Pacific—even in the isolated Jewish farm colonies on the prairies.

The history of the Zionist movement in English-speaking countries has recently benefited from the addition of two major works, Gideon Shimoni's study of Zionism in South Africa and Stuart Cohen's account of Zionism in the communal politics of Anglo-Jewry.[5] Added to the work of Yonathan Shapiro, whose authoritative analysis of leadership in the American Zionist movement was published in 1971, these books provide a comparative analytical framework of the Zionist experience in English-speaking countries in which any study of Canadian Zionism must be located.[6] In his *Jews and Zionism: The South African Experience (1910–1967)* Shimoni convincingly demonstrates that, because of unique factors prevailing in South Africa, Zionism there, from the 1890s to the present, assumed and retained a "remarkable prominence . . . , both as a communal institution and as a normative mode of Jewish identification."[7] Shapiro, who, in assessing the American experience in his *Leadership of the American Zionist Organization 1897–1930*, starts with the assumption that "the American version of Zionism served the function of providing an ideology of survival for the Jewish community," examines the power struggle among the contenders for leadership of the Federation of American Zionists as a manifestation of changes and innovations in Zionist ideology. He finds that as leadership passed from immigrant Yiddish-speaking intellectuals to native-born Americans, official Zionist ideology was transformed from orthodox Zionism, which emphasized that Jews were a separate political and cultural identity, to Palestinianism, the more limited goal of mobilizing Jews to help build Palestine as a Jewish national home.[8] Finally, in his *English Zionists and British Jews: The Communal Politics of Anglo-Jewry, 1895–1920*, Cohen explores the tension produced in

British Jewry by "the interaction between the message that political Zionism proclaimed to the Jews as a collective and the response of Jews as members of different units."[9] In this process, taking place over a span of twenty-three years, Zionism only gradually overcame the opposition of the British community's entrenched patriciate and those with alternative philosophies. And, although this achievement was accomplished, Cohen points out, by a successful strategy of "institutional infiltration" which resulted in the orderly transfer of the more powerful communal offices to the Zionists, it had the effect of weakening the single-mindedness with which the movement began.[10]

These three studies share a basic theme, as Cohen expresses it: "Individual communities developed distinctive patterns of political association which, despite their overall adherence to a recognizably Jewish political tradition, were framed as specific responses to the peculiarities of their different situations." In Cohen's view, "Jewish history is necessarily heterogeneous,"[11] and is largely determined by Jews—as far as possible—within local contexts. In South Africa, the circumstances were conducive to that community's becoming a bastion of an intensely loyal Herzlian Zionism which emphasized the political over the rival schools of practical or cultural Zionism. In the United States and Britain, on the other hand, such a clear-cut normative identification was not possible because of both demographic factors and pre-existing and competing political ideologies and structures. If these, then, are some of the major benchmarks of the Zionist experience in those three countries, it is appropriate to ask whether any of them are relevant to the history of Canadian Zionism between 1898 and 1920. To attempt to answer the question, it is necessary to discuss the context in which Canadian Zionism evolved and the career of the leading personality of the movement, Clarence de Sola, who, for so many years, headed the Federation of Zionist Societies of Canada, the country's principal Zionist organization. If he was not, as will be seen, a typical Canadian Jew, de Sola certainly became the exemplification of the movement as its titular leader, chief spokesman and major ideologue. Thus, through the prism of de Sola's Zionist career, one may not only see how the movement evolved but also examine some of the important features of Canadian Jewry during a period encompassing significant numerical growth and geographical spread as well as far-reaching social and economic changes.

Clarence Isaac de Sola was the third son of Montreal's renowned rabbi-scholar, Abraham de Sola, who from 1847 to 1882 served as the spiritual leader of the Spanish and Portuguese congregation She'erith Israel (Remnant of Israel). The de Solas were relatively well integrated into Montreal anglophone society. Abraham, who was educated in London, became a lecturer in Hebrew and Oriental Literature at McGill University in 1849—only one year after his arrival in Montreal—and ten years later he was awarded an honorary doctor of laws degree in recognition of his scholarly eminence.[12] He was a highly respected figure in the city's literary circles and achieved international recognition for his scholarly attainments, as well as for having received the honour of opening the 1872 session of the United States House of Representatives with prayer. Born in 1858 into this family of great learning and social prominence, Clarence de Sola also came into considerable wealth. His mother was the daughter of a well-to-do Quebec City merchant and the sister of Jesse Joseph, a very wealthy Montreal businessman.[13] Supported by a substantial independent income, the de Solas lived well. Clarence attended the elite High School of Montreal and lived with his family in a large house on a fashionable west-end street, close to his Jewish and non-Jewish friends. Although not as scholarly as his distinguished father, Clarence, according to his diary, maintained a rigorous and ambitious program of reading, mostly history. He closely followed domestic and foreign political affairs, especially British, and, like most late Victorians, he was fascinated with the great European and imperial conflicts. But he was by no means a one-dimensional man; he was, in his youth, active in a variety of sports, including boxing, fencing, lacrosse and football, and he regularly attended musical and dramatic events in Montreal.

As an upper-class Montrealer, de Sola attended the balls, dances and soirees given by his friends in the anglophone elite. He was not especially close to them but, judging from his diary, he was apparently at ease in their company, and shared much of their outlook, culture and prejudices. His closest friends, however, were Jewish and were drawn almost entirely from the small group of old, established and well-to-do families associated with the Spanish and Portuguese synagogue. Picnic outings, holidays, literary and social evenings almost invariably were confined to this intimate group of the younger Jacobs, Davises, Aschers, Mosses, Harts, Josephs, Kellerts and Samuels, the sons and daughters of well-to-do merchants, manufacturers and real estate developers who comprised the Montreal equivalent to New York's "Grandees" and "Our Crowd."[14]

De Sola's principal preoccupation after finishing high school in 1875, however, was business. After a number of early ventures, he became the agent of Belgian interests as well as a shipbuilding contractor and an entrepreneur in a variety of large-scale bridge, railway and harbour ventures across Canada. Enjoying important connections among Quebec federal Liberals, de Sola expanded his business activity in a prosperous manner during the Laurier government's tenure in office. His diaries reveal that, between 1900 and 1911, frequent trips to Ottawa and long discussions with cabinet ministers, and even with the prime minister himself, were part of de Sola's regular routine. Through his business connections in Belgium, he became that country's consul in Montreal, an honour which brought him into frequent social contact with Ottawa and Quebec politicians, the Montreal anglophone plutocracy, governors general and a wide variety of English and European nobility.

Even with considerable personal wealth, the distinction of a learned father and, most important, the intensely proud lineage of the Spanish and Portuguese Jews—a pride that might have kept him aloof from other Jews—de Sola began in the late 1870s to take an interest in the welfare of the Montreal Jewish community. In the 1880s and 1890s, this community was undergoing rapid and far-reaching transformation. During the 1880s, Montreal's Jewish population rose by over 170 per cent, several new synagogues were established and numerous organizations formed, while the city experienced the cultural diversity brought by these new arrivals.[15] De Sola joined the Young Men's Hebrew Benevolent Society—the Jewish philanthropic organization which was dominated by members of the established community—and in March 1881 he helped to organize a local branch of the London-based Anglo-Jewish Association. As a youth, he was only perfunctorily involved in these matters until 1882, when the plight of hundreds of Jewish refugees arriving in Montreal following the East European pogroms moved him profoundly. Until then, entries in his early diaries referring contemptuously to "Polacks"—by which apparently he meant all East European Jews in Montreal—suggest that his parental home and social milieu were not especially tolerant even of the Jews who had arrived during the 1860s and 1870s. The Polacks were nearly always regarded as troublesome people by the de Solas and those who spoke at meetings were seen as somewhat comic figures.[16] But after 1882, in the privacy of his own diary, never again did De Sola use expressions of contempt toward his fellow Jews. Deeply stirred by the outrages that year against Jews in eastern Europe, he was again shaken in 1903, in 1905 and, once more, by the events of World War One. Thus, despite his early arrogance, which was shared by many other members of the small Spanish and Portuguese group, as well as by Montreal's British-born Jews—of whom there was a small but noticeable number—de Sola was drawn sympathetically to his people regardless of their different backgrounds.

Besides developing a sympathetic view of Jewish peoplehood, he was also faithful to the Jewish religion. Throughout his life, he always kept the Sabbath, ate only kosher food, regularly attended synagogue, read the Tanach (Bible) regularly, studied Hebrew, taught young children in the Sunday school at the Spanish and Portuguese synagogue and took great pride in helping religion classes to build and decorate its *succah* (booth to honour the fall harvest festival). He carefully observed the holidays in the traditional Orthodox manner according to the Spanish and Portuguese *minhag* (custom). Clarence de Sola, like his brother Meldola, saw the Reform movement as essentially un-Jewish.[17] On the eve of Rosh Hashana, in October 1880, contemplating what he believed was the tendency of Reform to undermine Jewish traditions, he speculated on the need for an Orthodox synod to mobilize the upholders of true faith against these threats. He confided to his diary a vow to follow the tradition of his distinguished ancestors as "staunch and learned upholders of the principles of Judaism and the rights of our race. Can I not emulate the example of my forefathers? Can I not prove myself a true and worthy Sephardi? I shall try."[18] (Much later, when de Sola was planning a new home bearing the imprint of his personality, he wanted it designed in the Andalusian style "such as a Sephardic Jew might have lived in when the Sephardim were at the height of their power in Spain.")[19] Clearly, then, de Sola's Sephardic pride was coupled with a sense of responsibility to uphold the Orthodox Jewish traditions and to combat the forces of internal disunity within North American Jewry. Unity and pride combined to become de Sola's program of action in Canadian Jewish affairs and, from the early 1880s onward, he was, in a real sense, intellectually and emotionally ready for the challenge and the opportunity which Zionism would provide for the activist role he was to assume. And, as one of the major figures in the "established" Jewish community who had some sense of the increasing diversity of Montreal Jewry, he soon came to recognize the need to fuse together the disparate groups in Canadian Jewish life.

In the early 1880s de Sola came under the influence of Dr. Moses Gaster, the Chief Rabbi of the Sephardic congregations of England between 1887 and 1918. Gaster maintained regular correspondence with both Clarence and his older brother Meldola, rabbi of the Montreal Spanish and Portuguese synagogue following the death of his father. Rabbi Gaster was, in the 1890s, one of the few prominent rabbis in Britain who openly espoused Herzl's Zionism.[20] Although Gaster's correspondence with Meldola was devoted to religious questions, Clarence reported regularly to him on the progress of Zionism in Canada, and received in return news of the movement in Britain and Europe, as well as encouragement and advice.

Having launched upon their Canadian Zionist campaign, de Sola and his associates in Montreal and across the country worked assiduously in spreading their message. Rabbis Meldola de Sola and Abraham Kaplan delivered pro-Zionist messages from their Montreal pulpits, and Rabbi Aaron Ashinsky could be relied on to address the downtown Jews in Yiddish. From Toronto, Dr. John Shayne and, later, Sam Kronick carried the cause to English- and Yiddish-speaking audiences across southern Ontario, and in Ottawa Archie Freiman was active, while, in Winnipeg, Harry Weidman and others canvassed the burgeoning Jewish population of that city and other western centres. These men were only a few of the many who joined what to many was this Jewish revival. In Montreal, key figures such as Dr. Wortsman and, later, Reuben Brainin, successively editors of the *Kanader Adler* (*Canadian Eagle*), and Hirsh Wolofsky, the publisher, supported Zionism, although they were not always pleased with de Sola's autocratic manner and lack of cultural depth. Women also played a major role in this development; they formed their own associations and national connections, while early on they adopted their own special projects in Palestine and laid the basis for the Hadassah organization which emerged in 1918. Children and youth were organized into clubs called Young Judaea, and by 1917 a separate national association of that name was formed by Montreal law student Bernard Joseph, who, not long afterwards, joined General Allenby's Jewish Legion to free Palestine from the Turks.[21]

The Federation of Zionist Societies of Canada by the end of the first decade of the twentieth century attracted growing numbers of Jews to its constituent organizations. While it was not exactly a mass organization, the federation's total national membership rose from a few hundred in 1899 to 1,000 in 1903, to more than 2,000 in 1906, and to nearly 6,600 in 1920, when the total Canadian Jewish community numbered a little over 125,000 people.[22] Although this was the equivalent of one in every nine or ten adults—only a modest segment of the nation's Jews—it is important to note that the movement attracted a significant proportion of the members of the small Jewish communities located in the lesser towns and cities beyond the metropolitan centres of Montreal, Toronto and Winnipeg. Of the nearly 6,600 members in 1920, for example, the non-metropolitan communities, with only 23 per cent of the Canadian Jewish population, supplied nearly half.[23] In many of these centres, almost all the adult Jewish population were members of the federation. In these communities, where the Jewish populations were expanding rapidly during this decade of massive immigration, the largely lower middle-class shopkeepers, peddlers and tradesmen, who were overwhelmingly newly arrived immigrants, became members of the federation through local societies. Leading members of these new communities, such as Isaac Cohen of Kingston, Joseph Enzer of Fort William and Bernard Myers of Saint John, were all East European immigrants of the 1890s or early 1900s.[24] While no doubt many of these individuals brought their Zionism from Europe, as new arrivals they were susceptible to appeals for support from such leading Canadian Jews as de Sola, whose direction of the Zionist cause provided, in their eyes, a Canadian as well as a Jewish legitimacy to the movement. The federation, moreover, offered the only sustained and organized link between the various Jewish communities of Canada, not only binding them together for a common purpose but also supplying a forum where their representatives could meet. Thus, aside from the widespread intrinsic appeal which Zionism had for many Jews as a cause in its own right, the federation established the only nationwide organizational framework for Jewish expression in Canada.

While directing this expansion, Clarence de Sola and his Montreal associates had a well-developed sense of independence—which sometimes came across as hubris—from the American Zionists, who were beset by what de Sola considered to be far too much internal dissension and unnecessary duplication of organizations. In December 1901, de Sola advised Theodor Herzl to nip this problem in the bud, while pointing out that, because of weakness and confusion among Zionists in the United States, various local Zionist associations in Des Moines, Detroit and Syracuse had recently asked to join the Canadian federation instead of the American.[25] In a letter to Herzl's successor, Max Nordau, in February 1910, de Sola underscored the success of Zionism in Canada as opposed to the experience in Britain and the United States. According to de Sola, the "larger contribution per capita of our population than in any other country," had been due "to the fact that we have insisted all along on the strictest discipline in our ranks, with the result that our organization is strong and united, and schismatics have always found themselves in an utterly hopeless minority."[26] Not long afterwards, de Sola dispatched a somewhat acerbic letter to the Central Zionist Bureau in Cologne, pointedly disagreeing with proposed constitutional changes allowing the existence of more than one central Zionist authority in any one country such as Canada. De Sola wrote, "the greatest fault of the Jewish people to-day is their unwillingness to submit to discipline. In Canada," he boasted, "we have had a rigid, almost military discipline in our Federation."[27]

Although his letter reflected considerable arrogance, de Sola's belief that the Canadians were better organized was not his alone. As early as 1903, Herzl's adviser, Jacob de Haas—who, after visiting Canada and the United States, had a good basis of comparison—wrote to Herzl that "the movement here [in Canada] appears to be stronger and more solid than in the United States and altogether considerably different." Implying a comparison with unnamed American Zionist figures, he continued, "de Sola works very hard and is popular."[28]

Right from the beginning, it is clear that de Sola was determined to run his own show. In March 1899, in reply to a letter from Professor Richard Gottheil, the president of the Federation of American Zionists, requesting the Canadians to cooperate with their fellow Zionists in the United States, de Sola stated that the Canadians felt strongly "that the autonomy and individuality of [their] Federation should not be sunk or lost sight of. . . . As you must be aware," he lectured Gottheil, "the Canadian Jews have always maintained a very independent course in their communal affairs. . . . This feeling . . . is not dictated from any lack of good feeling towards our neighbours, but is simply the natural feeling of people living in a separate country, in which, to a certain degree, the sentiments and traditions are different from those of the neighbouring country."[29]

De Sola's philosophy of Zionism, as expressed in his addresses at Canadian Zionist conventions, never seems to have altered very much from the orthodox Basle program of Zionist aims to establish a Jewish national home in Palestine and the strategies adopted by the leaders of the world movement for its implementation. In a general sense, he was a loyal supporter of Herzl, perhaps partly because he was mesmerized by Herzl's personality and speeches, as well as by the respect and honours accorded to him in London at the Fourth Congress in the summer of 1900, and by the private visit he paid to Herzl in Vienna in the preceding June. Indeed, de Sola's very failure to attend any other congresses, even though Herzl, Nordau and Wolffsohn encouraged him to do so, is evidence of his willingness to accept decisions about strategies and tactics from those who, he believed, understood these matters better than he. At later Zionist congresses, in fact, the Canadian federation was more than not represented by English or American delegates or by any Canadian Jews who happened to be travelling to Europe. An examination of the Congress proceedings reveals that after presenting perfunctory reports Canadian delegates were never active in the debates.

This colonial attitude was not unique to de Sola or to the Canadian Zionists alone. Jews living elsewhere in the British Empire—in South Africa, for example, far from the dynamic centres of world Zionism—were also willing to accept direction from headquarters and work first to establish efficient organizations in their own countries, while providing what they could in the way of financial, moral and political support for the realization of their Zionist dream. To Clarence de Sola, the rising businessman who regularly negotiated contracts with Canadian federal cabinet ministers and senior civil servants, the discussions between Herzl and the Turkish Sultan, the Kaiser of Germany, the Emperor Franz Joseph and other European potentates were an entirely understandable and acceptable way of securing recognition of Palestine as the Jewish national home. He delighted in news of Herzl's high-level diplomacy and frequently embellished his letters and speeches to Canadians with information of this sort.

De Sola kept himself well informed of events in the Zionist world, moreover, through his correspondence not only with Rabbi Gaster but also with Zionist figures elsewhere, including, of course, those at the movement's headquarters in Vienna, Cologne and Berlin. He read the English Zionist press, as well as *Die Welt* and, more particularly, *The Maccabean*, the American Zionist monthly he circulated to Canadians to keep them informed of Zionist developments abroad. Once the Montreal-based *Jewish Times* became more favourable to Zionism in 1900, de Sola saw this publication as a more suitable vehicle for influencing the Canadian Jews, and he subsequently lost interest in the American-based *Maccabean*.

In response to the early anti-Zionism of the *Times*, which in 1898 considered the movement's "goals to be politically unattainable and economically unfeasable,"[30] de Sola and other Canadian Zionist spokesmen were at pains to point out that the Jewish state was meant to become a haven for Jews from countries where they were oppressed, not for American, Canadian and British Jews.[31] The issue of dual loyalty, loyalty both to Canada and to Jewish national revival, never seems to have bothered him. In a letter to one supporter, he stated,

> We regard the idea that the reestablishment of the Jewish state would throw suspicion upon the loyalty of Jews residing in other lands as too absurd to call for serious reply. To our minds, the Zionist movement aims at securing a home for Jews living in countries where they are suffering oppression. Those, who like ourselves, enjoy the same privileges as the other citizens of the countries we live in declare most emphatically our loyalty to the countries we live in notwithstanding that we are a nation.[32]

Despite the early concerns expressed in the *Jewish Times*, the question never at this time became a major issue in Canada.

As already noted, de Sola strongly favoured discipline and order, two elements which he found to be sadly lacking in Jewish public life. He believed that, with firm direction, Zionism could bring order out of this chaos and disunity which, in his opinion, had held Jews back for so many years. In a letter to de Haas early in 1903, shortly after several hundred delegates and observers from Halifax to Vancouver had attended the federation's third convention in Montreal, de Sola exulted, "how wonderfully our movement is uniting the scattered parts of our race."[33] He wrote in a similar vein to Jews in cities all across Canada. Encouraging Joseph Enzer of Fort William to form a local Zionist society, he wrote, "remember that one of the great aims of Zionism is to organize our entire race and solidify it under one governing body; hence there is a principle at stake in gaining the adherence of the inhabitants of even the smallest village." In this and in many other letters, de Sola carefully explained that the purpose of this unity was to achieve the goals of the Basle program, which included the obtaining of a legally secured home for the Jewish people in Palestine, the physical and economic development of that home-land and the awakening of Jewish national and spiritual consciousness through the development of Hebrew literature and everything that would raise the cultural level of the Jewish people.

Although cognisant of the importance of Zionism as an all-embracing Jewish revival—and though he seems to have accepted these nationalistic implications of the movement—de Sola also conceived of it in more practical terms. To a Jew in New Brunswick, de Sola pointed out that the aim of the Zionist movement was not to "restore the whole of the Hebrew race to Palestine. The object . . . is simply to restore to that country that portion of our race who are at present suffering from persecution, and who, as a consequence, are emigrating and seeking new homes."[34] More-over, he argued that "for an organized mass of people to flood these western countries under no direction," he continued, "and with no proper training for agriculture, or other means of living, will be disastrous, and must naturally only produce misery. The only feasible, practical and busi-ness-like solution to this situation is to settle these people in Palestine where they can be self-supporting in agricultural or other practical pur-suits." Thus, he saw Zionism as a practical solution to a problem facing the Jews of Canada on whom the burden of Jewish European immigration would otherwise fall, and whose financial resources would be inadequate to support the institutions and programs that would be necessary to assist them to settle and earn their living.

Although he often publicly stated, especially at annual conventions, that there were two tasks for Zionism in Canada—education and fund-raising—it is clear from his correspondence that fund-raising was by far the more important goal. Indeed, from the very beginning, the federation set fund-raising as its first priority. In addition to the shekel, the basic mem-bership fee for Zionists everywhere, and the sale of Jewish Colonial Trust shares, the Jewish National Fund to purchase land in Palestine was adopted early on as a Canadian special cause. Raising money, in de Sola's mind, was exactly the kind of role best suited to Zionists, because it was practical work. "Mere ebullitions of sentiment would prove inadequate unless supported by concrete achievements," he told the delegates to the national convention in January 1911.[35] "When we gather in Convention annually," he added, "the first thing that interests us is to see how much practical work our Federation has accomplished during the year, . . . above all, how much we Zionists have contributed in hard cash to the funds of the Movement." For most members of the federation's constituent associations, which were springing up in Jewish centres, large and small, across Canada, de Sola's prescriptions for Zionist action seemed an acceptable definition of what their functions ought to be. There were some internal tensions within the federation as to whether the mere gathering of money deserved as much attention as education or, as one dissenter, Abraham Fallick of Toronto, put it, "the proper understanding of Zionist principles and institutions."[36] But most members, like de Sola, emphasized that "Our Movement aims at an ideal but we are practical enough to recognize that it can only be attained through that which is material."[37] He would brook no opposition from "a man of no influence in the community, a comparatively recently arrived emigrant" who had dared to attack "the leading Jews in Canada, and the power and authority that they represent." Such leading Jews, he observed, contributed "about four-fifths of the . . . funds of the Movement every year in Canada [which] has been the cause of the success of Zionism in this country."[38] Thus de Sola made it abundantly clear not only where the priorities lay and that large donors were the ones who kept the federation alive in Canada, but also that fund-raising was virtually the only activity of note going on within the Canadian federation. Dissenters like Fallick and a few others who wanted to enrich its cultural program had to knuckle under or get out of the organization.

With his priority on fund-raising clearly established, De Sola was never prouder of the Canadian Zionists than in 1910, when at his suggestion they embarked on a scheme for the Jewish National Fund to purchase land for reclamation and settlement. This was exactly the kind of practical work that he wanted Canadians to undertake, and he took special interest in raising the necessary $10,000; once that amount was subscribed and collected, he had the federation take up a further land purchase arrangement the following year.[39] He also gave approval—although a guarded one—to the plans of a Winnipeg branch of the Ahuza movement to buy a 3,500-dunam tract of land at Sheikh Munis, north of Tel Aviv, where the Winnipeggers planned to settle and farm.[40] Negotiations for this purchase were well advanced when they were interrupted by World War One. The scheme eventually lapsed.

In fund-raising for various projects, in the size of its membership, in the adherence of women and youth, the federation was in a generally healthy condition by 1914. But the events of the war raised serious problems and, for a time, significantly altered the federation's hitherto unchallenged power, influence and legitimacy as a Canadian-Jewish communal institution and official spokesman of Jewry in the nation. The war also highlighted many of the major transformations in the social and intellectual life of Canadian Jewry that challenged the legitimacy of Zionism as

the sole vehicle for Jewish national aspirations. The war also contributed
to the emergence of discontent among young intellectuals in the Zionist
movement, who dissented from the philosophy espoused by de Sola and
his associates. The effects of the war on Canadian Jewry were profound.

By 1914 almost all the Canadian Jewish community comprised East
European immigrants who had arrived during the great migrations after
1900. Whether they were located in Glace Bay, Montreal, Brantford, Re-
gina or Vancouver, the hearts of these immigrants lay in the East, in the
Russian, Galician, Polish, Roumanian and Lithuanian towns and villages
where their close relations found themselves in the war zones. From 1914
to 1921, the Yiddish press, which by 1914 included three Canadian papers
that readers often supplemented with Yiddish dailies from New York,
carried news of starvation, forced migration and pogroms. Immediately
after the outbreak of war, Canadian Jews aided their stricken brethren
overseas, first through individual efforts, then through broader organizations such as the Ukrainian Jewish Farband, and finally, by 1915, nation-
wide associations such as the Canadian Jewish Alliance. The later association, as David Rome has demonstrated, provided the forum for demands
that a Canadian Jewish Congress be convened for marshalling the ethical,
moral and financial resources of the entire community to influence the
resolution of *all* Jewish issues that arose from the war, not only Zionism.[41]
In Montreal alone, three organizations arose, broadly representative of
major sectors of the city's Jewish socio-economic structure: the Canadian
Jewish Committee, "an uptown group"; the Central Relief, supported by
the Orthodox and the middle classes; and the People's Relief, which represented the working class.[42] From the standpoint of the Congress' proponents, Jewish claims at a postwar peace conference involved not only the
question of Palestine, but also the political rights of Jews still living in
eastern Europe. The advocates of the Congress were, therefore, directly
challenging the Zionist claims and assumptions that Jewish renewal lay
solely in the "upbuilding" of the national home. Until that ideal of messianic fulfillment would be reached, European war relief and Jewish civil
rights required immediate attention, and, though Zionists like de Sola
were certainly not hostile to these causes, Congress supporters believed
that the Federation would not give suitable priority to them.

Indeed, as early as 1905, de Sola and the federation had been so
sensitive to the tragedies of East European Jewry that, in the wake of the
Kishinev pogroms, the federation momentarily set aside its Palestine
causes and raised funds for relief of these Russian Jews.[43] But de Sola
believed that Congress advocates were too ambitious, and he refused to
help organize such a Congress. As he confided to his diary at the end of
March 1919, "I felt Palestine questions are being properly handled by the

Zionists and do not require Congress."[44] He also felt that "those questions that Congress might help to alleviate or solve—distress and persecution in Gallicia [*sic*], Poland, Russia &c. are not being approached or handled in a practical way by Congress." Like Judah Magnes, who opposed the American Zionists' taking part in the formation of an American Jewish Congress on the grounds that this would weaken Zionism, de Sola preferred to keep Zionism strictly oriented toward Palestine.[45] In refraining from Congress activity during the war, de Sola perhaps lost a major opportunity to deepen the Zionist appeal among the Jewish masses.

Besides the question of a Jewish Congress, the onset of war created serious political difficulties for all Zionists, especially for those living in countries like Canada which were combatants against Germany and its ally Turkey. Sensitive to the problems which might impede the realization of their aims in Palestine, and, in the immediate context, the protection of what already had been achieved, should the Zionist cause be identified with either side in the conflict, the world Zionist executive sought to remain neutral. De Sola was instructed to conduct Zionist affairs with circumspection. What is involved for Canadians was essentially the restriction on sending money directly to Palestine, so that money had to be forwarded indirectly through American relief organizations. But the war had the effect of seriously reducing fund-raising in Canada until about 1917 because of the uncertainty of the *yishuv*'s (Jewish settlement) fate and the emergence of other, more pressing concerns for Canadian Jewry. Moreover, at the outset of the war, de Sola and the federation, uncertain as to what they should be doing, appeared to contemporaries to be doing little, if anything, to preserve the movement's strength in Canada. Among those dissatisfied with de Sola's failure to provide more dynamic leadership to Canadian Zionism in 1914 and 1915 were young intellectuals like Abraham Roback, Louis Fitch and Hyman Edelstein, all of them associated with Montreal's *Canadian Jewish Chronicle*. The wartime period accentuated the Montreal Jewish community's vulnerability in French Canada, while it also highlighted the fact that Montreal Jewry was also beset by bitter intracommunal economic conflict and serious structural problems.[46] Taken together a variety of issues affected the lives of a significant and growing number of Canadian Jews to whom, it seemed, Zionism was not directly relevant. To the average Jewish garment worker in Montreal, Toronto or Winnipeg, for example, the affairs of the Amalgamated Clothing Workers Union were likely to be decidedly more important. And to those working-class Jews who might have been interested enough to join a Zionist group, the middle-class, English-language, fund-raising oriented, west-end led Zionist societies, which included clothing manufacturers (whom they considered to be sweatshop exploiters), would have been

less than satisfactory.[47] These individuals, most of them located in the
metropolitan centres and the larger secondary cities of Ottawa, Hamilton,
London and Windsor, tended to support the more idealistic and intellectually satisfying programs of the Poale Zion (Zionist Workers') and, for
the Orthodox, the Mizrachi, both of which were founded before World
War One and began to flouish in the 1920s outside the framework of the
federation.[48]

The war also accentuated the fact that certain features of Canadian
constitutional and political history had established for the Canadian Jewish community a context that differed significantly from that of American
Jewry. For example, loyalty to Britain's cause, which waxed positively
rhapsodic at times, provided Zionists with opportunities to identify their
purposes with Britain's imperial mission. As far back as 1903, when the
Uganda proposal (a temporary refuge for Jews in British East Africa) was
under consideration, de Sola had performed oratorical prodigies on the
subject of Zion's redemption under the British flag.[49] Fourteen years later,
when Allenby's armies were poised in Egypt for an assault against Palestine, de Sola saw the coming British liberation of Eretz Yisrael (The
Land of Israel) as the dawning of a new messianic age. He even announced at the fourteenth convention of the federation in 1917 that it was
now time for the re-establishment of the Sanhedrin as the supreme court
of Jewish law and governing council of the people of Israel.[50] Canadian
Zionists, therefore, unlike their American cousins, enjoyed the important
benefit of being able to identify their cause within the context of what Carl
Berger defines as British-Canadian nationalism and imperialism without
raising the implicit question as to whether or not adherence to Zionism
posed a serious problem for their loyalty to Canada.[51] Thus, when the idea
arose of forming a Canadian Jewish unit to fight in the imperial forces
conquering Palestine, de Sola, at first puzzled by the proposal, soon became one of its most ardent supporters. His work for this Jewish Legion
was one of his last acts on behalf of Canadian Zionism. Amidst considerable tension and acrimony within the organization, he relinquished the
presidency at the 1919 convention and died a few months later. He was
replaced by a provisional committee, which later selected A. J. Freiman of
Ottawa as de Sola's successor. The federation, renamed the Zionist Organization of Canada, undertook even more ambitious fund-raising ventures
during the 1920s, thus continuing in the mould established for it by de
Sola.[52]

The course of Zionism in Canada between the 1890s and the end of
World War One was not determined solely by individuals such as Clarence
de Sola or his associates in leadership positions of the Federation of

Zionist Societies of Canada. The movement's development was the outcome of special circumstances in Canada which shaped de Sola's outlook
and created an environment in which Zionism came to be the most important mode of Canadian-Jewish identity in that era. Aside from the fact that
Zionism enjoyed a kind of legitimation from its associations with British
imperialism, it also possessed the stamp of approval of various Canadian
federal cabinet ministers who made brief guest appearances at the federation's conventions. Although the war highlighted the emergence of non-
Zionist groups within Canadian Jewry, Zionism bore the imprimatur of at
least part of the Canadian Jewish elite that the de Sola brothers symbolized, and the support of this group—perhaps almost an aristocracy,
considering the family's genealogy, wealth and position in Anglo-
Montreal society—also lent legitimacy to the movement. And while not
all members of the mercantile elite in the metropolitan centres were active
Zionists—nor, perhaps, even members or contributors—none of them
were outspoken or active anti-Zionists. Nor, at this time, did any mainstream or elitist Jewish organization take anti-Zionist positions. A comparison of this situation with what occurred in the same period south of
the border demonstrates some of the unique and special features of Canadian Jewish life.

It is within this general context that one must place Clarence de Sola.
His contributions to Canadian Zionism were essentially organizational.
But, as well as directing the federation's affairs for so many years, de Sola
also supplied it with much of its strength and style. To him, Zionism was
more than a philanthropy, far more than traditional Jewish charity, or
tsedakah. He urged his associates in Montreal and around the country to
organise, influence other Jews, to share the dream and, above all, to raise
funds. It was to him a continuously inspiring ideal of Jewish national
reconstruction, and an especially vivid one to a practical man who himself
was a builder of ships, canals and railways during Canada's great early
twentieth-century economic boom. Zionism to him was justified, also,
because it provided the common ground on which all Jewish people could
unite. This national unity he regarded as a significant achievement, and,
compared to the more divided Zionist structure in the United States, de
Sola was indeed correct. But more than just geographical and organizational unity was present in the movement that he dominated. There was a
large measure of agreement on its first principles. Without minimizing the
importance of internal disputes over fund-raising priorities, or the fact that
by 1914–1918, the war and its aftermath had raised new and fundamental
issues of which de Sola, by now a tired old man, was not fully aware,
nevertheless it is fair to say that throughout most of his years as leader, de

Sola provided Zionism and Canadian Jewry with something approaching what Yonathan Shapiro termed an "ideology of survival," and a Canadian Jewish identity as well.

That it was indeed a flawed vision and a problematic leadership is clear. The primary goal of fund-raising was in accordance with the purposes laid down by the European Zionist leadership who were in a position to provide the Canadians with different purposes, which de Sola would probably have tried to follow. But this guidance was not forthcoming, and it would be unrealistic to have expected de Sola, who was a mere lieutenant in one of the smaller Jewish communities—and a relatively new and unformed one at that—to have done much more than follow orders from Vienna. In running the affairs of the federation, de Sola was often self-righteous, pompous, dictatorial, awkward and insensitive. With all that, however, as a full-hearted Zionist and a proud Jew, devout, serious and thoughtful, who believed in the inevitability of the Jewish national revival in the Land of Israel, he helped build a large nationwide organization which possessed a vigour, success and liveliness that aroused international envy and emulation. It is true that the organization overly stressed fund-raising, to the tragic detriment of education. But this was not entirely his fault. The message from Vienna, Cologne, Berlin and ultimately from Jerusalem to Canadian Zionists was always—and, unfortunately, still remains—"send us more money, and more and still more." If Zionism in Canada has become merely a vehicle for fund-raising, a role that, for many, is ultimately demeaning, it is partly because world Zionist leaders, with few exceptions, have failed to insist that the dream demanded much more of Canadian Jews than money alone. One can only speculate on the possible success of an additional goal—such as personal participation in the fulfillment of the Zionist program through *ali'ah* or emigration—on Canada's Jews, but there is no evidence that in those years it was even contemplated.

And, finally, to return to the historiographical context of this paper and the question of how Canadian Zionism compares with the British, American and South African experience, we may conclude that it resembles all three but seems to be most dissimilar to the British model. While it was in many ways close to the American Zionist philosophy which Shapiro defines as "Palestinianism," Canadian Zionism in the era dominated by Clarence de Sola had not experienced the same internal power struggles and ideological debate as had occurred in the United States, mainly because the general Canadian Jewish historical experience was so different. Zionism in Canada did not have to contend, as it did in both Britain and the United States, against already established Jewish organizations, nor did its leaders have to persuade others of the movement's legitimacy against or within an already defined Canadian Jewish identity. Being a much newer community, Canadian Jewry before the arrival of Zionism had no national coherence or articulated identity. In Canada, then, as in South Africa, Zionism—arriving, as it were, first on the scene—provided both an acceptable structure and an identity to Canadian Jewry. And yet, though similar in these respects, the Canadian experience of sharp class distinctions in the metropolitan centres by World War One differs from the South African model, where class distinctions were neither as sharp nor as sustained. But the fact that Zionism, in a variety of organizations, remained strong in Canada, in hinterland Jewish communities as well as in the metropolitan centres, is indicative of the extent to which it had become firmly entrenched as the normative form of Jewish identification in this country. In that context, then, we may justly conclude that Clarence Isaac de Sola made an important and lasting contribution to Canadian Jewish life.

NOTES

This study was prepared as part of a larger work covering four major themes in Canadian Jewish history, and was facilitated by support from the Multiculturalism Directorate of the Department of the Secretary of State, and by grants from the Social Sciences and Humanities Research Council of Canada. I am happy to acknowledge the helpful comments on this paper by my Queen's colleagues Lucien Karchmar and George Rawlyk.

1. David Vital, *The Origins of Zionism* (Oxford, 1975), p. 66.

2. Benjamin G. Sack, *History of the Jews in Canada* (Montreal, 1965), pp. 218–220.

3. Leon Goldman, "History of Zionism in Canada," A. D. Hart, ed., *The Jew in Canada* (Montreal, 1926), p. 291; *Encyclopaedia Judaica* (Jerusalem, 1972), XIV, p. 343; VIII, p. 1475.

4. Goldman, "History of Zionism"; Stephen A. Speisman, *The Jews of Toronto: A History to 1937* (Toronto, 1979), p. 201; Arthur A. Chiel, *The Jews in Manitoba: A Social History* (Toronto, 1961), p. 154.

5. Gideon Shimoni, *Jews and Zionism: The South African Experience (1910–1967)* (Cape Town, 1980); Stuart A. Cohen, *English Zionists and British Jews: The Communal Politics of Anglo-Jewry, 1895–1920* (Princeton, 1982).

6. Yonathan Shapiro, *Leadership of the American Zionist Organization, 1897–1930* (Urbana, 1971), passim.

7. Shimoni, *Jews and Zionism*, p. 2.

8. Shapiro, *American Zionist Organization*, p. 6.

9. Cohen, *English Zionists*, xiii.

10. Ibid., pp. 321–323.

11. Ibid., xi.

12. Carman Miller, "Alexander Abraham de Sola," *Dictionary of Canadian Biography* (Toronto, 1982), XI, pp. 253–255.

13. Annette Wolff, "Abraham Joseph," *Dictionary of Canadian Biography*, XI, pp. 454–456; Hart ed., *The Jew in Canada*, p. 331.

14. Stephen Birmingham, *"Our Crowd": The Great Jewish Families of New York* (New York, 1967) and *The Grandees: The Story of America's Sephardic Elite* (New York, 1971).

15. Louis Rosenberg, *Canada's Jews: A Social and Economic Study of the Jews in Canada* (Montreal, 1939), p. 12.

16. Public Archives of Canada, Microfilm Reel A913: Diary of Clarence Isaac de Sola. 21 April, 13 December, 1872.

17. Ibid., Reel A915, 31 March 1906.

18. Ibid., Reel A913, 12 October 1880.

19. Ibid., Reel A915, 13 May 1913.

20. Marvin Lowenthal, trans. and ed., *The Diaries of Theodor Herzl* (New York, 1962), pp. 453–454.

21. Louis Rasminsky, ed., *Hadassah Jubilee: Tenth Anniversary, Toronto* (Toronto, 1927), pp. 135–148, 174–178. Dov Joseph, interview with G. Tulchinsky, Jerusalem, 2 January 1980.

22. Central Zionist Archives, Jerusalem, K.K.L. 5/359, "Federation of Zionist Societies of Canada, Financial Statements and Record of Zionist Achievement in Canada, Submitted to the Seventeenth Convention."

23. Rosenberg, *Canada's Jews*, p. 308.

24. See Hart, *The Jew in Canada*, pp. 367, 567.

25. PAC, MG 28, U81, Zionist Organization of Canada, vol. 5, pp. 473–474.

26. CZA, A 119/200–202, de Sola to Nordau, 28 February 1910.

27. Ibid., Z2/39.

28. Ibid., Z1/244.

29. PAC, MG 28, U81, vol. 5, pp. 94–95.

30. *Jewish Times,* 30 September 1898. Zionism, the *Times* author continued, could easily arouse more anti-Semitism, because it was essentially unpatriotic.

31. Ibid., 3 February 1899.

32. PAC, MG 28, U81, vol. 5, p. 19.

33. CZA, de Sola to de Haas, 12 February 1903.

34. PAC, MG 28, U81, vol. 5, p. 201.

35. *The Maccabean,* XX (January 1911), pp. 266–270.

36. CZA, KKL 1/20 (1907–1913); A. Fallick to de Sola, 18 October 1908.

37. *The Maccabean,* XX (January 1911), p. 269.

38. CZA, KK 1/21, de Sola to the Chief Bureau of the Jewish National Fund, Cologne, 13 July 1908.

39. *The Maccabean,* 1911, p. 269.

40. Yossi Katz, "The Plan and Efforts of the Jews of Winnipeg to Purchase Land and to Establish an Agricultural Settlement in Palestine before World War One," *Canadian Jewish Historical Society Journal,* vol. 5, no. 1 (Spring 1981), pp. 1–16.

41. David Rome, "Early Documents on the Canadian Jewish Congress, 1914–1921," Canadian Jewish Archives, new series, no. 1 (Montreal, 1974), passim. See also H. M. Caiserman, "The History of the First Canadian Jewish Congress," in Hart, ed., *The Jew in Canada,* pp. 65–482.

42. Hirsch Wolofsky, *Journey of My Life: A Book of Memories* (Montreal, 1945), pp. 72–73.

43. De Sola Diary, Reel A915, 18 January 1906.

44. Ibid., 16 March 1919.

45. Arthur A. Goren, ed., *Dissenter in Zion: From the Writings of Judah L. Magnes* (Cambridge, Mass., 1982), p. 22.

46. Wolofsky, *Journey of My Life,* passim.

47. *Kanader Adler,* 22 December 1908.

48. For the history of the Poale Zion in Canada see *Di Poale Zion Bavegung in Kanada: 1904–1920* (Montreal, 1956). The Mizrachi movement was begun in Toronto in 1911 and spread to other parts of Canada; see Bernard Figler, "Zionism in Canada," in Raphael Patai, ed., *An Encyclopaedia of Zionism and Israel* (New York, 1971, 2 vols.), I, pp. 174–179. A Mizrachi convention of delegates from across North America took place in Montreal in December 1919; *Kanader Adler*, 5 December 1919.

49. *The Maccabean*, V (December 1903), pp. 363–365.

50. Ibid., XXII, pp. 57–58.

51. Carl Berger, *The Sense of Power: Studies in Canadian Nationalism* (Toronto, 1971), passim. See also Michael Brown, "Divergent Paths: Early Zionism in Canada and the United States," *Jewish Social Studies* (Spring 1982), pp. 49–68.

52. Goldman, *History of Zionism*, p. 304.

II
The Zionist Lobby and Canada's Palestine Policy, 1941–1948

DAVID J. BERCUSON

he Canadian Zionist movement traces its roots back to the late
1890s, when the Federation of Canadian Zionist Societies, fore-
runner of the Zionist Organization of Canada, was founded. In
1920 the federation asked the Canadian government to intercede with
Britain on behalf of the Zionist movement to have the east bank of the
Jordan River included in the projected Palestine Mandate.[1] The approach,
like that of most Jewish attempts to influence Canadian governments on a
variety of issues until late 1938, was quiet, unobtrusive and deferential. By
then, the pattern for Jewish political activity in Canada was well established. Lobbying was to be done through friends at court, Jewish or
otherwise, and was to be undertaken in a way that did not focus attention
on the Jewish community and so wear out its welcome in an overwhelmingly Christian country. The approach did not work then or later,
for the efforts of Canadian Jews to persuade the Canadian government to
change its approach to the Jewish refugees during the 1930s was a tragic
failure.[2] Zionists took note of that failure. When confronted by Britain's
1939 White Paper on Palestine limiting Jewish immigration, severely cur-
tailing Jewish land purchases and holding out the promise of an independent, Arab-dominated Palestine, they began to dramatically change the
way in which they approached the Canadian government.

The outbreak of World War Two doomed a generation of European
Jews and dramatically altered the dimensions of the Palestine question and

linked it to the fate of the Holocaust survivors. Zionists around the world stepped up their drive to open the gates of Palestine to Jewish refugees even before their worst fears about the destruction of European Jewry were confirmed. In Canada, the United Zionist Council (UZC), a new Zionist umbrella organization, established a public relations committee in May 1941, only one month after its first meeting.[3] The chairman, Harry Batshaw, was a Montreal lawyer, educated at McGill University and in France, who had been involved for at least a decade in a wide variety of Jewish and Zionist activities as well as Liberal party politics. One of his first moves was to establish a Pro-Palestine Committee, intended to be an organization of Christians and Jews friendly to the Zionist cause who would spread the Zionist message throughout the community and take part in Zionist efforts to lobby the federal government.[4] In addition to the Pro-Palestine Committee, a Canadian Palestine Committee, modelled after the American Palestine Committee and the Pro-Palestine Parliamentary Committee of Great Britain, was established to "give expression to the interest, sympathy and moral support of the Canadian people for the Jewish National Home,"[5] and was to be entirely non-Jewish in membership.

The public relations efforts of 1941 and 1942 were feeble and intermittent—a "modest beginning," Batshaw later reported.[6] But as news of the Holocaust leaked out of Europe to Palestine, and from Palestine to Zionists around the world[7] efforts to line governments and public opinion up behind the Zionist cause increased. In May 1942, in the midst of World War Two, delegates representing the Jewish Agency, the Yishuv, and the American Zionist Emergency Committee met at the Biltmore Hotel in New York City to reconsider Zionist aims. Zionist leaders, especially in Palestine and the United States, concluded that nothing less than full sovereign statehood was necessary if the Jewish national home was to have a future and if it was to serve as a haven from persecution. The Biltmore conference, largely at the urging of David Ben Gurion and assisted by Rabbi Abba Hillel Silver, the dynamic leader of the Zionist Organization of America, called for full Jewish Agency control over immigration into Palestine and demanded that "Palestine be established as a Jewish Commonwealth integrated in the structure of the new democratic world."[8] Henceforth statehood was the key objective towards which all efforts were directed and from which solutions to Jewish problems, such as immigration, would flow. Yet, Zionist public relations work in Canada virtually ignored the Biltmore conference declaration and Canadian Zionists continued to concentrate on the British White Paper and the humanitarian issues connected with it.

In September 1943, the National Council of the UCZ convened in special session in Toronto to form a revitalized National Public Relations Committee, still under Batshaw's direction. The Zionists aimed to win increased support from non-Jewish Canadians, including the clergy and "various political parties," in a drive to persuade Britain, through the Canadian government, to abandon the White Paper restrictions on Jewish immigration to Palestine.[9] A campaign was initiated to enlist members into the Canadian Palestine Committee and to establish committee branches across the country. In December 1943, Mackenzie King, prime minister and secretary of state for external affairs, was personally approached by A. J. Frieman to intervene with the British government to forestall the imposition of White Paper immigration restrictions in Palestine scheduled to go into effect in April 1944. Frieman claimed that the Canadian government was "not without responsibility in this matter" and could, because of its membership in the League of Nations, make "appropriate representations" to the United Kingdom government. Frieman's letter was somewhat intimate in tone and was clearly intended to appeal to the prime minister's friendship as well as his supposed sympathetic understanding of Jewish problems.[10]

King, however, was determined to keep his distance from the Palestine question and sought the advice of the Department of External Affairs before replying. The job of drafting an answer was given to Elizabeth P. MacCallum, a new member of the department and its only bona fide expert on the Middle East. Born in Turkey of missionary parents, she had graduated from Queen's University and had worked toward a Ph.D. at Columbia University in New York before she was lured away in 1925 to work for the Foreign Policy Association under the direction of James G. McDonald, who later became the first United States ambassador to Israel. During six years of intensive work, MacCallum published a book, *The Nationalist Crusade in Syria,* and wrote more than twenty papers for the association's information service concentrating on the Middle East. In 1942 she joined the European and Commonwealth division of the Department of External Affairs and specialised in the Middle East because "none of the men were interested."[11] She was shy, almost deferential, and precise and turned out carefully reasoned documents. At times she seems to have felt it her special duty to debate, in type and behind the closed doors of the department, the points raised by Zionists and their supporters in their briefs and memoranda to the government.

Frieman's letter offered the department, and the government, the opportunity to put its views about current British Palestine policy on the record and those views were largely based on MacCallum's reasoning. She rejected all of Frieman's arguments. In a carefully worded and detailed memorandum MacCallum claimed that "well-informed Canadian Jews, occupying positions of some responsibility" were uneasy about Zionist policy because it might detrimentally affect the interests of Jews in Palestine and elsewhere. Some of these "non-Zionist Jews" considered schemes to mount a mass emigration of European Jews to Palestine "a mistake," coming at the very moment when a reaction against Hitlerism was bound to "bring about a permanent improvement in the status of Jews" in Europe. It would be wrong, she maintained, to encourage the people of eastern Europe and the Balkans to plan for a postwar society without Jews. Mac-Callum believed that Canadian efforts to encourage Britain to abandon the 1939 White Paper would ruin the British effort to force Arabs and Jews to begin "direct consultation" on important policy questions affecting Palestine which was, in her opinion, the whole point of the White Paper.[12]

King's reply to Frieman, based on MacCallum's draft, should have dashed any hopes the Zionists may have had about getting the prime minister on their side. He told Frieman that the White Paper was not directed at limiting Jewish immigration but was actually aimed "toward creating political conditions which would facilitate peaceful development of the Jewish National Home." Seeking the withdrawal of the White Paper would be "to condemn in advance the effort to establish democratic procedures and the principle that both elements of the Palestinian population must be consulted about policies which closely affect their interest." The position of the Jews in Europe could best be secured through a victory of the Allied forces over Nazi Germany while the situation of the Jews in Palestine would be best served "by agreement among those whose interests are directly concerned."[13] King, thus, indirectly endorsed the White Paper and made it clear that Canada would not, for the moment, intervene in Palestine matters. If Frieman and his followers wanted the government to change its course they would have to use whatever political leverage was at their disposal to convince King that a significant proportion of Canadian voters were behind them.

In the months following the King-Frieman exchange the drive for public sympathy was stepped up as the Zionists intensified their efforts to mount a major, sustained, nation-wide drive for support among Jews and non-Jews with a carefully planned, long term, public campaign. There was little precedent for this among Canadian Jews and Harry Batshaw felt it necessary to explain this type of action to the January 1944 convention of the Zionist Organization of Canada. Public relations, he told the gathering, was crucial to the attainment of Zionist aims for a "publicly secured" homeland. The Balfour Declaration had been supported by hundreds of political and church leaders in Britain when it had been issued, he pointed out, and this support had been carefully cultivated by Zionist leaders in Britain.[14] Batshaw's work soon produced dramatic results with new initiatives across the country to rally Christian support for the cause of the Jewish National Home. The two organizations spearheading this work were the Christian Council for Palestine, directed by Henry Janes, a Toronto public relations consultant, and the Canadian Palestine Committee under Herbert Mowat, a former Anglican minister from Toronto. Janes and Mowat had been hired by the UZC—which paid their salaries and expenses—and they were responsible to the council. Janes proved less than adequate in his role and his organization failed to win widespread support among Christian clergy, its designated target group. His extravagant expense claims also led to dissatisfaction among leaders of the UZC and, eventually, to a parting of the ways by the summer of 1944.[15] Mowat, on the other hand, was a huge success. He was a tireless worker, an effective speaker and an enthusiastic, even passionate promoter of the Zionist cause. After a visit to Welland, Ontario, in the spring of 1945, the executive secretary of the local B'nai Brith lodge wrote of him: "Mr. Mowat certainly sold the non-Jew the idea of Palestine as the rightful homeland of the Jews. I don't know of anyone who is more qualified to speak to non-Jewish audiences on the Palestine question with such sincerity as Mr. Mowat."[16] He and his Canadian Palestine Committee were soon carrying a large share of Zionist public relations work.

In early 1944 the UZC in conjunction with the Canadian Palestine Committee, launched a major effort to convince Mackenzie King to place the Palestine question on the agenda of the forthcoming Commonwealth prime ministers conference and to press the British to lift the White Paper restrictions on Jewish immigration. On 27 March 1944, A. J. Frieman brought Dr. Nahum Goldmann to the East Block for a discussion with King. Goldmann was the Jewish Agency representative in Washington and was returning there from London. He stopped off in Ottawa because he was anxious to speak to King and Frieman made the arrangements. Goldmann spoke for less than an hour, summarizing the Zionist position on the White Paper and when the two men left, Frieman was convinced that King was "favourably impressed" and would be "kindly disposed" towards the Zionist position.[17] Three days later King told the House of Commons that he would see to it that the Palestine matter was brought up at the London talks.

On 31 March another Zionist delegation met King, this time at the behest of Mowat and the Canadian Palestine Committee. Mowat was accompanied by Henry Janes and nine members or supporters of the Canadian Palestine Committee, including CCF leader M. J. Coldwell, Social Credit MP J. H. Blackmore, Liberal MP Arthur Roebuck and Senator Cairene Wilson. Percy Benough, president of the Trades and Labour Congress, Aron Mosher, president of the Canadian Congress of Labour and Robert Pennell, president of the Toronto Board of Trade were also part of the delegation. S. J. Zacks, newly appointed co-chairman of the UZC public relations committee, Batshaw and two other representatives of the Zionist Organization of Canada also attended. After a brief introduction by Roebuck, Mowat outlined the aims and purposes of the Canadian Palestine Committee and claimed that it enjoyed wide support throughout Canada from the press and from organizations such as the National Council of Women. King claimed to be impressed by the delegation's "representative character" and succeeded in convincing them that he "would be helpful" at the forthcoming conference.[18]

Once King had made his commitment to bring the Palestine question up at the Commonwealth meeting, J. W. Pickersgill, head of the Prime Minister's Office, approached the Department of External Affairs for advice. MacCallum, in response, prepared a long and careful analysis of the background to the 1939 White Paper, its impact on the Arabs and Jews, and the likely direction of Britain's Palestine policy after the war. It was the most thorough history and analysis of the Palestine question yet written in the department and it presented a tough minded assessment of the difficulties Britain would face in the near future. MacCallum also pointed out that Canada, "recognized as a leader among smaller nations" would eventually be called upon to support "the efforts [of both Arabs and Jews] to achieve nationhood and political independence" and would, at the same time, be "expected to speak in defence of Jews who [would] wish to continue making their homes" in Europe and North America. It would be difficult, she believed, for Canada "to fulfill all three of these expectations" but she made no suggestions about future courses of action that Canada might adopt.[19] Hume Wrong, in charge of the European and Commonwealth division at External and MacCallum's immediate superior, drew the obvious conclusion: "I would myself be loath to see any strong advocacy by the Canadian Government of a particular solution to the Palestine problem. No matter what may be done about the White Paper, Palestine will remain, for a long time, a troubled area . . . in which it is most unlikely that Canada will have any very direct human interest."[20] Wrong, however, was needlessly worried about Mackenzie King meddling in Palestine affairs. The matter was not on the agenda for the Commonwealth meeting and the official, secret, minutes of the conference fail to record any mention of Palestine uttered by King or anyone else.[21]

The work of lobbying the federal government paralleled and reinforced the broader campaign to rally public opinion against the White Paper. In the summer of 1944, Dr. Carl Hermann Voss, executive director of the American Palestine Committee, spoke to a group of clergy in Montreal who then passed a resolution supporting the Balfour Declaration and demanding "maximum Jewish immigration" into Palestine. Mowat toured the Atlantic region to address service clubs, university faculty, and ministerial associations. In Halifax, Saint John and Yarmouth he spoke on Palestine and the Jewish refugees on local radio. In western Canada Zionist representatives addressed receptive audiences in Saskatoon, Edmonton, Calgary and Vancouver.[22] On August 4, Mowat, Roebuck and Zacks went back to Ottawa to meet Undersecretary of State Norman A. Robertson and Hume Wrong. It was known in Zionist circles that Churchill's government was examining solutions to the Palestine problem and was once again seriously considering partition of Palestine into Jewish and Arab states. Zacks, Mowat and Roebuck gave Wrong and Robertson a written brief opposing partition which Robertson promised to bring to Mackenzie King's attention, and they tried to find out what Mackenzie King had done at the Commonwealth meetings. Robertson claimed that King had raised the Palestine matter but he refused to disclose details of the discussions.[23] After leaving Wrong and Robertson, the delegation met several MPs from the major parties to explain their position on partition. The MPs—Rev. Daniel McIvor for the Liberals, Stanley Knowles for the CCF and John R. MacNicol for the Conservatives—spoke in the House later that day along with Roebuck in support of the anti-partition brief. Knowles also questioned King on his role at the Commonwealth meeting. The prime minister replied that the Palestine question had not been on the agenda, but claimed that he had placed it there, though he could not tell the House what had been discussed.[24]

King's lack of enthusiasm for Palestine matters did not discourage Sam Zacks. Even though he concluded in August 1944 that Britain would not try to solve the Palestine question until the war was over, he still believed the Canadian government could be convinced to help Zionists "force a decision earlier."[25] This was wishful thinking because the government was preoccupied with the thousands of tasks necessary for the daily conduct of the war and needed to maintain good relations with Britain. Nevertheless, the work of the Zionist public relations machine, carried out by the UZC and the Canadian Palestine Committee, was stepped up with cross-country speeches, radio addresses, luncheons, the distribution of literature and personal approaches to prominent Canadians beseeching them to join the Canadian Palestine Committee. Well-known political and public figures lent their support to the cause, including F. R. Scott, Chester Martin, Lady Eaton, Senator Salter Hayden and Senator Adrien Hughessen. In Quebec, Aimé Geoffrion, a well-known lawyer with important Liberal connections, Emil Vaillancourt and Jean Louis Gagnon also joined the committee.[26]

Until late 1944, Zionist public relations work had largely by-passed Quebec, which represented somewhat of a dilemma for the Zionists and the Canadian Palestine Committee due to an assumption that French-Canadian views on Palestine would be biased by deeply rooted anti-Semitic feelings. Batshaw set out to remedy this with the help of David Rome of the Canadian Jewish Congress. They approached Paul Guerin, a journalist with *La Presse* who also ran a small clipping and public relations bureau, to seek his views on the best way to spread the Zionist message in Quebec. After a number of meetings, the three decided to concentrate on a low-key campaign that would include the distribution of press releases to French newspapers and to a select list of Québécois. At the same time approaches would be made to "leading French-Canadian liberals" to enlist them for membership in the Canadian Palestine Committee. Batshaw worried about the danger that anti-Semites in Quebec might support Zionist objectives on the basis "that they would like to see even Canadian Jews go to Palestine," and he had little doubt that Zionist public relations work would "meet with greater resistance" in Quebec than was experienced in Ontario.[27]

For most of the war Zionist public relations work in Canada concentrated on rallying public opposition to the White Paper and attempting to enlist the Canadian government as an ally in the cause. Almost no effort at all was spent countering anti-Zionist propaganda since there was so little. As long as the truce between the British and the Yishuv remained in effect in Palestine, Zionists could emphasize the tremendous efforts put forward by the Yishuv on behalf of the Allied war effort. But when that truce began to break down and attacks on the British started to mount, the UZC and the Canadian Palestine Committee faced a difficult problem. Most Canadians were ignorant about, and apathetic towards, the Palestine question but they were not ignorant or apathetic about Britain, a close war ally, ancestral home of many Canadians and Canada's legal, constitutional and political mother country.

The problem first cropped up in the fall of 1944, when two members of the Stern Gang assassinated Lord Moyne, the British minister resident in Cairo. The murderers were quickly caught, tried and executed. The assassination brought immediate and unfavourable press reaction in a number of Canadian cities and prompted a soul-searching by some Canadian Zionists. When news of the killing broke, Mowat was about to leave for a speaking tour of western Canada but was urged to stay home by a representative of the Edmonton Zionist Council who told Rabbi Jesse Schwartz, secretary of the Zionist Organization of Canada, that if he were a Christian he would tell Mowat and the Zionists "until you set your house in order and root out this gang even if it involves sacrifices of blood, lay off for a little while begging for sympathy."[28] But even before this message was received, Mowat moved quickly to cover his tracks with a press release that denounced the "Sternist terrorist organization." They could not be a greater obstacle to Zionist aims, insisted Mowat, than if they "were in the pay of the bitterest enemies of the Jewish National Home."[29] Mowat's tour went ahead and, as usual, produced positive results, particularly in Winnipeg where a speech to the local press club brought an immediate improvement in press coverage of Jewish and Zionist news.[30] The adverse press reaction to the Moyne killing was thus but a temporary setback to Mowat and the UZC. In January and February 1945, many new members were added to the Canadian Palestine Committee and Sir Ellsworth Flavelle accepted Mowat's invitation to become national chairman, lending a prestigious and well known name to the organization.[31] Another meeting was arranged on 24 January between Robertson and Wrong of the Department of External Affairs and a joint Canadian Palestine Committee and Zionist Organization of Canada delegation.[32]

Meetings between Zionist leaders and government officials usually produced little more than promises that the Canadian government would forward their petitions and position papers to London, and the January 1945 meeting was no exception. But this time Zionist pleas for Canadian intervention in Britain's enforcement of the White Paper came just as knowledge of the Jewish catastrophe in Europe was becoming widely disseminated. The epitomy of bureaucratic sangfroid, Robertson thereupon took an uncharacteristically sympathetic view of the Zionist position, although he had little experience with the Palestine question and considered MacCallum's 1943 views on the White Paper "objective and realistic." But after the January 1945 meeting he told King that "the position of the surviving European Jews will be very difficult." Their property had been seized and their livelihoods destroyed, Robertson noted, and if European governments were trying to restore Jewish property, taking it away from those who had held it during the war, a recurrence of anti-Semitism might occur. In his view, therefore, "the cause for permitting the largest possible movement of Jewish refugees into Palestine [was] on compassionate grounds alone a very strong one." Despite these apparently personal sympathies, however, he knew just how complicated the Palestine question was and he "did not think that the Canadian Government would wish to press a particular policy for meeting one specific problem upon the United Kingdom Government."[33] His budding sympathy was, therefore, considerably tempered by his desire not to complicate Anglo-

Canadian relations by urging a reluctant Britain to adopt a pro-Zionist position.

In the spring of 1945, as Hitler's armies crumbled in Europe and the victorious allies prepared to meet in San Francisco to draw up the United Nations charter, the UZC intensified its public relations and lobby efforts with a three pronged campaign aimed at increasing the membership of the Canadian Palestine Committee, placing the Zionist program before as many members of Parliament as possible, and pressing the government to adopt a pro-Zionist stance at San Francisco and at the Commonwealth prime ministers meeting scheduled to precede it. In the month of April alone, seventy-six MPS, MLAS and senators, from all parties and provinces, joined the Canadian Palestine Committee, including Ian Mackenzie, minister of veterans' affairs, and J. G. Gardiner, minister of agriculture.[34] A delegation headed by Sir Ellsworth Flavelle met again with Robertson and presented a brief which claimed that Canadian governments had been sympathetic to Zionist aims since 1912 and were bound to support the Balfour Declaration because of Canada's membership in the League of Nations at the time the Palestine Mandate was awarded.[35]

On 25 April the United Nations conference opened at San Francisco and Mackenzie King headed the Canadian delegation which also included Gordon Graydon, Conservative party house leader (Conservative party leader John Bracken did not yet hold a seat in the House), and M. J. Coldwell, leader of the CCF, as well as seven alternate delegates, most of whom were members of the Department of External Affairs. Sam Zacks, Saul Hayes and Sam Bronfman also attended as part of a large gathering of non-governmental delegates representing Jewish organizations from around the world, who made up one of the largest groups at the meeting. The Zionists among them were particularly concerned with the question of how the United Nations, as successor to the League of Nations, would dispose of former League mandates and particularly the Palestine Mandate, which was the only Class A mandate left.

At San Francisco the deliberations focused on proposals for a United Nations Organization that had been drawn up by the great powers at the Dumbarton Oaks conference in October 1944. Those proposals dealt, among many other matters, with trusteeship territories to be administered by the United Nations or assigned to United Nations member countries for administration. If Palestine should come under the administration of the United Nations Trusteeship Council, the policies of that council would obviously be applied to it. Zionists and Arabs knew this and set out to influence the policies to be established to guide the Trusteeship Council in future. The Arab delegations did not focus specifically on the Palestine question but concentrated instead on an effort to force the Trusteeship Council to recognize only the rights of the largest single group in each trusteeship territory. Success would have dealt a serious blow to the legality of the Zionist position in Palestine, since the Jews were in a minority there. The Zionists countered this with a campaign to have the specific rights of the Jewish people in Palestine, as defined by the Balfour Declaration, built in to any future trusteeship decisions on Palestine. In fact, however, they need not have worried about the Arab proposals because Britain, France and the United States strongly opposed the Arab proposals and wielded considerable power at the San Francisco meeting. The Arabs had no chance of success against these colonial powers who were jealous of protecting their own interests and possessions around the globe.[36]

The Zionist lobby at San Francisco spent considerable time and effort to line up the support of the British Commonwealth countries, Canada among them. Canada was, in fact, active in several important areas at the San Francisco meeting,[37] but on trusteeship matters Canada, in contrast to New Zealand and South Africa,[38] remained in the background and "took no active part in the discussions,"[39] despite the Zionist public relations work of the previous three years. Canada had no colonial dependencies and stood smugly aloof. Once again the efforts of Zionists to convince the Canadian government to involve itself in the Palestine question, however obliquely, had failed.

By late 1945 Britain and the United States began to search for a political solution to the Palestine question. The Anglo-American Committee of Inquiry and the Morrison-Grady commissions were formed to investigate and to recommend solutions for this increasingly complex problem even as Irgun and Stern Gang attacks in Palestine mounted and the Haganah made efforts to bring Jewish displaced persons into Palestine in defiance of the White Paper. In Canada the UZC and the Canadian Palestine Committee redoubled their efforts to expand their membership, line up prominent Canadians behind their efforts and influence government policy. The job was made more difficult by the open war that raged in Palestine between the British and the underground fighting organizations because the press in Canada generally reacted with considerable editorial fury to every new attack. Canada had just fought a major war as a staunch ally of Britain and Anglophilic feeling ran deep in the country. Zionists and Jews were castigated by some newspaper editorial writers for their lack of gratitude to Britain for saving European Jewry from Hitler's gas chambers.[40] Zionist leaders perceived a definite rise of public anti-Semitism[41] and feared this would adversely affect their efforts to convince Ottawa to be more friendly to the Zionist cause and to put pressure on Britain to allow the displaced persons to enter Palestine legally.

Those efforts were a total failure. Despite petitions, letters, newspaper advertisements, private meetings and radio broadcasts from Jews and non-Jews alike, the Canadian government, for the most part, stayed clear of the Palestine question. And when it did get involved, it was for the purpose of helping Britain stem the flow of illegal immigrants to Palestine by trying to block the sale of war surplus Canadian ships to individuals or organizations that were likely to transfer those ships to the Jewish Agency. The Department of External Affairs was highly embarrassed when it learned that ex-Royal Canadian Navy ships were plying the Mediterranean waters under the Panamanian flag, bringing illegal immigrants to Palestine.[42] External Affairs and Canada's political leadership had no intention of muddying the waters of Canadian-British relations over Palestine, which was not considered to be of direct interest to Canada.

Canada eventually did get directly involved in the Palestine question in the spring of 1947 when it was named as a member of the United Nations Special Committee on Palestine. But that had nothing whatever to do with Zionist lobbying efforts in Canada and was due, rather, to the determination of the United States to draft Canada for this special, and somewhat hazardous duty. The United States wanted a committee composed of small countries, with relatively weak Jewish communities, which had had nothing to do with Palestine.[43] Canada qualified on every count. The irony here is that the very neutrality on Palestine which Canada had so scrupulously observed in the past was now the major qualification for its sudden plunge into Palestine via UNSCOP. Canada's secretary of state for external affairs, Louis St. Laurent, had not wanted to get involved in UNSCOP; but both he and the Canadian delegation to the United Nations Special General Assembly in New York were outmaneuvred by the Americans. Nevertheless, since St. Laurent failed to avoid involvement, he and King chose the next best course and named Supreme Court Justice Ivan C. Rand to serve on UNSCOP as an independent observer who was not bound by, and who would not bind, the Canadian government.[44]

On 31 August 1947, UNSCOP issued its report. Seven out of eleven members, including Rand, recommended that Palestine be given its independence as quickly as possible and that it be partitioned into a Jewish state and an Arab state tied together by an economic and monetary union to last no less than ten years. Jerusalem and its environs were to become a separate area administered as a United Nations trust territory under a governor appointed by the United Nations Trusteeship Council. The recommendation was clear, if somewhat idealistic, and Canada, as a member country of the United Nations, and one with considerable influence in the postwar world, would finally have to take a leadership role. This was the signal for a new intensification of Zionist political lobbying in Canada.

The UZC and the Canadian Palestine Committee, this time joined by the Canadian Jewish Congress, were quick off the mark and issued public statements congratulating Rand on his contributions to UNSCOP and urging the Canadian government to follow his, and UNSCOP's, recommendations.[45] These public declarations were buttressed by private meetings with a number of Liberal MPs in which Jewish constituents urged the government to support partition. Rand's role was generally played up, as if to remind Ottawa that it could not ignore the opinions of this respected jurist. Moshe Shertok, unofficial foreign minister for the Jewish Agency Executive, noted at one point,: "This is most satisfactory! We should by all means play up Rand with the Canadians, so as to strengthen their noblesse oblige complex."[46] Using this, and other arguments, the Zionist lobby directed what George Ignatieff later remembered as "very strong . . . pressure" on the government and particularly on undersecretary of state Lester B. Pearson.[47] At one point defence minister Brooke Claxton told Ignatieff, who was a member of the Canadian delegation to the UN General Assembly in the fall of 1947: "Don't forget George, I don't mind how you vote but . . . don't forget that I have no Arabs in my constituency and I have I've forgotten how many Jews."[48]

Strong pressure there undoubtedly was, and Jewish votes in a handful of constituencies (two or three in Montreal, two or three in Toronto, one or two in Winnipeg) may have been given some consideration in the government, but Canada did not support partition to curry favour with Jewish voters as a result of Zionist lobbying. Jewish influence in the Liberal party and in the government was strictly limited, as the failure of the campaign to convince the Canadian government to allow Jewish refugees to enter Canada clearly shows; in the fall of 1947 the government had still not lowered the barriers completely.[49] Jewish votes, J. W. Pickersgill later recalled, could often be taken for granted because the Liberals knew that Jews would not vote for the Conservatives and, although the CCF may have been an alternative to some, the leadership of the Jewish community was integrally tied to Liberal politics.[50] It was simply not in the nature of the Canadian political game that David Croll or Sam Bronfman or Lazarus Phillips or Harry Batshaw would abandon the one political organization that gave them some entré, however limited, to government and which obligingly provided a token handful of safe Jewish seats so that Liberal Jewish MPs could sit in the House of Commons. The government's decision to support partition was based on "practical and realistic considerations."[51]

When the Canadian delegation to the UN General Assembly departed for New York in mid-September it was given no specific instructions as to what position to take on the UNSCOP recommendations but was told, instead, to support "any proposals which appear . . . likely to bring about a solution to the Palestine problem provided that there [was] reasonable evidence that they can be put into effect." The delegation was reminded that Canada was not bound by Rand's views although it ought to bear in mind that "a distinguished member of the Supreme Court of Canada had arrived at certain conclusions after careful consideration of the issues involved."[52] After several weeks of listening to discussion on the matter and sounding out the views of various delegations, particularly those of the United States, the Soviet Union and the United Kingdom, the delegation, led by R. G. Riddell, and with the exception of Elizabeth Mac-Callum, prepared a draft statement to be read by J. L. Ilsley, Canada's minister of justice and head of the delegation, in the Ad Hoc Committee on Palestine. It cautiously supported partition as "the only solution practicable at the moment" and as a basis for further discussion at the United Nations.[53] St. Laurent, who unlike Claxton had almost no Jewish voters in his constituency, brought the draft to the cabinet which approved it on October 14 and a slightly revised statement was made later that same day.[54] The final version was, if anything, even more hesitant in its support of partition than the Riddell draft.[55]

Over the next few weeks the Canadian delegation, led by Lester Pearson, worked hard to find a formula which would reconcile basic differences between the United States and the Soviet Union on plans to implement partition; Pearson contributed significantly to the final partition plan draft put before the General Assembly. When the final vote was taken on 29 November Canada supported partition as "the best of four unattractive and difficult alternatives."[56] In a secret report circulated within the Department of External Affairs some weeks later, the reasons behind Canada's actions were clearly outlined. First, there was no "practicable alternative" under discussion because the alternative Arab plan of a unitary Arab-controlled state was totally unacceptable to the Jews, and the Arab states "at no time indicated" that they would consider any other plan which "offered control of immigration and land regulations to the Jews within a Jewish area." Second, partition was supported by the USSR and thus offered the only possibility of a solution to the Palestine problem which might prevent Soviet intervention in the area. Third, failure to adopt partition might discredit the Jewish Agency and thrust "Jewish extremists" into the leadership of the Jewish community in Palestine. This might cause a civil war among the Jews that would "place an even more severe strain on United States–United Kingdom relations." Finally, partition "gave to the Western powers the opportunity to establish an independent, progressive Jewish state . . . with close economic and cultural ties with the West generally and in particular with the United States." The

Canadian delegation had believed that if the UN failed to do anything, it would be thoroughly discredited and that partition was the only plan which was likely to receive the two thirds support necessary for adoption.[57] Since the delegation basically recommended policy to St. Laurent, whose views were not challenged in the cabinet, it is clear that considerations far more important and central to Canadian interests than Zionist lobbying formed the foundation of Canadian policy in this important decision. Canada did not support partition because of Zionist lobbying or because of the Jewish Agency's condescending use of Ivan Rand's name; it backed partition for reasons of high policy. In this instance official Canadian views and the aspirations of Canadian Zionists were parallel but unconnected.

That was not true of many other key decisions made by the Canadian government on Palestine in the months that followed. In March 1948, Senator Warren Austin, American ambassador to the United Nations, announced that in the face of the violence that had broken out in Palestine, the United States was temporarily retreating from its support of partition and desired a special session of the UN General Assembly to consider placing Palestine under a trusteeship and to impose a ceasefire between Jews and Arabs. The Zionist movement in Canada and elsewhere naturally opposed the move, but Canada supported the calling of the special session in order to see if any alternative to partition existed which could produce a "constructive result," in St. Laurent's words.[58] Nothing came of this session, but Canada's willingness to even consider abandoning partition in the event that American-British cooperation on something else might be achieved, is a clear indication of how little influence Zionist lobbying, or Jewish votes, had on Canadian policy.

A similar case arose after 15 May 1948, when an independent State of Israel had been declared. In the months following that declaration, Zionist lobbying, through the UZC and the Canadian Palestine Committee, concentrated on convincing Ottawa to recognize the new Jewish state and support its admission to the United Nations. All the stops were pulled out in an intensive campaign but no results were obtained for over seven months.[59] The Canadian government was unwilling to get too far out of step with the United Kingdom, which refused to recognize Israel,[60] for fear that Canada would undermine its potential role in trying to build bridges between the United States and the United Kingdom in the Palestine issue.[61] By this time Canadian foreign policy had become very much tied up with the founding of the North Atlantic Treaty Organization and Canadian policy-makers feared that NATO was being endangered by the wide policy divisions which separated Britain and the United States over Palestine. Thus the conciliation of those two pillars of the western alliance, always the major cornerstone of Canadian foreign policy, played the dominant role in shaping Canadian Palestine policy in the summer and fall of 1948.[62]

If the political pressure of Zionist lobbying can be said to have had any effect at all, it was on Canada's extension of de facto recognition of Israel on 24 December 1948. The first public sign that this was in the air came on 22 November when Pearson, in a speech to the First Committee of the United Nations General Assembly, listed "certain facts which must be accepted" if peace was to be restored. The first of these was "the emergence of an independent Jewish state in Palestine."[63] This statement led Shertok to believe Canada would support Israel's admission to the United Nations as part of the extension of de facto recognition when the matter came before the Security Council in December.[64] When the issue came to a vote on 17 December, however, Canada abstained and that action helped defeat the resolution.[65] Shertok and other members of the Israeli delegation were surprised and disappointed at Canada's action and urged that Canada help offset the impact of the Security Council vote by extending recognition to Israel.[66]

Canada's 17 December abstention was not a reversal of Canadian policy. It came because of the particular wording of the admission resolution which appeared to call on the Security Council to enforce the boundaries laid out in the 29 November 1947 partition resolution of the General Assembly. The Canadian government rejected this notion and viewed the 29 November resolution as a recommendation only. Canada wanted to leave the boundary open because it was clear that as far as the Arabs and the Israelis were concerned the November 1947 partition boundaries were not acceptable. Better then, it was reasoned, to leave the matter for the United Nations Palestine Conciliation Commission.[67]

On 21 December Pearson recommended to cabinet that de facto recognition be granted and cabinet approved; Shertok was informed on 24 December.[68] This may have been the one time that the Canadian government acted out of concern for Jewish votes and under the influence of the Zionist lobby, because the Jewish community in Canada was certain to be highly vocal in its displeasure that Israel had been barred from UN membership because of a Canadian abstention.[69] The short time span between the abstention and the cabinet decision—four days—did not allow a full public relations effort to be mobilized, however, and if this consideration was in the minds of cabinet ministers, it was a matter of potential, not actual, pressure.

From the beginnings of the campaign by Canadian Zionists to mobilize a broad range of public opinion and to focus the concerns of Canadian Jews on the Palestine question until Canada's de facto recognition of

Israel, the Zionists and their allies lobbied the government to take a pro-Zionist course. The presence of that lobby is undeniable but it is not a priori proof of its effectiveness. In fact, the Zionist lobby had little or no impact whatever on Canada's Palestine and middle east policy during this period. The Canadian public, for the most part, remained basically apathetic about Palestine to the very end[70] and Canadian public opinion was heavily behind Britain even though Canadians, no less than the British themselves, were often not sure where Britain stood. This public attitude gave the government all the freedom it needed to make its decisions on the basis of how it viewed the conflict in Palestine within the larger context of Great Power relations and Canadian national interests. Jewish votes and Zionist lobbying made no difference to Canadian policy.

NOTES

1. Zachariah Kay, *Canada and Palestine: The Politics of Non-Commitment* (Jerusalem, 1978), pp. 56–57.

2. Irving Abella and Harold Troper, *None Is Too Many: Canada and the Jews of Europe, 1933–1948* (Toronto, 1982).

3. Central Zionist Archives, Jerusalem (CZA), Zionist Organization of Canada Minutes and Correspondence, File S5-786, Minutes of United Zionist Council Meeting of 8 April 1941.

4. Ibid., National Council Minutes, 26 May 1941.

5. Canadian Jewish Congress Archives, Montreal (CJCA), Palestine Collection, "A Proposal for a Canadian Palestine Committee."

6. CZA, Files of the Political Department, File S25-1998, "Summary of Report Delivered by Harry Batshaw K.C. . . . at the 27th Convention of the Zionist Organization of Canada."

7. CZA, Zionist Organization of Canada Minutes and Correspondence, File S5–786, Lauterback to Jesse Schwartz, 9 December 1942; 2 February 1943.

8. Zvi Ganin, *Truman, American Jewry, and Israel, 1945–1948* (New York, 1979), p. 8.

9. CZA, Files of the Political Department, File S25-1998 "Summary of Report Delivered by Harry Batshaw, K.C. . . . at the 27th convention of Zionist Organization of Canada."

10. Public Archives of Canada (PAC), Department of External Affairs Records, RG 25, G1, Vol. 1839, File 583/2, Frieman to King, 3 December 1943.

11. Interview with Elizabeth P. MacCallum, July 1980.

12. PAC, RG 25, G1, Vol. 1839, File 583/2, "Memorandum for Mr. Glazebrook . . . ," 17 December 1943.

13. Ibid., King to Frieman, 24 December 1943.

14. CZA, Files of the Political Department, File S25-1998 "Summary of Report Delivered by Harry Batshaw K.C. . . . at the 27th Convention of the Zionist Organization of Canada."

15. PAC, Zacks Papers, MG 30, C144, Vol. 1, Zacks to Schwartz, 14 April 1944.

16. Ibid., Vol. 3, Carrel to Zacks, 24 April 1945.

17. CZA, Central Office London Files, File Z4-14731, Frieman to Weizmann, 31 March 1944.

18. CZA, Files of the Political Department, File S25-7496 "Report to Members of Public Relations Committee," n.d.; PAC, King Papers, MG 26, J4, Vol. 381, File 3971 "Memorandum re Meeting of the Prime Minister with a Delegation of the Canadian Palestine Committee . . . ," 7 April 1944.

19. PAC, King Papers, MG 26, J4, Vol. 310, File 3308 "Postwar Policy and the 1939 White Paper," n.d.

20. Ibid., "Memorandum for Dr. Gibson," 8 May 1944.

21. Minutes of the Commonwealth Prime Ministers Meeting are found in King Papers, Vol. 322, File 3407.

22. CJCA, Palestine Collection, Batshaw to "Fellow Zionists," 24 July 1944.

23. CZA, Files of the American Section, New York, File 25-1123, Batshaw to Goldmann, 7 August 1944.

24. Ibid., Confidential Memo re "Interview with the Under Secretary of State for External Affairs . . . , 4 August 1944."

25. Zacks Papers, Vol. 3, Zacks to ? 21 August 1944.

26. CJCA, Palestine Collection, Minutes of the United Zionist Council, 12 October 1944.

27. Zacks Papers, Vol. 1, Memorandum re Eastern Division's Public Relations, 8 December 1944.

28. Ibid., Wershof to Schwartz, 10 November 1944.

29. CJCA, Palestine Collection, Press Release from the Canadian Palestine Committee, 11 November 1944.

30. Zacks Papers, Vol. 3, Dorfman to Zacks, 22 December 1944.

31. CZA, Files of the American Section, New York, File Z5-1123, Report of Herbert A. Mowat for January and February 1945.

32. Ibid.

33. King Papers, Vol. 310, File 3308 Robertson to King, 1 February 1945.

34. Ibid., "Additions to Canadian Palestine Committee Since April 1, (1945)."

35. Kay, *Canada and Palestine*, pp. 116–117.

36. Eliahu Elath, *Zionism at the UN: A Diary of the First Days* (Philadelphia, 1976) pp. 5–10, 14–15.

37. See John W. Holmes, *The Shaping of Peace: Canada and the Search for World Order, Vol. 1, 1943–1957* (Toronto, 1979), pp. 245ff.

38. Elath, *Zionism at the UN*, pp. 38–39 and other diary entries.

39. Holmes, *Shaping of Peace*, p. 254.

40. See, for example, *Calgary Herald*, 22 July 1946.

41. Zacks Papers, Vol. 2, Schwartz to Zacks, 7 April 1947.

42. David J. Bercuson, "'Illegal' Corvettes: Canadian Blockade Runners to Palestine, 1946–1949," *Canadian Jewish Historical Society Journal* (Fall, 1982).

43. PAC, RG 25, b-3, Vol. 2152, "Palestine and the Special Assembly of the United Nations," 22 April 1947.

44. Canada, House of Commons, *Debates*, 2 June 1947.

45. CZA, Files of the American Section, File Z5-4871, "Statement Issued by United Zionist Council," 5 September 1947; CJCA, *Congress Bulletin*, September 1947, p. 19.

46. CZA, Files of the American Section, Z5-485 II, Gelber to Members of the Jewish Agency Executive, 17 September 1947. The Shertok quote is from a note pencilled by him on the document.

47. Peter Stursberg, *Lester Pearson and the American Dilemma* (Toronto, 1980), p. 72.

48. Ibid.

49. Abella and Troper, *None Is Too Many*, pp. 238–279.

50. Interview with J. W. Pickersgill, July 1980.

51. PAC, RG 25, File AR 35/1, Vol. 3, Pearson to Robertson, 30 December 1947.

52. King Papers, Vol. 429, File: "1947, Saber to Scythes" Draft letter from the Prime Minister to the Secretary of State for External Affairs, 10 September 1947; PAC, Privy Council Office, Records RG 2/16/Vol. 10, Conclusions of Cabinet Meeting of 11 September 1947 (henceforth Cabinet Conclusions).

53. Department of External Affairs, Historical Section Files (DEA) File 5475-CD-40C, Canadian Consulate General, New York (CCGNY) to Secretary of State for External Affairs (SSEA) 14 October 1947.

54. Cabinet Conclusions, 14 October 1947.

55. DEA, 5475-CD-40C, "Text of a Statement Made on October 14, 1947 in the Ad Hoc Committee on Palestine. . . ."

56. CJCA, "Statement on Palestine: Rt. Hon. J. L. Ilsley, Canada," 26 November 1947.

57. PAC, RG 25, Rile AR 35/1, Vol. 6, "The Policy in Regard to Palestine of the Canadian Delegation to the Second Session of the General Assembly," 27 December 1947.

58. House of Commons, *Debates*, 29 April 1948.

59. Zacks Papers, Vol. 2, Appeal to "Key Members of National Public Relations Committee," 2 June 1948; *Globe and Mail*, 17 May 1948, p. 5; Israel State Archives (ISA) RG 93.03, File 16, Box 69, Comay to Israeli Delegation, UN, 13 July 1948; DEA, 5475-CD-5-40, Memorandum for the Action Under-Secretary of State for External Affairs, 2 December 1948.

60. DEA, 47B(S), SSEA to High Commissioner for Canada in the United Kingdom, 18 May 1948; Cabinet Conclusions, 26 May 1948.

61. DEA, 47G (S), "Palestine Recognition of Jewish State: Policy of Commonwealth Governments," 9 September 1948.

62. Escott Reid, *Time of Fear and Hope* (Toronto, 1977), pp. 52–53.

63. R. A. MacKay, ed., *Canadian Foreign Policy 1945–1954: Selected Speeches and Documents* (Toronto, 1970), p. 144.

64. DEA, 5475-CR-2-40, Canadian Delegation, UNO, Paris to SSEA, 26 November 1948.

65. ISA, RG 93.03, File 19, Box 2414, Comay to Pearson, 18 December 1948.

66. Ibid.

67. Department of External Affairs, *Statements and Speeches,* No. 48/65, "Application of Israel for Membership in the United Nations," Text of Mr. Riddell's Speech, 17 December 1948.

68. Cabinet Conclusions, 21 December 1948.

69. MacCallum interview.

70. According to one informed observer this was true as late as December 1948. National Archives, Washington, RG 59, General Records of the Department of State, 867N.01/12-3048, Steinhardt to Secretary of State, 30 December 1948.

12

The Origins of Organized National Jewish Philanthropy in the United States, 1914–1939

MARC LEE RAPHAEL

Until the outbreak of World War One, largely as a result of the vitality and generosity of western and central European Jewry and the smallness and disunity of the Jewish community in the United States, American Jewry played a minor role in serving East European Jewish philanthropic needs.[1] But during the war, the threat of death and destruction to the Jews in Europe (millions of whom stood directly in the path of the contending armies), the precarious situation of the Jews in Turkish-controlled Palestine,[2] the enormity of the needs of eastern Europe, coupled with the critical problems of survival for Jews in London, Paris, Vienna, Berlin, Amsterdam and elsewhere on the continent, led to the first massive nation-wide fund raising efforts by American Jews. The techniques which the philanthropic leadership developed in the campaigns of World War One would be those which still dominated Jewish philanthropy seventy years later, when American Jews would pledge nearly $600 million.

Between 1914 and 1918 the Jews of eastern Europe were especially vulnerable. They had no institutions or resources to protect them against foreign armies or popular hostility and their women were left with little means of support when their petty trader/artisan husbands went off to war. As Jewish refugees from the towns, villages and smaller cities crowded into the larger cities, especially in Poland, tens of thousands were in need of food and clothing.

The machinery for providing massive assistance to overseas Jewry simply did not exist in 1914, and had to be created. The Union of Orthodox Jewish Congregations organized first by forming, on 4 October 1914, the Central Committee for the Relief of Jews Suffering Through the War. But these immigrants, who sought to direct funds primarily to Palestine and eastern Europe, were quickly engulfed, perhaps co-opted, by the American Jewish Committee and its highly acculturated German Jewish aristocracy. They brought together forty organizations, many of which had quickly sprung into action in response to European appeals, at New York's Temple Emanu-El three weeks later. This group, dominated by the Committee, established a committee of five (three AJC men; one Central Committee man; one socialist), instructed the five to ask one hundred prominent Jews to form a new committee—the American Jewish Relief Committee—dominated, on the twenty-five-member board, by the Committee leadership, and got the AJRC off the ground with a budget of $100,000.

The immigrants, however, quickly and to everyone's surprise, rejected membership in the AJRC and insisted on soliciting funds on their own. A People's Relief Committee, organized in 1915 and headed by Meyer London, did the same; it would raise $800,000 by 15 July 1917, while the Central Committee, by the same date, would raise over $2,000,000, retaining about 30 per cent of this sum for direct distribution to *yeshivoth* and institutions in eastern Europe and Palestine as well as to organizations (and even individuals) specifically designated by contributors. The Central Committee did, however, agree to join the AJRC in creating an organization which would identify needs and allocate and distribute funds collected separately by the German Jews (AJRC) and the East European Jews (CC), and later (November 1915), by the People's Relief Committee. Thus was the American Jewish Joint Distribution Committee, or Joint, born (27 November 1914), a momentous event for the subsequent raising, allocating and distributing of massive sums of money.[3]

By the end of 1915 local and state committees had raised about $1,500,000 for distribution overseas: the Central Committee conducted nationwide campaigns in synagogues and through stamp sales; the PRC worked the unions; while the AJRC accumulated files of potential contributors throughout the nation and, equally important, designated state/local committees to solicit these persons not only by mail but, sometimes, in person. One leader, Nathan Straus, was so exhilarated by the success and overwhelmed by the needs that he called for a $5 million campaign in 1916—to be launched by his $10,000 gift.[4]

To make such a venture possible, mass appeals were launched, beginning with the $1 million Carnegie Hall "kick-off" in New York City on 21

December 1915, and followed by similar extravaganzas in other cities which raised $4,750,000 by the end of 1916.[5] Rabbi Judah Magnes, after a fact-finding visit to Europe on behalf of the Joint in 1916, proposed a $10 million campaign for 1917, and the CC as well as the AJRC introduced yet more techniques which would subsequently become integral parts of national Jewish philanthropy. These included assigning quotas to each community (New York City's was $5 million), organizing lists of prospects by occupational categories and soliciting within each grouping with volunteer "regiments," creating women's committees to solicit wives, staging Jewish cultural events (especially concerts) in which a percentage of the proceeds went for overseas relief, and using newspapers, theatres and visiting speakers in imaginative ways. By the end of 1918 the Joint had allocated nearly $15 million, a sum far beyond anything done before by American Jewry. It had introduced techniques, many the brainchild of Jacob Billikopf, the former head of the federations in Milwaukee and Kansas City and the director of the World War One campaigns, which would dominate subsequent Jewish philanthropy.[6]

For the future of mass Jewish fund-raising, two developments during the war years loomed large. First, the AJRC and CC organized campaign rallies and solicited individuals in dozens of towns and cities throughout the United States. Much like the nonsectarian "war chest" drives conducted at the same time, an elaborate, systematic canvassing machinery reached across the land and made personal contact with the top prospects individually, and with the masses in rallies. At the end of the war Jacob Billikopf could boast, with truth, that "there is not a city in America where there is a single Jewish inhabitant in which, at one time or another, we have not made an appeal."[7]

What helped greatly to assure generous collections of money were organized teams, with captains appointed by federation leaders, distinguished leaders sent on whirlwind campaigns, and friendly competition, chronicled in the Anglo-Jewish and Yiddish press. These campaigns enhanced the prestige of Jewish philanthropy, created new heroes, confirmed the emerging thesis that centralised fund-raising could amass more money with less annoyance to givers than several independent drives, and launched philanthropy into the forefront of American Jewish priorities.

Secondly, the JDC provided one of the earliest meeting grounds, in the area of Jewish philanthropy, for German and Russian Jews. Although the chairman from 1914 to 1932, Felix M. Warburg, felt most comfortable with fellow members of the German-Jewish aristocracy, and this group did dominate the executive of the Joint, the inner circle of men that determined its policy in the formative years of the organization was one-third East European. Joseph C. Hyman, the actual executive head of the organi-

zation (acting secretary, secretary, executive director and finally executive
vice-chairman), was from an East European Jewish family, while Joseph
A. Rosen, an ex-Menshevik revolutionary, headed the Joint's Russian
work. Warburg, Paul Baerwald, James N. Rosenberg and Bernhard Kahn
were able to work rather easily with them.

The Joint's secretary, Albert Lucas, was secretary of the Union of
Orthodox Jewish Congregations, while on the subcommittee of eight
which received and digested every report on conditions and needs abroad
and then made recommendations, three were East European, three were
strongly pro-Zionist, and all eight seemed to have worked cooperatively.
In addition, of the fifty-seven men on the Joint board, a sizeable number
were Orthodox, including at least one rabbi (Moses S. Margolies, chief
rabbi of Boston and then rabbi of the Orthodox congregation, Kehilath
Jeshurun, in New York City). Many, such as Harry Cutler and Harry
Fischel, had official Zionist connections, were intimately connected to the
East European Jewish community, and conducted their business in a
rather friendly manner with the cosmopolitan bankers of the board.[8]

This spirit was also true of Warburg. With respect to the Zionists, for
example, while he never accepted the Palestine first arguments of
Weizmann, neither did he accept the anti-Zionism of the Joint's largest
financial supporter, Julius Rosenwald. Warburg was a non-Zionist who
could work well with fiery Zionist leaders and their opponents.

So the Joint represented a meeting place for all of American Jewry,
even if one group had more control than the other. As a result, American
Jewry achieved a degree of collaboration and organizational impetus that
made the organization of the Joint a major step toward the eventual
maturation of American Jewry. No small credit for such a step should go
to Warburg, who, according to one communal professional, "walked with
his head high above" the "small Jewish politics of the period [which]
raged about him."[9]

Billikopf and the others who helped organize the Joint's campaigns of
1916 and 1917 did not begin with a tabula rasa, of course. Efforts to coordinate charitable activities within individual American Jewish communities
began to emerge in response to the tremendous needs of the East European Jewish immigrants. In 1895 and 1896 federations of Jewish philanthropies—central organs for raising and distributing local funds to
(overwhelmingly) local organizations—were organized in Boston and
Cincinnati respectively, and then in other large communities during the
next two decades. But not until after the successful campaigns of World
War One were such federations established in all the large communities—
usually by the captains of the war relief drive—as well as in many intermediate and smaller ones.

During and immediately after the war, the collection of funds provided an early model for today's highly organized, specialized, computerized, half-billion-dollar American Jewish fund-raising. The federations and welfare funds thoroughly canvassed the community, compiled lists of potential contributors (noting either their previous gift or potential gift), sent out a solicitation letter with a subscription blank, appealing to those on the list for funds, and followed up the letter with personal visits. The funds raised in federation drives supplemented the overseas campaign, helped to support local health, education, welfare, cultural and community-relations organizations, and sustained national agencies enhancing Jewish identity and protecting Jewish rights.

Federations captured the imagination of businessmen. Modelling themselves on the most progressive business and organizational structures, they promised efficient coordination and organization of the communal welfare machinery, immunity from multiple solicitation, economical collection and distribution of funds, and the development of a broad base of support which would relieve the pressure on the small circle of givers.

The most dramatic change in these federations during the 1920s occurred in response to the lingering needs of overseas Jewry—needs felt vividly in 1922 with the three-year $15 million emergency relief drive, and again in 1925 with another drive for $15 million both chaired by David A. Brown and conducted throughout American Jewish communities on behalf of European, but not Palestinian, Jews. The Central Committee, AJRC, People's Relief Committee and JDC remained intact for these drives, and the mechanisms for raising $6 million from New York Jews or $1 million from Chicago Jews in both campaigns were those established a decade earlier. In addition, several federations began, for the first time, to raise funds for, and allocate dollars to, overseas agencies in Europe and Palestine, while in other communities a welfare fund began to accomplish this purpose.[10]

In one year, 1926, Columbus, Detroit, Indianapolis, San Francisco and Oakland initiated such funds, while in Cincinnati, Omaha, Cleveland and Minneapolis, within the next five years, welfare funds, combining national, overseas and local allocations, were established under federation auspices.[11] In yet other communities, although no new organizations were created, federation allocations began increasingly to include the Joint, United Palestine Appeal, Polish *yeshivoth,* Palestine schools and Jerusalem orphanages. The ideal was, of course, that each agency so funded would cease its local solicitations and leave contributors with only one appeal annually; in fact, however, tensions between local federations and several overseas (that is, Palestine) organizations continued for many years as the latter continued to send appeals to various communities.[12]

The problem which resulted from the emergence of welfare funds and the expansion of federations was predictable: local allocation committees felt completely unqualified to judge the merits of remotely based overseas (and even national) agencies, while individuals, when solicited privately by an overseas organization, often turned to their local federation for information about the agency.

In addition, the federations obviously needed some type of coordinating body to bring their leadership together, share common concerns, problems and successes, and engage in common planning. The first person, to my knowledge, to suggest such an organization was Abraham H. Fromenson, at that time executive secretary of the National Farm School. In 1914 he proposed a "Federation of federations" that would enable the "representatives of the various communities whose philanthropic work is organized" to "have a means of coming together at stated intervals for the discussion of common problems, ways and means of increasing contributions, methods of administration, and consideration of the financing of existing national institutions as well as the advisability of permitting the launching of new philanthropic enterprises." Although for many years nobody reacted positively, or, for that matter, in print at least, negatively to Fromenson's suggestion, when federation executives finally created an organization for "coming together" it was to accomplish every one of his goals.[13]

The Great Depression, and not an overseas event, provided the catalyst for the creation of a coordinating organization for the federations. As executives of the sixty-one American and two Canadian federations, together with those who headed the five welfare funds, met often during 1930 and 1931 to discuss the impact of the economy's collapse on local agencies, they discovered the advantages that could accrue from joint consultation and coordination vis-à-vis national and overseas concerns. An editorial, on 20 March 1931, in the first issue of *Notes and News,* the publication of the Bureau of Jewish Social Research, the agency to which all the federations and welfare funds reported, bemoaned the absence of centralized information about fundraising. A year later, on 8 April 1932, an editorial decried "the lack of centralized effort in coordinating fundraising activities for non-local activities."

In 1931 and 1932 more than one hundred Jewish communities were holding at least two and about eighty conducted three annual campaigns: one for local causes, one for the Joint, and one for the United Palestine Appeal, an organization founded in 1925 by Zionist supporters who complained that too large a proportion of the Joint's funds were going to European Jewish communities. Not only were there multiple campaigns, but they were intensely competitive. Abba Hillel Silver, a prominent

Cleveland rabbi, consistently refused, throughout the 1920s, to campaign for European Jewish causes. When he refused, for example, to join the National Committee of the United American Jewish Campaign for Foreign Reconstruction and Russian Colonization, he argued that "mass colonization in Russia [is] a stupendous blunder" and that "Russian colonization will pass; Palestine will remain." He and other Zionists bitterly attacked the UAJC emphasis on Russian Jewry's reconstruction, rejected innumerable appeals to either join the JDC causes or refrain from attacking these causes, and felt that the Joint leadership, and especially David A. Brown, had betrayed them in the three-year campaign of the 1920s by concentrating all their energies on eastern Europe and thus neglecting Palestine. With multiple campaigns, and accusations from one side to the other, there was much about overseas distribution the federations and welfare funds did not know.[14]

At the May 1932 National Conference of Jewish Social Service in Philadelphia, representatives discussed at some length the dilemma of the Depression, the great value in joint planning and the need to coordinate information on national and overseas agencies. They agreed to establish a Council of Jewish Federations and Welfare Funds which would coordinate such information, and a committee was formed for this purpose.[15]

Twenty-five "representative" communal leaders formed this organizing committee, and at the end of October 1932, in Cleveland, the CJFWF was formally launched with agencies representing fifteen cities. The general assembly elected an executive committee of fifteen and instructed it to meet semi-annually, elected William J. Shroder of Cincinnati the president, and announced its main task to be aiding Jewish federations to make intelligent and informed decisions about national and international Jewish organizations.

This immediately became the CJFWF's most important function. The executive committee met in New York City in February 1933 and prepared detailed budgets of every national and overseas organization which solicited in communal campaigns. The first report of June 1934, for example, detailed the American Jewish Committee, American Jewish Congress, Joint, Hadassah, Jewish National Fund and Hebrew Sheltering and Immigrant Aid Society budgets; the second report of that same month analysed the American Palestine Campaign, B'nai B'rith, the Hebrew University and the United Jewish Appeal; the September 1934 report provided descriptions of the Jewish Welfare Board and several smaller agencies' budgets; the fourth report, December 1934, studied the Jewish Telegraphic Agency, ORT and Mizrachi. Each report made crystal clear what percentage of an organization's budget came from the federations, what the increases requested (if any) were for, and, before long, began to recommend specific quotas to communities. From the start, the CJFWF held enormous power in determining communal allocations in both national and overseas funding.[16]

By the time the CJFWF emerged, the Germans and Russians, or, if one wishes to argue that such distinctions were rapidly fading, the Joint and the Jewish Agency for Palestine, had agreed to conduct an experimental $6 million joint "Allied Jewish Campaign" in every federated and welfare fund city during 1930. The split would be 58 per cent and 42 per cent, the JDC receiving $3.5 million and the Jewish Agency $2.5 million. This was a coup for the Zionists, by now increasingly potent, as a separate campaign would never yield so much (the Zionist campaign of 1928, for example, yielded less than $1 million).

David Brown, the veteran of several JDC campaigns, had already headed the Palestine Emergency Fund campaign of 1929, an indication of the triumph of his philanthropic skills over ideology, and he would head the Allied Jewish Campaign too. In 1930 even Abba Hillel Silver, the fierce opponent of the Joint in many earlier campaigns and an exceptionally popular keynote fund-raiser, agreed to address gatherings under AJC sponsorship. His rousing campaign address in Buffalo, in January 1930, devoted as many words to Jewish suffering in eastern Europe as to the needs of Palestine Jewry. Louis Lipsky, president of the Zionist Organization of America, was so carried away by the cooperative spirit that he proclaimed, in his campaign kick-off address, that the "Zionist movement aims not only to redeem Palestine for the Jews but also to strengthen Jewish life wherever possible."[17]

Although the founding of the Allied Jewish Campaign did not signal a permanent linking of all overseas fund-raising, the reason was financial rather than ideological. The combined campaign coincided with the beginning of the Depression, and the campaign raised only a small part of the expected sum: $2.5 million in pledges and only $1.5 million in cash by December 1930.[18] The accusations which flew from one side to the other, and which led to separate campaigns in 1931, 1932 and 1933, were largely the complaints of organizational leaders caught in a situation where desperate needs far outweighed available resources. It was easier to blame each other than the more mysterious economic forces at work. Nevertheless, the joint drive had created important communal values and laid the foundation in many cities for enduring cooperation on behalf of Jewish causes.

By 1934 the two sides—those seeking to build Jewish life in eastern Europe and other Jewish centers, and those committed to constructing a Jewish homeland in Palestine by linking the backs, hearts and minds of those Jews in eastern Europe and elsewhere—felt that economic conditions could sustain a joint campaign. The modest $3.2 million UJA campaign, however, raised only $2.2 million and when the JDC received its share—a paltry $1,290,000—its leaders found it hard to believe it could not have done better alone.[19]

Nevertheless, they agreed to another try, but in 1935 the UJA found only one city, Cleveland, meeting its assigned quota, and only $1.6 million raised in the entire campaign. This was, for example, two million dollars less than the Joint had raised in 1928, and the executive board voted at the end of the campaign to discontinue joint appeals. It felt that a significant number of quite wealthy men would give 100 per cent of their gifts to the Joint (for European Jewry), and resented the 55/45 or 60/40 split with what one board member called the "Palestine component."

The Zionist leadership, however, did not agree so quickly that the best strategy was to pursue an independent course. It reasoned that dual campaigns encouraged the biggest donors, still the older German-Jewish wealth, to make a single gift to European Jewry, and 45 per cent of those gifts was far more attractive than nothing. But the Joint had made its decision for 1936, despite Zionist overtures, and, as it turned out, for 1937 and 1938 as well, and Zionist pleas to reconsider were either ignored or rebuffed.

The decision to unite once again—a decision which has endured—came less from any internal process than from two shattering overseas developments. The infamous *Kristallnacht* of 10 November 1938 and Göring's decision to demand a 7 billion mark indemnity crystallized the growing realization among Joint leaders that, in spite of their ideological differences with Zionists, only a combined appeal could mobilize the resources necessary to meet the tremendous needs. And for the Zionists, the realization that immigration to Palestine had dwindled severely in 1937 and 1938 and that enormous sums of money would be necessary to get Jews out of Europe, led them to seek the support of non-Zionists. Neither did so, however, enthusiastically. A Joint executive claimed the Zionists were "fanatics, dancing to the tune of dreamers," while a ZOA leader stated that the JDC "ministers to the pathological phobias of a few New York Jews." Nevertheless, the common agenda drew them together, though their own priorities would be vigorously, even bitterly, defended.

Much of the credit for this 1939 merger to form the permanent UJA goes to the Council of Jewish Federations and Welfare Funds, which doggedly pursued the leaders of each faction as well as some of their constituents. Every federation/welfare fund director clearly understood (and the discussions at their general assembly reflected this) that a combined campaign would be more efficient and more profitable than the tension-filled and competing double campaigns of the past several years. Everyone had experience working together, the needs were so great everywhere that compromise seemed possible and even essential, and the Council dangled to each side a $20 million campaign for 1939. The only condition the CJFWF sought to impose (successfully) was that the precampaign allocation percentages would be binding on all 225 CJFWF community campaigns. The annual battle over allocations, repeated in each city, had exhausted federation leaders, and they sought a *regnum* in the name of compromise. As the CJFWF president explained succinctly, our request is "based on the desire to avoid friction arising from competition for funds in welfare fund cities; fundamentally it was based on the belief that a fair agreement would produce maximum giving." Both sides agreed; the Council launched a massive program in 1939 to train campaign leaders and workers in harmony; and the 1939 UJA raised an impressive $16.2 million. The Council's sense that maximum fund-raising needed a European and a Palestine component, and the acceptance by both sides that this was vitally necessary, was given a hard push by events in the international arena. At the same time, the continuous experience and expertise of the national and local philanthropic apparatus provided the organization to make organized national Jewish philanthropy an immediate success.

NOTES

1. On the limited role of American Jewry in overseas philanthropic affairs before 1914, see Moshe Davis, "Jewish Religious Life and Institutions in America," in L. Finkelstein, ed., *The Jews* 3d. ed., vol. I (Philadelphia, 1960), pp. 509–510.

2. The seriousness of Palestine Jewry's plight was brought to the attention of some American Jewish leaders very early, as when Henry Morgenthau cabled from Turkey on 31 August 1914, requesting $50,000 to aid these Jews. Although reports vary on how the money was raised (see note 4), it was quickly in Morgenthau's hands.

3. Oscar Handlin, *A Continuing Task* (New York, 1964); Herbert Agar, *The Saving Remnant* (New York, 1960); "Jewish War Relief Work," *American Jewish Year Book* 5678 (1917–1918), pp. 194–226; Naomi W. Cohen, *Not Free to Desist* (Philadelphia, 1972), pp. 81–90; Yehuda Bauer, *My Brother's Keeper* (Philadelphia, 1974), pp. 3–8; Morris Engelman, *Four Years of Relief and War Work by the Jews of America 1914–1918* (New York, 1918).

4. The Anglo-Jewish press of nearly every city followed the campaign closely; I used the *Philadelphia Jewish Exponent*. See also, for the Straus reference, Handlin, *Continuing Task*, p. 26.

5. One million dollars was collected on one day, 27 January 1916, as President Wilson proclaimed it Jewish Sufferers Relief Day.

6. See note 4. For the 1918 "Honor Roll" of contributors to the Jewish War Sufferers Campaign, see *Jewish Charities* IX, no. 3 (July 1918), p. 58.

7. Jacob Billikopf, "Campaign Methods," *Jewish Charities* IX, no. 11 (March 1919).

8. Joint Distribution Committee Papers, Box 18, American Jewish Historical Society (Waltham, Mass.).

9. David Farrer, *The Warburgs: The Story of a Family* (New York, 1975), pp. 96–108; Agar, *Saving Remnant*, p. 31.

10. *Jewish Daily Bulletin*, passim.

11. Harry Lurie, *A Heritage Affirmed* (Philadelphia, 1961), p. 105.

12. Federation allocations from this period, city by city, are in the Council of Jewish Federations and Welfare Funds Papers, AJHS.

13. *Jewish Charities* v, no. 2 (September 1914), p. 28.

14. David Brown to Abba Hillel Silver, 22 October 1925 and 26 January 1926; Silver to Brown, 16 September 1925 and 2 February 1926; Silver to Louis Marshall, 29 October 1925, in Personal Correspondence, 9–4–1, Abba Hillel Silver papers, The Temple (Cleveland, Ohio).

15. The decision of May 1932 was the culmination of discussions which took place among federation executives at Cleveland (January 1931) and Pittsburgh (November 1931), conferences the previous year in response to the 1929 presidential address of Samuel A. Goldsmith at the Atlantic City convention of the National Conference of Jewish Social Service.

16. The budget reports have been published and are at the American Jewish Archives, AJHS and Blaustein libraries.

17. "Allied Jewish Campaign," Mss./Ty 20–5, Abba Hillel Silver papers; *Jewish Daily Bulletin,* 9–11 March 1930.

18. *American Jewish Year Book* 33 (1931–1932), p. 30.

19. For the documentation for this, and the subsequent paragraphs, see the notes to chapter 1 in my *A History of the United Jewish Appeal,* Brown Judaic Studies 34 (Chico, Calif., 1982).

13
A Tale of Two Communities

The Growth and Decline of Small-Town
Jewish Communities in Northern Ontario
and Southwestern Louisiana

GERALD L. GOLD

North American Jews are usually thought of as an urban minority even though many small towns in both Canada and the United States, particularly trading centres, have included influential historic Jewish minority communities. These rural Jewish minorities, however, have declined drastically in the past forty years and, in many instances, formerly thriving communities have disappeared entirely. Rural Jews, in their role as tradesmen rather than as capitalists, have often played an active role in their communities by influencing the economic decisions that led to particular regional developments. The early involvement of Jews in the definition of communities also gave them a "pioneer" status and a commitment to their region equal, at least, to their ethnic commitment to Judaism. This is particularly the case for Jews who moved into frontier communities in the nineteenth century, at the very time when elites in those communities were defining a relationship to the surrounding rural hinterland. Later Jewish settlers, of course, did not share this pioneer status. Moreover, there were often enough Jewish families in small towns and service centres for some Jews to become concerned with the institutional aspects of being Jewish in a Christian environment and at some point to develop Jewish institutions.

There is also considerable evidence that, before the Second World War, despite their status as outsiders or "strangers," Jews living in small towns fared better in everyday inter-ethnic relations than did their urban counterparts. Because of this apparent increased tolerance as well as the historical role of Jewish traders, a critical examination of Jewish communities should also consider Jews in small rural communities and the factors that led to their collapse.

Through the comparative study of Jewish communities in Timmins in Northern Ontario, and in Opelousas in Southwestern Louisiana, this paper examines the eclipse of small Jewish settlements and identifies those factors which led to their growth and decline. This is not a demographic inquiry where the disappearance of small-town Jews is explained in terms of migration to urban centres and a consolidation of ethnic institutions in large cities. Instead, the decline of rural Jewish life is here considered to be a phenomenon for which there is no single explanation. The demographic explanation is plausible from the perspective of urban Jewish institutions, for which the idea of a small-town Jewish community is a contradiction in terms for it would offer few Jewish services and more significantly, few other Jews who would be part of a common pool of marriage partners. This contradiction may be the reason why researchers have accorded a low priority to small-town Judaism. The oft-cited research by Peter Rose on small-town Jews in New York State is important to the study of ethnic relations, but Rose's study does not specifically inquire into the role of Jewish minorities within a regional context.[1] Collections of articles on American Jewry that appeared in the postwar years follow Rose's emphasis on inter-ethnic relations and on psychological adaptation to a minority status. For example, Sklare's first collection on American Jewish social patterns includes an insightful research report on small town Jews. Later research relegates the small-town Jew to a status of irrelevance; but his second volume includes only a few passing references to rural or to small-town minorities.[2] None of the American studies indicate that there may be significant differences in the adaptation of small-town Jews in Canada as compared to the United States.

Though Opelousas and Timmins are examples of a more general trend, they represent in their timing and in the origin of their settlers, contrasting patterns of Jewish settlement in small communities. Opelousas is the first of the two communities to have a Jewish minority and represents the many Central European Jewish small-town communities where "Jewish merchants kept store and traded in freshly-picked cotton."[3] The Opelousas Jews were French speakers who arrived before the influx of large numbers of eastern European Jews at the turn of the century. As in other Central European Jewish communities, Judaism in Opelousas was focused on a Reform congregation that sought a maximum possible integration with the surrounding community. By contrast, the Jews of Timmins were born in Russia and Poland and arrived in the Canadian north before or just after the First World War as part of a group of Orthodox Russian Jews. While they constantly attempted to integrate themselves into the northern frontier society, they also sought to retain their distinctiveness. Whereas both minorities participated in majority institutions, the larger Timmins community developed institutions that emphasized Jewish distinctiveness and, ultimately, most Jews left Timmins to better maintain their Jewish identities. The Jews of Opelousas, however, did not respond in a concerted manner to the integrative pressures of their environment. Though they were a smaller community, and could not maintain a full complement of Jewish institutions, the assimilation of many Opelousas Jews into elite Protestant families places the distinctiveness of North American Jewry into a context that must account for chronology and place of settlement.

The two communities were similar in that both have been trading centres for a frontier society where a French-speaking minority is the largest ethnic group. In each region, the definition of Jewish ethnicity is partly related to how this French-speaking minority has interacted with the dominant economy. Thus in Northern Ontario, Jews were prominent in forestry and in the retail trade, both of which were also essential to French Canadians. In South Louisiana, Jews were instrumental in establishing a cotton and grain trade that has been pivotal to the livelihood of French-speaking Cajun farmers. At the same time, the Jewish minority in each region was part of a wider society in which the role of Jews was defined differently than it was at the community level. In the north, the Jew was one of many ethnic minorities, all of whom were, in varying degrees, at odds with the dominant Anglo-American interests which owned the mines and mills. In the south, Jews found themselves incorporated within the landholding elite whose interests also became the interests of Jewish traders.

Each of the minority communities maintained different relationships with Jewish communities elsewhere. The northern Jewish community related strongly to the Jewish institutions that were established by the influx of Russian and Polish Jews who began arriving in Canada at the end of the nineteenth century. Their southern counterparts, however, were prominent within the dominant planter society that ruled the South after the American Civil War—though they were never completely accepted by that planter elite. From the beginning of the expansion of settlement and the introduction of new primary resource technologies, each group developed its own structures for separating themselves from the wider community. This institutional completeness[4] within each rural Jewish minority was strongly affected by the presence of and interaction with other ethnic groups. Also of importance is the attitude of the dominant society towards

minorities and, in particular, Jewish minorities, and the status of the minority as Jews within a network of Jewish ties.

THE JEWS OF OPELOUSAS:
LANDOWNERS IN FRENCH LOUISIANA

The first Jews settled in Opelousas in the decade before the Civil War
at the time that Samuel Haas, an immigrant from France, began what was
to become a prosperous merchandising and agricultural business in a town
that was, with the neighbouring bayou port of Washington, the fringe of
the old plantation belt and the edge of a cotton-growing frontier.[5] The
Opelousas Jews who were integral participants in the ante-bellum frontier
economy were similar to other southern Jews who, though "deeply sensitive to the human character of their [sic] negroes,"[6] were not in visible
opposition to slavery. The point is a significant one in that throughout the
history of Opelousas, Jews supported the white side of a racial conflict that
began with Reconstruction and which continues to be the major line of
ethnic demarcation in the present-day community.

Haas was one of about ten Opelousas Jews who were active leaders of
mainstream elite institutions such as the St. Landry parish police jury
(council for St. Landry parish), the parish school board and the Masonic
lodge. Moreover, it is this group, including personalities such as Alphonse
Levy, who launched the Southwest Louisiana Land Company, that was
responsible for the development of many new railroad-centred towns such
as Crowley, west of Opelousas. Where Levy and his co-investors introduced the rice and cotton industry to the thousands of Cajun sharecrop-
pers who had already settled the frontier between the Mississippi delta and
the Texas border.[7] Though few of these communities ever included significant Jewish minorities[8] the thirteen Jewish families which Kaplan reports
in Opelousas in 1885[9] became brokers between rural Cajun farmers and an
emerging national market for cotton and rice. These families remained in
Opelousas through the 1920s. They formed the nucleus of a group that had
much in common culturally, even though they were too much a part of
their planter milieu to be involved in the creation of separate Jewish
institutions. Most were francophones, many from Alsace, giving them a
linguistic bond with both the dominant French-speaking elites of Opelousas and Washington. French also provided a linkage with the French-
speaking white Cajuns and black Creoles who filled the unilingual agricultural communities of the surrounding prairie. Interviews and historical
research in Mamou Prairie, twenty-five miles to the west of Opelousas,
demonstrate that although Opelousas Jews owned up to two-thirds of all
agricultural land, depending on the period and locale under study, there

was no anti-Jewish sentiment among Cajuns, nor was there any identification of landowners *as* Jews except by Cajun merchants in smaller towns
and service centres for whom the Jews were competitors. As seed and
merchandise distributors and as land speculators, the Jews of Opelousas,
working through French-speaking agents, accumulated considerable
wealth in land and in what was to become profitable oil and gas leases,
while their children left the region to become doctors, bankers, oil-
speculators and politicians.

In short, the Opelousas Jews were perceived of as part of the elite
group who were responsible for the settlement and development of their
region, rather than as a distinctive ethnic and religious minority. There is
good evidence to indicate that this is also the way in which they perceived
themselves despite a persistent ideological Judaism among the older settlers.[10] At the turn of the century, a Masonic lodge was of higher priority
than a synagogue. A short-lived and active B'nai Brith chapter started in
1920, in a period in which a number of service organizations began in the
towns and villages of the region. A synagogue was opened in 1929 with ten
families and sixty-five members, though regular Jewish services were not
held there from 1942 until the 1970s. With the high rate of intermarriage
and the virtual absence of Jewish newcomers, Kaplan concludes that the
bonds that once tied Jews together in Opelousas eroded to the point that
the multiple civic ties of Opelousas Jews are with the community at large
rather than with Jewish institutions. For young Jews in Opelousas there
were no Jewish networks with which they could connect or which could
provide a Jewish context to the education that they were often receiving
from hired outsiders.[11] In recent years, this situation has begun to change
in Opelousas as migrants arrive with new business interests and as
Opelousas becomes part of the oil economy of the neighbouring city of
Lafayette.

By 1980, except for a few descendants of a family with considerable
agricultural interests, almost all of the original Jewish families had emigrated from Opelousas or married into the local non-Jewish population.
Rather than disappear, the Opelousas Jewish community was rekindled as
a community of several dozen families of relatively new arrivals whose
economic interests and social networks are vested in the oil economy of
the city of Lafayette, twenty-six miles to the south. The new Jewish residents, primarily second and third generation Americans of eastern European origin, many of whom came from cities in the north and east of the
United States, are active in businesses that are not dependent on the
expansion of an agricultural frontier.

Pre-1960 Opelousas fits a southern American pattern in which "organizational pressure" impelled Jews in trading centres to belong to a con-

gregation (founded in 1875, in the Masonic Hall) but not necessarily to be visibly active Jews. As Reform Jews, their Judaism set aside any notion of separation from the majority and their religion was thought to be a religious tradition in which the "informality and intensity of Jewish worship was replaced by a liturgical model of Protestantism housed in a temple."[12] In the South this implied almost total integration into the local community. Interestingly, where religious accommodation was required at an elite level, this was done by Jews becoming Protestants, and where the same accommodation occurred in farming communities, Jews became "Cajun" Catholic farmers. Hero captures this accommodation by joining Kaplan's narrative on Opelousas with his own intimate familiarity with elites in Southern Louisiana.

> Isolated in the local communities and profoundly dependent upon local good will and friendly relations with local white Gentiles, most of these Jews adapted themselves to prevailing values and habits. They played poker with the sheriff, fished with the county judge, hunted with the planters, and became leaders of the local Chamber of Commerce, Rotary and other service groups. Evangelical ministers and laymen were often persistent and, since the church was a social as well as a religious organization, a considerable fraction of Jews or their children joined the Presbyterian, Methodist or Episcopal, or other church which included influential members of the community. Having few Jewish choices, sons and daughters frequently married Gentiles. Even if they did not change their own religious affiliations, their children generally became Protestants [though not Catholics—even though the latter were dominant in the Opelousas planter elite].[13]

In Opelousas Jews left to marry in urban centres such as New Orleans or they took their mates from within their own social class, marrying outside of their religion. Those who married as Jews had children who invariably married Gentiles. A few attempted to retain a Jewish identity in Opelousas. Some refused to marry, retreating to a self-imposed isolation. Marriage statistics support this strong tendency toward exogamy: from 1925 until the 1950s, when Kaplan did his field research, only two of eighteen marriages involving a Jewish partner were marriages between Jews, and one of these ended in divorce.[14]

Observant Jews who married into the Opelousas community were unable to maintain a Jewish lifestyle. This was the fate of one of Kaplan's female informants whose "Jewish ideological system was unravelling itself, layer after layer. . . . In a few years it became evident that the mother no longer possessed any of the rigid distinctiveness, which had meant so much to her when she first arrived in Opelousas."[15] Even her subsequent marriage to an Orthodox Jew did not prevent the secularization of this woman's family and the marriage of her six children with non-Jews.

TIMMINS: THE PEDDLER AND THE BUNKHOUSEMAN

At least until the 1950s the erosion of Jewish institutions in Opelousas and the intermarriage of the Jewish community has no parallel in the Jewish community of Timmins, a town in northeastern Ontario that is part of a region locally referred to as the "Porcupine Camp." The comparison is more appealing because Timmins Jews have not been thought of as part of a class group by other collectivities, even though Timmins Jews have often gone to great efforts to emphasize their integration in mainstream organizations. The Timmins Jews are also descendants of the later Ashkenazic immigrants who have concentrated in cities and who were not present during the dispersal of German Jews along the southern and western frontiers of settlement.[16] It would be inaccurate, however, to present their adaptation to small-town life as separatist and rigidly Judaic in that in both communities there is a compromise to life in the small community.

The Jews of Timmins arrived as labourers for the Temiskaming and Northern Ontario Railroad which reached the silver mines of Englehart in 1906, and the lakes and pine forest of the Porcupine Camp in 1910. Most became merchants and service people for the mining camp, though some families, such as the Feldmans, were involved in the contracting and forest work that accompanied the development of the mines. Where the miners were eastern European and "ethnics" working for Anglo-American capitalists, the Jews were also eastern European and fellow ethnics, though none of them ever worked in a mine-shaft. The ability to read, even in Russian or Ukrainian, and a knowledge of trading, gave the Jewish immigrants skills that most of the miners did not have. A few had acquired a higher education in Russia or Poland, and others accumulated capital and homestead land in Englehart and New Liskeard before arriving in the Porcupine. Their status as intermediaries, merchants and brokers rapidly became important and Jews were able to assume positions of status within the frontier mining town and to acquire the trust and confidence of ethnic miners who often lived in their bunkhouses.

This intermediary status is captured in the remarks of a descendant of one of the first settlers. Her birth, in 1910, and survival of the disastrous Porcupine fire of 1911, makes her a "pioneer," a status that she insists rises above any ethnic affiliation.

> We had a store in South Porcupine [Golden] after the 1911 fire and a big bunkhouse in the back that slept around 40 men. Most of these were Russians or Ukrainians. They felt more comfortable with someone they could trade with in their own tongues. Dad wrote letters for them and read the letters they received from home. Many a bride set out for her future life from my parent's home.

Many of the first of the approximately two dozen Jewish immigrant families who were established in the Porcupine by 1920 were recruited together on Ellis Island; they were Russian Jews who were willing to take railroad work. But many others followed the expansion of the mines, seeking work in the towns. It is significant that none of the half-dozen living representatives of this first period identify themselves as Ukrainians, Russians or Poles, all of whom have well organized ethnic communities in Timmins. The majority refer to themselves as Jews and few have intermarried with Gentiles.

The first settlers imported rabbis for religious occasions such as the Jewish New Year and, as of 1912, their dead were buried by a hevra kadisha that was established in Kirkesdorf, near distant Kirkland Lake. There were plans for a synagogue ("Zion Hall" as the town's one newspaper reported the event in an "ethnic" metaphor), the temporary headquarters of which became the "Hebrew Congregational Hall" in 1925. But an emphasis on Jewish institutions would be a misreading of the first twenty years of Jewish life in the Porcupine when a growing concentration of Jews in the town of Timmins sought membership in mainstream institutions such as the Elks, the Moose, the Eastern Star and eventually, the Masons. The spouses of these pioneers became officers of organizations such as the IODE (Imperial Order of the Daughters of the Empire). When a well-known Jew died in 1929, the newspaper reported extensively on his various activities, adding that he was "born in Russia [but that he must be regarded as] a loyal Canadian [and after all other honours an] esteemed leader of the Jewish community." Though the Russian and Ukrainian origin of Jews was de-emphasized, there was not yet a distinctive Jewish institutional presence.

Ethnic institutions did not emerge until more families moved northward, escaping economic difficulties that were less visible in gold mining centres such as Timmins. The establishment of a synagogue, a school and other Jewish institutions came in the 1930s, at a time when all ethnic communities in the Porcupine consolidated their institutions. Significantly, three years after the opening of the B'nai Israel congregation in Timmins in 1928, the members of the congregation organized an annual Purim Ball explicitly designed to include the entire community. To underscore this objective, the role of Queen Esther was played by a Gentile, Miss Mary Smith. This situational dimension to Judaism, where acceptance by the community was a priority and where communication between all ethnic groups continued throughout the prewar years, though not without several incidents for which there is no parallel in Opelousas.

The sensitivity of some Timmins Jews to Canadian Jewish alarm with events in Europe was demonstrated by several events that were publicized in the local newspaper. The first recorded action was in 1920, when several Jews in this new community offered public support for the Balfour Declaration on Palestine. There is no other record of protest until 1933, when Jewish efforts to mobilize public opinion became more visible when concern was voiced for the plight of German Jews. In 1938, after *Kristallnacht,* anti-Nazi sentiment was mobilized into political action by visiting student Rabbi David Monson. The endorsement of voluntary associations was used by Monson as part of his campaign to mobilize the 122 Jewish families of Timmins to take explicit action to alleviate threats to European Jewry. Monson spoke repeatedly to church groups and service organizations, such as the Kiwanis, in an attempt to mobilize the Canadian government to take political action that would assist overseas Jews. Though it is now apparent that the political support he garnered in the north was part of an effort that would have had little impact on the racist immigration policies of the King government, Monson's campaign attracted unexpected support because it coincided with the rise of the Socialist Consumer's Cooperative and the Communist Workers' Cooperative among miners in Timmins[17] in the Porcupine Camp. Though Rabbi Monson received the backing of the Workers' Cooperative in the distribution of 25,000 anti-Nazi leaflets, the radical organizations were not supported by most of the Jewish merchants, who sided with the status quo in Timmins.[18] Merchants continued to maintain their close ties with the Anglo-Saxon political elite of Timmins and Monson's campaign, though supported by Jews, was not continued as fervently after his departure in December 1938. No ethnic group was then a threat to the Jews of Timmins, not even the majority French, whose leader, Father Theriault, resisted participating in the anti-Semitism that was then current in Quebec.

Despite this heightened awareness of international issues, the Jews of Timmins were also, like their southern counterparts, committed to a modus vivendi with the other ethnic groups in their community.[19] Also like the Jews of Opelousas, they maintained extensive ties with nearby large cities and relied on the Judaic services of those cities. But, unlike Opelousas, most Jews of Timmins retained a Jewish distinctiveness and situational separateness. Their town, founded within the living memory of some residents, and reinforced by a steady stream of migrants from the cities to the south, developed a rooted Jewish community. Moreover, few Timmins Jews married into the local Gentile population. An active Young Judea spread the pool of potential mates across all of the small centres of northeastern Ontario. Cantor Linder provided Timmins with a resident rabbi; there were three kosher butchers, two kosher bakeries which closed on the Sabbath and three Hebrew teachers. Cantor Linder was able to supervise the maintenance of an Orthodox Jewish environment through acts that ranged from the ritual killing of chickens (he was a *shoichet*), to the preparation of the dead for burial at the community's hevra kadisha. The Timmins community remained stable until the 1950s, when Timmins itself experienced out-migration that corresponded with a gradual decline in mine production and which lasted until 1964. At the beginning of the 1950s the seventy-eight members of the Timmins B'nai Brith chapter, founded in 1936, were able to issue a souvenir book, emphasizing the presence of a group of Jewish merchants and professionals in the community. They were able to provide services such as the Boy Scouts for a Jewish collectivity and a Jewish presence within the community. A researcher working in that period might have assumed that small-town Judaism would survive in Timmins.

Yet the economic decline of the town led to a steady out-migration of children and their parents. By the 1970s, a community of more than one hundred families was reduced to less than twenty and by the end of the seventies, to less than six. The synagogue was proudly opened when Timmins and the Porcupine Camp was a spawning ground of ethnic communities and institutions. Its closing marked the end of the first phase of a Jewish institutional presence in Timmins. The Timmins Jewish community still nurtures old friendships and meets regularly, even with its former rabbi, but those meetings are eight hundred kilometers to the south, in Toronto.

NOTES

1. Peter I. Rose, *Strangers in Their Midst: A Sociological Profile of the Small Town Jew and His Neighbors.* (Cornell University, Ph.D. dissertation, 1959).

2. E.g., Sidney Goldstein, "Mixed Marriages in the Deep South," p.126 in *The Jews: Social Patterns of an American Group,* Marshall Sklare, ed., (Glencoe, Ill., 1958).

3. Lloyd B. Gartner, "Immigration and the Formation of American Jewry, 1840–1925," in *Jewish Life in the United States: Perspectives from the Social Sciences,* ed. J. B. Gittler (New York, 1974), p. 39.

4. Raymond Breton, "Institutional Completeness of Ethnic Communities and Personal Relations of Immigrants," *American Journal of Sociology* 70 (1964), pp. 193–205 and "Stratification and Conflict between Ethnolinguistic Communities with Different Social Structures," *Canadian Review of Sociology and Anthropology* 15, no. 2 (1978), pp. 148–157.

5. These historical data from Opelousas are drawn from Benjamin Kaplan, *The Eternal Stranger: A Study of Jewish Life in the Small Community* (New York, 1957). Kaplan's ethnographic account, based on interviews, documents and other secondary materials, is the only systematic pre-1960 study of a small Jewish community in Louisiana. When Opelousas was revisited by the author in 1980, many of Kaplan's respondents were dead or unavailable. His data were supplemented by my interviews with Jewish residents of the contemporary community and by references to Cajun householders interviewed in 1976–1980 in the adjacent region of Mamou Prairie where many Jewish families from Opelousas have been absentee landlords.

6. Bertram W. Korn, "Jews and Slavery in the Old South, 1789–1865," in *The Jewish Experience in America: Selected Studies from the Publications of the American Jewish Historical Society Vol III—The Emerging Community*, ed. Abraham Karp (New York, 1969).

7. Mary Alice-Fontenot and Paul B. Freeland, *Acadia Parish, Louisiana: A History to 1900* (Baton Rouge, 1976), pp. 264–267.

8. Interviews with community leaders in nearby Ville-Platte suggest that towns without a Jewish minority had the reputation of being effective in excluding Jews. There are, however, few reports of anti-Semitism either in Kaplan's ethnography or in our interviews in Mamou Prairie. This confirms the finding that there is little anti-Semitism in the South where Jews are of relatively high social status and support majority opinion on critical issues such as integration (Leonard Reissman, "The New Orleans Jewish Community" in L. Dinnerstein and M. D. Palsson, eds., *Jews in the South* (Baton Rouge, 1973), p. 303.

9. Kaplan, *The Eternal Stranger*, p. 94.

10. A survey of graves in the Hebrew Rest Cemeteries of Opelousas and Washington shows that nineteenth-century tombstones, such as those of the Haas family, are either entirely or partially inscribed in Hebrew. In comparison, twentieth-century inscriptions include little or no Hebrew.

11. Kaplan, *The Eternal Stranger*, pp. 101–103.

12. Gartner, "Immigration and the Formation of American Jewry," p. 39.

13. Alfred O. Hero, Jr., "Southern Jews," in Dinnerstein and Palsson, eds., *Jews in the South*.

14. Kaplan, *The Eternal Stranger*, p. 96.

15. Ibid., p. 97.

16. Data on Timmins Jews are derived from interviews in Timmins and in Toronto (1981–1984).

17. Peter Vasiliadis, *"The Truth Can Sometimes Be Very Dangerous": The Worker's Cooperative of Northern Ontario.* (Toronto, 1983), pp. 43–47.

18. These data are based on a census of Jews in Timmins taken by Rabbi David Monson in 1938.

19. There was one notable exception. Throughout the war, Sol Sky, of South Porcupine, spoke for the Soviet war effort. Sky's neighbors, the clients of his general store, were predominantly Finns. Significantly, Sky and his supporters lived several miles from the core of Jewish settlement in Timmins.

14
Anti-Semitism in Canada in the Interwar Years

IRVING ABELLA

In June 1934 there occurred one of the most bizarre strikes in Canadian history, and for the Jewish community the most telling. Samuel Rabinovich, a young medical student who had graduated first in his class at the University of Montreal, was offered an internship at Notre Dame Hospital. On the day he was to begin work all fourteen of his fellow interns walked out, refusing, as they put it, to work with a Jew. They picketed the hospital and refused to accept even emergency cases, their newly sworn Hippocratic oath notwithstanding. They were soon joined by fellow interns from five surrounding Catholic hospitals, as well as by the clergy of neighbouring parishes.

It was a sensational event and the French-language press gave it front-page coverage. The interns were all interviewed and their story told sympathetically. None of them wished to spend a full year working with a Jew—who could blame them, asked *Le Devoir*—and all of them were concerned that Catholic patients would find it "repugnant" to be treated, or even touched, by a Jewish physician. To the support of the indignant interns came such organizations as the Jean Baptiste Society, the Association of Young Catholics, various county councils and cooperatives, as well as prominent members of the Catholic clergy.

Within a few days the hapless Dr. Rabinovich submitted his resignation, the hospital promised never to hire any Jewish doctors, and the University of Montreal Medical School agreed to restrict the admission of

Jewish students. Jews, a Quebec paper gloated, have now learned their place and "it is not in Quebec."[1]

The infamous *grève des internes* was one of the literally hundreds of anti-Semitic incidents that were a hallmark of Canadian society in the years between the wars. There were far worse. Only one year after the strike, a group of men surrounded a crowded synagogue in the Laurentian resort town of Val David and set it on fire. Fortunately, all the worshippers escaped, though their sanctuary and all of its holy books were destroyed. In neighbouring towns such as Ste Agathe and Val Morin Jews were being constantly harassed, taunted, assaulted and even arrested. In Montreal through the 1930s Jewish funeral cortèges were often pelted with rocks thrown by children from Catholic school yards.[2]

English Canada, of course, was not immune from anti-Semitism. In August 1933, in Toronto, for example, there occurred the notorious Christie Pits riot when hundreds of youths terrorized a Jewish baseball team in a battle that lasted for six hours and in which scores were injured as Jewish reinforcements arrived and combatants poured into the neighbouring streets. For most of the time, the Toronto police refused to intervene—their chief wished to give "Christian boys enough time to teach the Jews a lesson"—and in the end only two arrests were made. There was also violence in the streets of Winnipeg and Vancouver as Jews and anti-Semites confronted one another.[3]

These, of course, were isolated incidents. Canada was not Nazi Germany. Yet it is difficult to deny that the Canada of the 1920s and 1930s was not a country permeated with anti-Semitism. After surveying the Jewish scene in Canada, a committee of the Canadian Jewish Congress reported in 1937:

> During the past few years we have witnessed an amazing growth of anti-Semitism. Manifestations of an intensified anti-Jewish sentiment have been springing up everywhere. . . . The minor and more spectacular evidences of this programme against the Jews have been the many instances in which Jews have been barred from hotels, beaches, golf courses and parks. While the many sign posters in front of parks and beaches to the effect that Gentiles only are admitted may be disturbing and do much to awaken anti-Jewish feeling, these are not the most serious effects of anti-Semitic propaganda. The most pernicious results of this movement have been the startling increase in the number of individuals and companies who refuse to rent living quarters to Jews; the spreading policy of not employing Jews; the boycott of all Jewish firms; the sporadic attempts by various organizations to involve Jews in disturbances and in violence.[4]

For Canadian Jews in these years, quotas and restrictions became a way of life. According to a study commissioned by the Canadian Jewish

Congress, few of the country's schoolteachers and none of its principals were Jewish. The banks, insurance companies and the large industrial and commercial interests, it charged, also excluded Jews from employment. Department stores did not hire Jews as salespeople; Jewish doctors could not get hospital appointments. Not only did universities and professional schools devise quotas against Jewish students, but they did not hire Jewish faculty. For most of this period there was not a single Jewish professor in the entire country. The report added that it was almost impossible for Jewish nurses, architects and engineers to find jobs in their fields. And some only succeeded when they adopted Christian surnames—at least until they were unmasked.[5]

If the Jew found it difficult to find a job or get an education, it was even harder for him to find a place to live or to vacation. Increasingly, restrictive covenants were placed on various properties prohibiting their sale to Jews, and at beaches and resorts throughout the nation signs were springing up banning Jews. A Toronto beach sign warned: "No Jews or Dogs allowed." So-called swastika clubs of young hoodlums were formed to intimidate Jews and keep them away from "restricted" beaches. The threat of violence in these areas was so great that Jewish leaders took the unusual step of warning the community "not to hold large gatherings in any portion of the city where such a gathering is liable to arouse the animosity of certain classes of the non-Jewish population." Indeed, so threatening did the situation appear that a Jewish member of the Ontario legislature warned his co-religionists:

> Unless something is done quickly the Jewish people may well meet the same fate in Canada that the Jews are meeting in Germany. . . . No fire is so easily kindled as anti-Semitism. The fire is dormant in Canada, it has not yet blazed up, but the spark is there. Germany is not the only place with prejudice. Look at Quebec.[6]

And indeed it was in Quebec where the Jew was most threatened. In English Canada there were no powerful institutions or movements advocating anti-Semitic behaviour, but in Quebec both the Roman Catholic Church and its lay allies in the French-Canadian nationalist movement were aggressively anti-Jewish. As a leading Toronto rabbi put it: "In Quebec anti-Semitism is a way of life. In the rest of Canada it is more an afterthought. Here it is much more subtle. There it is widespread and demonic."[7]

To the French-Canadian nationalist of this period, the Jews—indeed all foreigners—were a threat. Surrounded by the pervasive, all-encompassing American way of life, and in their own country dominated by an apparently narrow-minded English-speaking majority, French Canadians have always felt threatened. Their way of life, traditions, language, culture and religion were, at least in their eyes, constantly under attack, and never more so than in the 1920s and 1930s. The economic crisis, the migration from farms to cities, the obvious diminution of Quebec's political influence in confederation, the conscription crisis, the social repercussions of World War One and the defeat of those struggling to maintain francophone rights in the West and Ontario were keenly felt by French-Canadian leaders.

Thus the French-Canadian nationalism of the period was essentially negative and defensive in nature. Exclusionary and inward-looking, it felt itself under constant attack by such hostile ideologies as democracy, liberalism, socialism and materialism. In a society as homogeneous as Quebec, in which homogeneity was a prime national concern, the étranger, the foreigner, was the great enemy. According to one student of the period, this "traditional wariness of a minority people determined to persist as a cultural entity crystallized in the crises of the interwar period to give rise to a full-fledged nativism."[8]

To the French Canadian, Catholicism and national survival were inseparable. The nationalist movement, its press, its youth movement and all its activities operated around the axes of the church. And anything which tended to undermine the influence and role of the church was anathema. Most dangerous of course were modernism and materialism, and their purveyor—the Jew. He was perceived to be the propagator of the American way of life and the major source of social disruption and moral decay.

In the writings of almost every leading church and nationalist figure in Quebec, the Jew was commonly depicted as a parasite, the bearer of a germ spreading an insidious disease that was undermining the national health. The only remedy for disease was eradication and quarantine. Therefore the Quebec elite worked strenuously to bar all Jews from Canada and to ostracize those already there. They led anti-immigration crusades, lobbying strenuously and working indefatigably to keep Jews out. For those living in Quebec, the call went out for a total boycott. "If we do not buy from them," thundered *Action Catholique,* an official church journal, "then they will leave."[9] From this sprang up the notorious "Achat Chez Nous" movement, sponsored by leading church officials, which urged French Canadians to buy from their co-religionists and to stay away from Jewish storekeepers who, in the words of *Le Devoir,* "have cheating and corruption in the bloodstream." Though it originally began as a nationalistic weapon for the economic advancement of French Canadians and a legitimate form of self-defence, it soon turned into a campaign to boycott all Jews. As one senior clergyman told his fellow priests, "It is to free us from Jews and usurers."[10]

The movement had the total support of the church, most of the press and of course of local merchants. As the Restaurant Association journal warned, "Do you want to be poisoned? Buy your food from Jews."[11] The leading propaganda organ in this movement, however, was the prestigious *Le Devoir*, which argued in articles and editorials that the Jews were the economic enemy of French Canadians, and a "constant menace" to the merchant. The paper further charged that Jews often changed their names to conceal their identity and to deceive "the consumer who is not even aware that he is dealing with Jews." Furthermore, they open their stores on Sunday and "thus injure loyal citizens who observe the Lord's Day."[12]

Quebec's leading Catholic ideologue, Abbé Lionel Groulx, said of the nationalist movement that it was meant to resolve the Jewish problem. "If they could only subsist from each other," he wrote, "they would be forced to disperse."[13] Even a member of the Quebec cabinet, C. J. Arcand, charged that "a disloyal element" was trying to take over. "The control of business in Quebec," he charged, "rests in the hands of those who are not of us."[14] To leave no doubt against whom the boycott was directed, several years later, during the war, on a cross-country tour to propagate a better understanding between Canada's two races, the respected theologian and scholar, Abbé Maheux reassured an attentive Vancouver audience not to worry. "Our slogan 'L'achat chez nous' does not mean you! It does not mean do not buy from English-Canadians. It means do not buy from Jews."[15]

A study of the popular and clerical French-Canadian press reveals a catalogue of sins for which the Jews were held responsible that is both extensive and contradictory. They were, for example, commonly accused of being the agents of both capitalism and communism, frequently in the same tract. They were charged with being "unassimilable"; conversely they were castigated for assimilating too well, in that they were seen to be climbing the social ladder too quickly and through devious means. To add to the confusion, even though the Jews were depicted as steadfastly refusing to declare their allegiance to Canada, the French Canadians did not want to accept that allegiance in any case.

Furthermore not only were Jews undesirable and unassimilable, but according to most nationalistic writing they were also responsible for the moral decay and chaos of the period. According to Abbé Groulx, "The Jews bring us popular corruption through the cinema and fashion. . . . The Jews have passed from the adoration of the true God to the adoration of Satan. . . . The Jewish people exist and we must understand by this the hate of Christ and all Christian people."[16]

Another Catholic newspaper was more frank: "The Jewish-American cinema has stained the soul of our young women and has brutalized our young men by developing a taste for stupid luxury."[17] The official voice of the church was even more blunt. "Hollywood is Jewish," said the *Semaine religieuse de Québec,* in 1927. Jewish cinema "is an instrument for brutalizing Christians . . . it spares nothing, not the brain, not the heart, not the body. It attacks youth and prepares a generation of stupified animals. . . . In our so-called Catholic country we permit this vast school of Jewish demoralization next door to our own churches and Catholic schools."[18]

Another theme which permeated the Catholic and nationalist press was of the Jew as subversive, as a conspirator plotting to dominate in both the national and international spheres. The *Action catholique,* indeed, defined communism as the modern form of Judaism.[19] Huot, a prominent churchman writing in the Church's own paper pulled no punches: "The existence of the Jews is justified only as witnesses to the Christ epic. . . . The Jew is perfidious because he adores the blasphemous Talmud, because he has plotted for centuries against Christian states, because he has founded the socialist movement, because the Bnai Brith is associated with Freemasonry, and because Jewish bankers have financed the Russian Revolution."[20]

It is important to remember that these men were neither cranks nor fringe members of Quebec society, but its leaders, teachers, and élite. Whether they truly believed in a worldwide Jewish conspiracy against Catholic values is irrelevant for they found the Jew a useful scapegoat who could be blamed for all the moral and economic chaos of Quebec in the 1920s and 1930s. By painting such a repugnant and malevolent portrait of the Jew, the nationalist could argue that a nativist movement would clear their society of its enemies, restore order and return to their over-eager hands the reigns of power. And all this could be done by getting rid of the Jew. Psychologically, as the sociologist Everett Hughes has argued, the Jew in Quebec was a symbol, and as such "bore the brunt of attacks that the French Canadians would have liked to launch against their English Canadian dominator."[21]

Ironically, most of these writers and clerics denied they were anti-Semitic, seeing nothing unjust in their animosity toward the Jew. Indeed, their leader, Abbé Groulx, wrote that anti-Semitism was both unchristian and foolish, yet warned his readers in the same article that Jews were parasites and undesirable, and, along with most of his colleagues, congratulated Hitler for his efforts to curb the influence of Jews in Germany.[22]

Many church and nationalist leaders were also accommodating to the ideas and activities of the Quebec fascists and their party, the Parti National Social Chrétien, led by journalist Adrien Arcand. Though Arcand's group was based on a European model, its anti-Semitism was home-bred, nurtured by the writings and teachings of the province's intellectual elite.

Arcand was permitted—often encouraged—to speak in churches and Catholic schools while Catholic newspapers even reprinted some of his most monstrous speeches. Following services at a church in Rimouski, the parish priest handed to the congregation a newspaper with a reprint from Arcand's newspaper, *Le Chomeau*, which stated:

> Jews are like cockroaches and bugs. When you see one you can be sure that there are dozens around, and when you see a few around in the cities and in all the streets don't be fooled. There are more around. It is too bad we cannot exterminate them with insecticide.[23]

There were of course those in Quebec society who did not join in this anti-Jewish campaign. Chief of these was the elderly Henri Bourassa who had recanted his earlier anti-Semitism—at one time he used the pages of *Le Devoir* to denounce the Jews as "bloodsuckers" and to applaud the Russian pogroms of 1905—and was now using his seat in the House of Commons to denounce the outrages of his fellow Quebecois. Jean Charles Harvey and Oliver Asselin also joined with Bourassa to denounce the irrationality of anti-Semitism. But theirs were voices in the wilderness. Amongst Quebec church and nationalist leaders they stood alone. As David Rome has pointed out:

> What is most discouraging about this sad epic is its unanimity. Through the decades we do not find a single voice that can be labelled representative of a single sector of the otherwise variegated Church to speak out against anti-Semitism or on behalf of the Jewish group—not a single priest or nun or brother, not a single Catholic organization.[24]

Two of the major disseminators of anti-Jewish propaganda were *Action catholique* and *Semaine religieuse*, both official publications of the church, and key sources of authorized thinking within the diocese. According to Rome, "They functioned as a signal, if not an order of what was permissible, religiously and morally. . . . They spewed filth which will long stain the Church. Issue after issue brought anti-Semitic poison to faithful readers who transmitted it to their own credulous audience."[25]

What is most surprising to today's students about this concentrated campaign against the Jew is its irrationality. The Jewish community in Quebec was tiny and both politically and economically impotent. It made up just over 1 per cent of the province's population, and in only one county—Montréal-Gésu—did Jews number more than one to each thousand residents. Most Jews were recent immigrants and like most French Canadians, ill-educated, poor, powerless and oppressed. To one French-Canadian scholar this very phenomenon explained the anti-Semitism of the French Canadian. "As the province became increasingly industrialized and urbanized, the French Canadians reacted vehemently against the Jew who vied with them for their historical role as "premiers parmi les dominés."[26]

No issue better symbolized the Catholic and Nationalist distrust of the Jew than did the school question. Since confederation, for purposes of education Quebec's Jews were considered Protestants. Their children attended schools run by the Protestant school boards and all Jews were forbidden by law from becoming—or even voting for—members of the boards. Understandably, this had for long been a festering sore for the Jewish community. Attempts by various provincial governments to rectify this anomalous situation were always beaten back by a determined opposition from the church. Finally, in response to continued Jewish agitation, in 1930 the government of Louis-Alexandre Taschereau hesitantly introduced legislation which would allow Jews to create a committee to deal with the Protestant and Catholic school boards regarding the education of their children. However, it would still not allow Jews to either vote for or be elected to these boards. It was a moderate measure, providing the Jewish community with far less than it wanted, and far less than it had been promised. Nevertheless, it was far more than the Church was prepared to accept.

The introduction of the bill raised a storm of protest throughout the province. This "pernicious act," thundered *Action catholique,* was the first step in creating a secular school system in the province. "It will allow the Jews to undermine our schools," it warned. "This is an attack on Catholicism and on the values all French-Canadians cherish." Even Cardinal Rouleau of Quebec entered the fray, publicly cautioning the premier that the bill would destroy an educational system "which is for us a safeguard and a security."[27] At the same time Camillien Houde, later the mayor of Montreal, told the provincial legislature: "If the Jews don't like it, they can get out."

So fierce was this anti-Jewish campaign and so well received that the Taschereau government hurriedly repealed the bill—"a triumph," crowed *Action catholique,* "over the foes of Christianity." The non-partisan journal which reviewed the year's events, the *Canadian Annual Review,* saw it in a different light:

> The recent legislation places the Jews of Montreal in a position which is intolerable, unfair and contrary to the tradition of the Province of Quebec which recognizes equality for minorities and majorities.[28]

This same coalition of anti-Jewish forces came together to battle another piece of legislation. In 1932, the Jewish MLA Peter Bercovitch introduced a bill into the Quebec Assembly which would enable any person who considered that his racial or religious group had been the object of libel to obtain an injunction against the person committing the libel. The bill was designed to control the vicious anti-Semitic propaganda campaign that was sweeping the province. Though the legislation was directed at the scurrilous Arcand's fascist publication, both *Le Devoir* and *Action catholique* denounced the bill as an insult to French Canadians. It was the latter, argued *Le Devoir,* not the Jews who were being libelled and, in any case, the Jews deserved everything they got.[29] Predictably, the bill was defeated.

Throughout the remainder of the 1930s—and throughout the next decade as well—a well-organized coalition of nationalist and Catholic groups kept up their campaign against what they termed "Jewish pretensions." When public meetings were held by Jews and their supporters to protest against the Nazis, counterprotests were held by these nationalist organizations. Although Maurice Duplessis, premier of Quebec from 1936, was never openly anti-Semitic, he tolerated—perhaps even encouraged—the anti-Jewish activities of Arcand's fascists and other groups and spoke out energetically against the admission of Jewish refugees.[30]

It would of course be incorrect to maintain that anti-Semitism existed primarily in Quebec. In fact it was widespread throughout the country. Such organizations as the Social Credit party, the Native Sons of Canada and the Orange Order were rife with anti-Semitic feeling. Throughout the 1930s anti-Jewish outbursts on the editorial pages of some of the nation's newspapers, as well as from Protestant pulpits, became more frequent. For example, Rev. J. W. Inkster of Knox Presbyterian Church, located in the heart of Toronto's Jewish district on Spadina Avenue, would regularly warn his congregation of the "invidious Jew"; and his sermons were often reported in the city's press, particularly in the *Toronto Telegram,* a paper not overly friendly to the Jewish people.[31]

Worst of all, at least from the point of view of those Jews desperate to get out of Nazi-infested Europe, it had permeated into the upper levels of the Canadian government. Few capital cities anywhere, said Joe Garner, a senior British official and later high commissioner to Canada, were more subtly anti-Jewish than was Ottawa. As an atheist he worried on his arrival whether he could eat, sleep or drink in a city in which so many hotels, clubs and restaurants were restricted to Christians, until he was reassured that the restriction only applied to Jews.[32]

While Mackenzie King was worrying privately that too many Jews would pollute Canada's bloodstream, his government was ensuring that no more Jews would be coming. While few were as openly anti-Jewish as his deputy minister at Immigration, Frederick Blair, who warned anyone who would listen that Jews were cheaters and liars who always destroyed whatever country allowed them in, many others, such as Vincent Massey, Ernest Lapointe and O. D. Skelton, privately expressed their anti-Semitism and allowed it to affect their policies about Jewish immigration. It is perhaps no wonder that, of all the Western democracies and of all the immigration countries in the world, Canada had by far the worst record in providing a sanctuary to the Jews of Europe in the 1930s and 1940s.

Why was Canada so anti-Semitic? There are various reasons. To some extent the massive anti-Semitic propaganda of the Nazis had its impact. Some were taken in by it and by such American hatemongers as Henry Ford, Father Coughlin, Gerald L. K. Smith and dozens of others. They formed such anti-Jewish groupings as the Canadian Union of Fascists and the Swastika Clubs. It was also a time of depression and the search for scapegoats invariably ended at a Jewish doorstep. Jews were also publicly seen and denounced as troublemakers. The prominence of Jewish names in the left-wing movement seduced many gullible or malevolent Canadians into believing that most Jews were Communists.

In addition, many Canadians were reacting to the three decades of almost unlimited immigration. The rapid rise of nativism in the 1920s came out of a concern for the type of Canada these millions of uneducated, illiterate aliens would produce. For many, the Jew, since he tended to live in cities and therefore was the most visible of immigrants, symbolized this mongrelization. Anti-Semitism to many, therefore, was simply an extreme form of Canadian nationalism. Also, many immigrants, particularly from Eastern Europe, had brought over traditional anti-Semitic phobias. An anti-Jewish tradition of many generations could not be dissolved overnight.

Obviously, many hated Jews for religious reasons. Much of the anti-Semitism in Quebec and in fundamentalist areas of western Canada originated from religious teachings. Jews had killed Christ, had refused to repent or convert to Christianity and, therefore, were damned.

All of these were factors contributing to the anti-Semitism which permeated Canada in these years. One factor, however, stands out, and that was a feeling amongst many Canadians, especially the opinion-makers—the politicians, academics, writers, businessmen and journalists who set the tone for a society—that the Jew simply did not fit into their concept of Canada. Theirs was to be a country of homesteaders and farmers; and despite what the Jews were doing in Palestine at the time—turning a desert green—few Canadians felt that Jews could make successful agriculturalists. Those immigrants who did not farm were expected to go into the woods, or mines or smelters, or canneries, or textile mills, or join the construction gangs needed to build and fuel the great Canadian boom. And most Canadians felt that Jews did not fit this pattern, that they were city people, in a country attempting to build up its rural base, that they were peddlers and shopkeepers in a country that wanted loggers and miners. They were seen as a people with brains in a country that preferred brawn, as a people with strong minds in a country that wanted strong backs.

What is most astonishing about this anti-Semitism is how few and powerless were Canadian Jews at this time. They made up just over 1 per cent of the population and had no political or economic clout and could be seen as a threat only by the paranoid. Equally surprising was the silence of the churches in the face of this frightful and oppressive anti-Jewish feeling.

Yet for many Canadians the Jew was a symbol. To many English and French Canadians he represented a foreign culture and tradition which would undermine their customs, beliefs and way of life. Every single public opinion poll taken in the years before 1945 showed that the Jew, along with the Oriental, was the immigrant least wanted by the Canadian peoples, but he was also in the 1930s and the 1940s the immigrant most in need of a place to go. The attitude of the Canadian people ensured that Canada was not to be that place. The countless numbers of Jews fleeing the Nazis would have to find a sanctuary elsewhere. Few did.

NOTES

1. *Le Devoir,* 10–24 June 1934, *Canadian Jewish Chronicle,* June 1934; Oliver Asselin, *"La grève des internes," L'Ordre,* June 1934.

2. Canadian Jewish Congress (CJC) Archives, Montreal, file on Anti-Semitism, Quebec, 1935–1939; see also *Canadian Jewish Chronicle* for the 1930s.

3. CJC, file on Anti-Semitism, Canada, 1933–1938; see also Lita-Rose Betcherman, *The Swastika and the Maple Leaf* (Toronto, 1975); Stephen Speisman, *The Jews of Toronto, A History to 1937* (Toronto, 1978).

4. CJC, *Report on Anti-Semitic Activities in Canada,* 1937, pp. 4–6.

5. Ibid., 1938.

6. Reported in the *Toronto Star,* 24 April 1933.

7. C. J. C. Rabbi Maurice Eisendrath, *Statements on Anti-Semitism in Canada,* June 1938, p. 1.

8. C. R. Abelle, " 'La *Question Juive'*: Nativism in French Canada, 1930–39," research paper, (York University, 1981); see also Michael Oliver, "The Social and Political Ideas of the French Canadian Nationalist" Ph.D. dissertation, (McGill, 1954); F. Dumont, ed., *Les idéologies au Canada Français, 1930–39.* (Quebec, 1978); Victor Teboul, *Mythes et images du Juif au Québec* (Montreal, 1977); Arthur Silver, "Some Sources of Anti-Semitism in Quebec," *Jewish Dialogue* (Summer 1971).

9. *Action catholique,* 30 May 1935.

10. Abbé Grondin, quoted in Robert Rumilly, *Histoire de la province de Québec,* vol 16 (Montreal, 1955), p. 172.

11. *Le Restauranteur,* September 1933.

12. See A. J. Belanger, *L'apolitisme des idéologies québecoises, le grand tournant de 1934–36* (Quebec, 1974), p. 71.

13. *Action nationale,* April 1933.

14. *Canadian Jewish Chronicle,* 2 November 1934.

15. Cited in David Rome, *Clouds in the Thirties* vol. 2 (Montreal, 1977), pp. 12–13.

16. *Action catholique,* October 1932.

17. *La revue nationale,* August 1929.

18. *Semaine religieuse de Québec,* October 1927.

19. Ibid., December 1934.

20. *Semaine religieuse de Québec,* April 21, 1921.

21. Everett Hughes, *French Canada in Transition* (Chicago, 1943).

22. *Action nationale,* February 1934.

23. Rome, *Clouds in the Thirties,* vols. 1–6; CJC, files on Anti-Semitism, Quebec, 1935–1939.

24. Rome, *Clouds in the Thirties,* vol. 3.

25. Ibid.

26. Paul Cappon, *Conflit entre les Neo-Canadiens et les Francophones* (Quebec, 1974), p. 123.

27. *Action catholique,* April 1930, November 1930: Public Archives of Canada, Weinfeld Papers, Rouleau and Mgr. Gauthier to Taschereau, 15 March 1930.

28. *Canadian Annual Review 1930–1* (Toronto), pp. 158–159.

29. *Le Devoir,* 28 January–5 February 1932; *Action catholique,* January 1932.

30. See R. Rumilly, *Maurice Duplessis et son temps* (Montreal, 1973); Conrad Black, *Duplessis* (Toronto, 1979).

31. Cited in Irving Abella and Harold Troper, *None Is Too Many: Canada and the Jews of Europe 1943–1948* (Toronto, 1982), p. 282.

32. Canadian Jewish Congress Central Region Archives, Toronto; Joint Community Relations Papers, file articles, "Clippings on Anti-semitism, 1938."

15
A. M. Klein

The Poet and His Relations with French Quebec

PIERRE ANCTIL

T he life and work of the Montreal poet A. M. Klein abounds in antinomies. From the diligent study of the law to the outpouring of poetic emotion, Klein was able to swing easily from one literary genre to another, from a critical analysis of *Ulysses* to the autobiographical novel, from polemics and pamphlets to the inspirational Hebrew psalm. Thirsting for all sources of inspiration and searching out in himself all the potentialities of his art, Klein ended up by making a series of clean breaks—some dramatic, such as his departure from McGill University, others, minor, numerous, and simultaneous—without affecting the quality of his art. Finally, the poet, perhaps overly affected by the events of the turbulent era of the 1940s, produced a work, *The Rocking Chair and Other Poems,* which is difficult to understand in its entirety, for it has its literary roots entwined in several millennia of biblical and talmudic tradition. To fully appreciate Klein's work, the reader must be well versed in Judaic studies and in several languages, know how to appreciate all literary genres and be an expert on the subject of the immigration of the Ashkenazi Jews from eastern Europe—a formidable assignment indeed.

Before becoming too discouraged by such an agenda, let us look at the social milieu, which Klein wholeheartedly embraced, and to which he remained faithful throughout his life. Although he was not born in Montreal, he spent nearly his whole life in the Jewish community of that city. If the poet felt the heritage of the *shtetl* intensely within him and pulsated to the call of Jewish Palestine, it was above all in the Québécois community that he lived his life in its various phases—of McGill University, of the faculty of law at l'Université de Montreal, in the Montreal Jewish Public Library, with his neighbours in Cartier riding, and his successive homes in the Mount Royal district. At every moment of his life, Klein was both Québécois and Jewish, deeply concerned with his personal well-being and the well-being of the Jewish people, yet living in the midst of a great metropolitan society impregnated with an incipient Qubecitude. Even though he was Yiddish-speaking, how could he have escaped the multicultural milieu that still distinguishes Montreal today, a milieu in which he ended up feeling so much at ease?

Quebec also was the home of a francophone people who, in the thirties and forties, had not as yet discovered the term "Québécois" to describe themselves. Living in the country since the beginning of the seventeenth century, a rural and Catholic minority people since the English conquest, the French Canadians made up almost 60 per cent of the population of Montreal at the time of Klein's arrival and possessed the political and institutional power that made them one of two dominant groups, along with the Anglos. They were ever present in the poet's social world, and although he could not help but perceive them through the lens of his Jewishness, we cannot draw from this any conclusion regarding his understanding of the Québécois. Perhaps he had an intuition that these two peoples shared a difficult experience in common in their recent history, and that they had acquired little in a world where neither force of arms nor strength of numbers belonged to them.

In Klein's work, support for the Franco-Québécois cause constitutes one of the turning points. In a sense, the publication of *The Rocking Chair and Other Poems* in 1948 marked the abandonment of the theme that had been dear to him until then: the poetic exploitation of his Jewish identity. After *The Rocking Chair,* Klein almost abandoned poetry to devote himself to literary analysis, and later, to writing his only novel, *The Second Scroll.* Furthermore, the period immediately following World War Two saw a profound transformation of the relations between the Jewish community and the intellectual and political elite of francophone Quebec. The world of the habitant and the snowshoe burst into the poet's work precisely at this point following the tensions of the thirties, when Jews and francophones learned to coexist on a new basis. One can therefore assume that Klein did not write *The Rocking Chair* in a void, on a mere impulse, but that he responded specifically to a sympathetic undercurrent or at least to the lack of hostility which began to develop between the two longstanding Montreal neighbours—the Jews who had emigrated from the distant Polish or Russian plains, and the Québécois who had emigrated from the countryside of the St. Lawrence valley.

Indeed, there is nothing especially Québécois in *Hath Not a Jew* (1940, nor even in *The Hitleriad* (1944), which remains a book almost exclusively preoccupied with the death pangs of the Holocaust and the anguish of genocide. Until then, Klein relished using archaisms and terms which were learned or specifically Jewish, which made his poetry obscure or, at best, difficult to follow. It seemed as if Klein, having come to English late, attempted, by great display of scholarship, to make up for lost time and to invest his poetry with all the historic depth of the language of Shakespeare. Once he had completed this task, there would have been few persons within the Montreal Jewish community who could claim to have a better knowledge of Elizabethan English than Klein. The poem "The Rocking Chair" upsets this mode of writing and introduces into Klein's poetry a gentle contemplation of daily life, which he describes as a kind of lingering, perpetual experience:

> It seconds the crickets of the province. Heard
> in the clean lamplit farmhouses of Québec,—
> wooden,—it is no less a national bird;
> and rivals, in its cage, the mere stuttering clock.
> To its time, the evenings are rolled away;
> and in its peace the pensive mother knits
> contentment to be worn by her family,
> grown-up, but still cradled by the chair in which she sits.
> (*The Rocking Chair*, p. 1)

Certainly, some of the poetic erudition of the first volumes remains in this new work, but this time it serves to mark the cultural distance between the Jewish poet and the object of his interest: French-Canadian civilization. Without a trace of animosity, Klein shows in *The Rocking Chair* that he is no longer discussing himself or his ancestors, but, the unexpected other. In this book, the expression "fleur de lys" or "autre temps," by their strangeness, correspond to such erudite references as "White Levites at your altar'd ovens," or such biblical allusions as "Our own gomorrah house, the sodom that merely to look at makes one salt?" Furthermore, one poem in particular of this period, "Parade of St. Jean Baptiste," is studded with an especially scholarly and obscure vocabulary, for the simple reason that in the writing of this poem, Klein wanted to use only words common to both French and English: "This is one of a series of experimental poems making trial of what I flatter myself to believe is a 'bilingual language' since the vocabulary of the poem is mainly of Norman and latin origin." Without doubt, he thus made sure that his reader would perceive the distance separating him from the Québécois theme, to which the poem was dedicated, without ever having to depart from the historical fastness of the English language.

Of course, Klein remains Jewish in his *Rocking Chair* and more especially as he approaches a subject where the mystical and daily life perpetually coexist, as in his famous poem, "The Cripples." And then, after all, this taste for word games, this desire to merge the vocabularies of different languages, had already been practised by Jewish writers in the Italian peninsula and in the Arab world several centuries before Klein's birth. Above all, the poet had direct access, through his own experience, to a feeling which gave him empathy with his francophone compatriots; like them, he belonged to a culture in which family values had an enormous importance and formed an anchor of protection against the siren call of the outside world.

Notwithstanding, Klein had a completely external knowledge of French Canadians, and of their ways and customs. Completely at ease in the language of Molière, thanks principally to his studies in law undertaken in 1930 at l'Université de Montréal, an institution which was, at the time, exclusively francophone and Catholic, and also because of a short stay in Abitibi in 1937–1938, Klein nevertheless had few French-Canadian friends, and he certainly had no close friends in that community. Furthermore, his vision of francophone Quebec in *The Rocking Chair* remains oriented toward outdated and folkloric aspects of the culture. All the same, Klein had frequented francophone circles often enough to be capable of conveying superb portraits of French Canadians, such as M. Bertrand, the dandy yearning for Parisian culture, or Hormidas Arcand, the anti-semite. Klein was also capable of composing, as in "Sire Alexandre Grandmaison" and in "Annual Banquet: Chambre de Commerce," complete descriptions of a distinctive world of the forties. In "Librairie Delorme" the poet succeeds admirably in portraying the atmosphere of Montreal's famous Ducharme (antique) bookstore. When reading the poem, one could almost see prospective customers filing into the small shop:

> . . .an abbé, perhaps, beatified with sight
> of green Laurentia, kneeling to church-bell.
>   (*The Rocking Chair*, p. 44)

However, the most successful evocation of the francophone milieu of Montreal in this volume is found in the poem "Political Meeting." Accustomed as he was to political debates and a fervent follower of partisan rhetoric since his student days at McGill, Klein had followed the flamboyant career of Camillien Houde with a certain amount of interest and apprehension, especially because this man symbolized, more than anyone else at the beginning of the forties, the very idea of the francophone—an idea that commanded attention through the power of Houde's speeches. The populist mayor, born in the poor neighbourhood in the east end of Montreal, campaigned at the time against conscription and the involvement of French Canadians in a war that was being waged in Europe. Klein was quick to grasp the possible anti-Semitic implications of such a position, and he denounced it on several occasions in his editorials, written for the *Canadian Jewish Chronicle*. Taking this ideological reservation into account, one feels in "Political Meeting" that the character of Houde has succeeded, up to a certain point, in casting a spell on the poet, who feels, perhaps vaguely, that the orator also wishes to defend his people in the face of the agony of the war, which was close at hand:

> praises the virtue of being "Canadien"
> of being at peace, of faith, of family,
> and suddenly his other voice: "Where are your sons?"
>
> He is tearful, choking tears; but not he
> would blame the clever English; in their place
> he'd do the same: maybe.
>
> Where *are* your sons?
>
> The whole street wears one face,
> shadowed and grim; and in the darkness rises
> the body-odour of race.
>
> (*The Rocking Chair*, p. 16)

Several critics of Jewish origin were inclined to recognize, in *The Rocking Chair*, the mark of the Jewish education Klein had received early in his life, even if this collection of poetry, unlike the first collections, did not bring an especially Jewish theme to the fore:

> because the parallels are so great between the Jews and the French Canadians. The French Canadians saw themselves as almost a biblical people with a language and religion that separated them from the majority around them. Quebec was a kind of Palestine, a French ghetto in North America.
>
> Like the Jews, French Canadians are also concerned, almost preoccupied, with survival. It is a constant theme for the poets of both peoples.[1]

However, I do not believe that this parallelism between the two peoples, although it was very real, was the author's only motivation when he began the composition of his Québécois poems. I would maintain, rather, that at the end of World War Two Klein was looking for a new channel for rapprochement with his francophone compatriots, and that the writing of *The Rocking Chair* was in this sense a catharsis for him. This motivation, closely linked to the circumstances of the time, is revealed when one studies the history of the collection itself, and when one examines the situation in which the Jewish leadership of Montreal found itself following the peace of 1945. This does not diminish the quality of Klein's poetic inspiration in any way, but it places his actions in a social context to which the author was very sensitive, and which could not fail to affect him in his writing.

In July 1947 Klein published seven of his Québécois poems in the journal *Poetry,* of Chicago.[2] When one considers how little attention the author received in Quebec, even within his own community, one could certainly assume that all of the poems would have ultimately gone unnoticed in Montreal. Shortly afterwards, Klein was offered the Edward Bland Memorial Fellowship, a prize awarded by a black American organization to a collection of poems of high literary quality, whose contents have had an impact on social relations. In its October 1947 edition the *Congress Bulletin,* the official mouthpiece of the Canadian Jewish Congress, announced Klein's award and republished the prize-winning poems under the new title *Poems of French Canada.*[3] Not content with having published the seven poems in this form, the directors of the Congress published the poems again, at the end of the year, in a pamphlet, with yet a different title: *Seven Poems.* In an internal memo dated November 25, 1947, David Rome, editor of the *Bulletin,* wrote to Saul Hayes, the executive director of the Congress:

> I wish to report to you that our release of Mr. Klein's poems has met with a response which, frankly, I had not anticipated. *La Presse* made even more of the story than I had expected. We are receiving a number of requests for copies from Jewish, French Canadian and English members of the public. We are sending some of them the *Congress Bulletin* which contains these poems.
>
> It is also suggested that the pamphlet should be sent to our list of priests and to doctors, government officials, etc., in Quebec and among those who read French. In order to do this, we would have to reprint the poems.[4]

All evidence suggests that Klein had struck a responsive note with his Québécois poems, to the point where the leadership of the Congress had been touched by it and perhaps it had also affected those people who worked at maintaining and developing positive institutional ties with the Jewish community and the general public.

The work of the public relations people of the Canadian Jewish Congress to publicize these poems bore fruit very soon. In November 1947 David Rome wrote, probably in a letter of introduction to the poems themselves:

> You may agree with me that it is significant that poems which so exactly and understandingly reflect the French Canadian scene should be written by a Jewish writer who is acknowledged by his community as its literary spokesman. The appearance of these poems is indicative of a very desirable development in Canadian group relations.[5]

The Congress was quickly overwhelmed with praise for Klein's work, which seemed to indicate that the publicity campaign had been well managed and that Klein's poems were well received in all circles, including the clergy, as the text of this letter, signed by Claude Sumner, a francophone Jesuit of the Collège Jean-de-Brébeuf indicates:

> It is indeed very significant that these poems, which reflect so accurately the French Canadian life, should have been written by a Jewish author. They reveal, not only a careful observation, keenly intent upon the facts and details of the French Canadian scene, but a remarkable insight which enables the writer to reach and even penetrate the *soul* of the men and women he describes. Such accurateness implies on his part a sensitiveness in perfect consonance with his subject, a great sympathy, a comprehension wide open to all things of beauty.[6]

The Congress published Klein's poems a fourth time in 1948, in a pamphlet entitled *Huit poèmes canadiens,* adding to them this time a preface in French and the text of the laudatory book review that had appeared in *La Presse* the previous year, written by Jean-Marie Poirier. In addition to the seven poems already published, an eighth poem, "Parade of St. Jean Baptiste" was added, which had appeared first in the February 1948 edition of *Canadian Forum,* and which developed the same theme in a more detailed manner. The distribution of these small brochures must have been very efficient, for in January 1948, a journal as clerical in nature as *Les carnets viatoriens* took note of their publication: "Here is a song of exceptional value. Its moderate and touching tone, tender and yet virile, humbly interested in the vision of every object in its surroundings, its sense of poetic appearance and of the words which express it; all of this touches the soul and delights the mind."[7]

Even the very serious *Action universitaire* of Montreal complimented Klein, praising his dual role of a poet and a man sympathetic to French Canada:

> French Canadian life has obviously attracted him, there he has found a stamp of humanity capable of nourishing his inspiration. It is not that everything appears idyllic and admirable to him; we do not ask so much of him, good heavens! In Klein's writing, there is a certain tendency to view things in both an ironic and amused manner at the same time, which allows

him to recreate charming cameos, in which individual characterizations approach caricature, without ever displaying a trace of bitterness or mockery.[8]

Between 1947 and 1949, David Rome probably did more to make
Klein known in Quebec than did Klein's publisher in Toronto, the Ryer-
son Press, which published the collection of Québécois poems under the
title of *The Rocking Chair and Other Poems,* in the summer of 1948. One
can appreciate the magnitude of Rome's efforts among the Québécois
public when one remembers that in 1952 Klein earned the literary prize of
the province of Quebec for *The Rocking Chair and Other Poems,*[9] an honour which never would have been conferred on him if his work had not
reached the francophone literary milieu of the time. Left to himself, the
poet, a man of solitary and modest temperament, would have undoubtedly
been unable to obtain the same results in such a short time.

Nevertheless, Klein had not always harboured such feelings of openness towards the francophone community, which he rediscovered at the
end of the forties. During the thirties and even earlier, he had felt an
iciness in the relations between the two neighbouring communities, and
like other people among the Jewish community, he was troubled by it.
Even if a great deal has been written on the subject of Canadian anti-
Semitism during these last years, in certain circles the specific character
and extent of this phenomenon is still poorly appreciated, particularly with
regard to Quebec.[10] Klein's personal experience and the testimony of his
work appear to be symptomatic of the general state of intercultural relations which had existed for more than a century between Jews and francophone Québécois. A polemist and writer for the *Canadian Jewish Chronicle* since the beginning of the thirties, Klein wrote scathing articles
attacking francophones who had been stricken with the virus of anti-
Semitism. We shall cite a passage from one of these articles, an editorial of
8 July 1932 entitled "The Twin Racketeers of Journalism," which surely
was directed at Adrien Arcand and Joseph Ménard:

> To give it a touch of modernity, however, the editors brought their
> defamations up to date by reiterations of the notorious *Protocols of the Elders
> of Zion.* They filled their papers with slanders as headline, garbled quotation
> as footnote, and forgery as space-filler. The contents of their pages, more-
> over, when analysed, proved that what its publishers could not invent or
> copy, was supplied to them by a syndicate of anti-Semitic propaganda,
> trafficking in synthetic venom and co-operative hate. Its headquarters
> seemed to be Germany: when Hitler sneezed, they caught cold. Thus the
> pest of Jew-hatred, like the bubonic plague, was being brought from conti-
> nent to continent, through the medium of rats.[11]

It is interesting to note in the anthology recently published by M. W. Steinberg and Usher Caplan, that the poet put an end to his violent attacks on Quebec anti-Semitism precisely at the end of World War Two, after he had denounced a whole series of anti-Jewish incidents, including riots against conscription and the partial burning of the Quebec City synagogue in 1943. Of the twelve editorials concerning Quebec chosen by the editors of *Beyond Sambation*, eight were written about anti-Semitism in Quebec, and they were all written before 1946. On 29 December 1944, in "The Tactics of Race-Hatred," Klein warned the readers of the *Canadian Jewish Chronicle* to distrust people who apply the term "anti-Semitic" to French Quebec as a whole: "Either the pious defence of a discriminated minority is being used as an instrument of denigration against the French-Canadian minority; or the crusader, adopting the tactic of 'Stop thief,' is pointing to Quebec anti-semitism only to draw attention off his own."[12]

After 1945 Klein thus adopted a new attitude towards the Quebec francophone community. Was this simply an isolated gesture, a whim on the part of the poet, who could have been affected by his own intuitions? Several factors seem to indicate that Klein joined a movement of rapprochement after the war that was still tentative but well under way, one which he did not lead or anticipate. In its edition of 30 May 1947, the *Congress Bulletin*, in an important article, gave voice to the new perception which was developing among the Jewish leadership concerning the general nature of its relations with the Franco-Québécois:

> Since the last Plenary Session, in January 1945, there have been a series of developments whose import cannot be exaggerated. This is not to say that racial or religious prejudice has disappeared from this part of Canada (Québec) any more than from any other part. Nor is it implied that there has been a volte face or a change of policy or of doctrine among this section of the Canadian people (the French Québécois). Rather might it be said that the friends whom we have always had among them have become more active in the presentation of their views. It might also be that the Jewish community of Canada has learned with the passage of time and with experience the means of presenting its case more effectively before French Canada and of winning its support.
>
> The change has been very great although its symptoms are intangible.[13]

In an article entitled "The State of Anti-Semitism in French Canada" David Rome presented the readers of the *Bulletin* with some new facts on this issue, and advanced an interpretation of the dynamics between the two communities, which heretofore had been undisclosed. Rome noted, among other things, that the large majority of the francophone press condemned anti-Semitism from then on, and that they granted the Jewish community the space it was entitled to for the printing of press communiqués sent out by the Canadian Jewish Congress on this subject and that the Catholic Church of Quebec encouraged the francophone press in these activities. Above all, Rome noted that *Le Goglu,* a particularly anti-Semitic periodical that had resurfaced after 1945 and invoked Christian justice as its authority, had been publicly condemned by influential Catholics, including some priests. Elsewhere in his article Rome described several minor but significant developments in the attitudes of francophone Catholics, which led him to conclude, with a great deal of enthusiasm, that "it is not too much to say that the pro-Jewish statements which have appeared in the press of this country have no parallel in the entire literature of Catholicism in two thousand years."[14]

A short time earlier, on 5 May 1947, Louis M. Benjamin had discussed the same theme in the *Congress Bulletin,* and he had treated the subject in the same way, proceeding from the same information gleaned here and there from current events: "A change in the relationship of the French and the Jews of Québec is coming about. There are now definite signs of a rapprochement between our people and the Gallic population of this province. This is evidenced in many ways."[15]

Although these articles appeared anonymously in this type of publication, somewhat like the editorials in the anglophone newspapers of Canada, they were perceived as being the official position of the mother institution—in this case, the Canadian Jewish Congress. The new language used by the *Congress Bulletin* around 1947 with regard to the francophones of Quebec went well beyond the simple level of personal opinion, in importance and in subject matter; in fact, it involved the entire community and indicated new priorities of concern among the traditional Jewish leadership. In October 1949 in the official report of the eighth plenary session of the Canadian Jewish Congress, one chapter reiterated the same views developed two or three years earlier on the subject of French Canada, and granted them the endorsement of a biennial general assembly.

Whatever the relative weight of such opinions on the part of any Jewish organization may have been, it was still up to the Canadian Jewish Congress to invest a great deal of time and energy in the attempt to bring the two communities closer together in those decisive years. At the time the Congress was the most respected Canadian Jewish institution, and it was also the institution which was most closely listened to outside of the Jewish community. It actively undertook the building of the friendship between the two peoples on a renewed basis. Klein must have been acquainted rather early on with this new spirit, since the items on the agenda of the Congress had to be freely circulated among the collaborators and staff of the Congress. Indeed, the poet was very close to the Congress

through his privileged relationship with the philanthropist Samuel Bronfman, who had been the president of the organization since 1939 and was a
dominant figure in the Montreal Jewish leadership in the postwar period.
In addition, Klein maintained close ties with David Rome and Saul Hayes
through his para-professional activities linked to his writing and his re-
sponsibilities as a lecturer at the Jewish Public Library and other Jewish
organizations.

However, this openness on the part of the Jewish community was not
accomplished without due consideration, and without sufficient evidence
of good faith on the part of both parties. Certain attitudes of the Quebec
francophones had thus paved the way for a mutual understanding. Without such efforts, the good intentions of the Jewish community would have
been in vain, due to a lack of reciprocity. David Rome was not mistaken
when he asserted in 1947 that the Jews had Catholic and francophone
friends, whose importance and influence began to be felt. In order to
judge the contrast in attitudes between the thirties and the end of the
forties, it may be useful to cite a little-known text of M.-Ceslas Forest, a
Dominican priest who taught a course on social ethics at l'Ecole des
sciences sociales, economiques et politiques de l'Université de Montréal.[16]
Published in 1935, "La Question juive au Canada" perfectly summarizes the
opinion held by educated and informed francophones of the time, and this
was in line with the doctrine and Catholic ethics practised since the mid-
nineteenth century and earlier. The author's opinion remains explicit and
it lays the foundation of an entire school of thought, which was very
widespread at that time: Quebec is a Christian state in its law and in its
institutions, and this character must be protected against all attacks: "By
becoming Canadian citizens, the Jews have accepted to live in a Christian
country. There, the promised freedom finds its limit. Their demands,
however legitimate they may be, must never interfere with the character of
our institutions and our laws."[17]

This way of thinking had been applied in Quebec to the question of
Jewish schools, a problem that had been debated practically since the
period of mass immigration in the 1880s. On this basis alone, the Catholic
clergy had insisted in 1930, and even earlier, on the exclusion of Jewish
people from le Conseil de l'instruction publique (Public Education Council), which would have placed Jews on equal footing with Christians in the
area of education. As Forest recalls, "All the same, one cannot require a
Christian state to provide religious education for non-Christians in their
non-Christian faith."[18]

This attitude, adopted by the Catholic hierarchy of Quebec, engendered a social climate which rapidly became awkward during the thirties,
when one takes the presence of a small number of notorious anti-Semitic

agitators among the francophone population into account, including Adrien Arcand and Joseph Ménard, to mention only the most well known. During this period, however, the Catholic clergy did not undertake any anti-Jewish campaigns in Quebec, for it was restrained by its own adherence to the principle of Christian charity, which remains universal in its application: "There are not two sets of morals: one which governs our relations with the Jews and the other which governs our relations with the rest of humanity. There is only one set of morals, and its regulations are clear: one is never permitted to wrong others by unjust means."[19]

Nevertheless, the Catholic Church and its adherents did nothing to bring an end to the racist banter of the anti-Semites, who declared themselves to be fervent Catholics and claimed to be defending their religion and their nationality by their actions. During the thirties, not one official representative of the Catholic Church of Quebec openly opposed anti-Semitism, in whatever form it appeared. Yet another obstacle blocked the way to a better understanding between Jews and francophone Québécois: it was felt that people of Mosaic religious persuasion had no national allegiance "in exile," and that they mocked the country where they had settled, or the customs which were practised there: "We do not see why we should upset the management of our educational system just for this group of immigrants who has never sincerely adopted its new country."[20]

Poised in a position of national withdrawal and cultural survival on one hand, and imprisoned in the narrowest interpretation possible of the duties of Christian ethics on the other hand, the vast majority of Quebec francophones had witnessed with a growing indifference the deterioration of their relations with the Jewish community. This is precisely the situation that would undergo a change after the war without, of course, an official or public announcement of this change, or the majority of the population being immediately aware of it.

In May 1945, in a clerical journal called *Relations,* which had exhibited anti-Semitic tendencies some years earlier, a young Québécois Jesuit published an article on the Jewish minority and education, "La minorité juive au Québec," which was still of interest. In this brief study, Stéphane Valiquette merely noted some known facts and statistics, and the reader would not have been able to find the slightest evidence of hostility, or the smallest reservation concerning the presence of these immigrants and descendants of non-Christian immigrants in Quebec, where there were approximately seventy thousand such people at the time. Even better, Valiquette had gone to the very source to obtain his information, to the offices of the Canadian Jewish Congress, where he had enjoyed warm contacts with the leadership for a long time.

In fact, the biography of Father Valiquette compresses in itself almost all the direct ties the Catholic clergy had maintained with the Quebec Jewish community. Born in 1912 at the corner of Rachel and Saint-Dominique streets, in the heart of Montreal's traditional Jewish ghetto, Valiquette lived in an orthodox Jewish milieu during his entire childhood, even acting as a "shabbes goy" for several years at a corner synagogue.[21] This early experience must have profoundly affected the young Valiquette, who never forgot his Jewish brothers once he entered the Jesuit noviciate in 1931, and who wanted to maintain his contacts with them. In 1937, through his own superior and with the permission of other authorities, he obtained an interview with H. M. Caiserman, who was the secretary-general of the Canadian Jewish Congress. This act was in itself remarkable for the time, even more so because Valiquette, by acting in this way, was fighting the inclinations of the vast majority of francophone clergymen, who were indifferent if not hostile to any organized form of rapprochement, and who were readers of the often anti-Jewish Catholic press. In the entire Jewish community of Montreal, only the Reform rabbi Harry Joshua Stern had had any contact with a Catholic priest: the Jesuit Joseph Paré of the Collège Sainte-Marie; and this meeting occurred by chance during an Atlantic voyage in 1929. Stern and Paré developed an admiration for one another over the years, and together they organized meetings between Christians and Jews on several different occasions during the thirties—meetings which, however, did not involve institutional or superior Catholic authorities. Valiquette would go much further than this; as of 1939, he began to speak before members of the seminary of the diocese of Montreal, to inform them about the Jewish community of Montreal and to discuss what their attitude towards this community should be. In 1944, the same year in which he was ordained as a priest, Valiquette completed a thesis on liberal Judaism, with the help of Rabbi Stern.[22]

Valiquette and a small group of clergymen committed to his cause came to the fore in the months following the end of the war. In 1945 the well-known Canadian fascists who had been imprisoned by the federal government for the duration of the war regained their freedom, and some of them soon started their outcry against the Jews. Around 1946, Le Goglu was published again, under the direction of Joseph Ménard, reproducing the same anti-Jewish slander and attempting to regain its audience of the thirties. This time, however, the social climate had changed. But what interests us here is the fact that the Catholic Church of Montreal had in the meantime created a commission to serve the needs of the non-Catholic citizens of Montreal. Founded at the end of 1940 by Mgr. Charbonneau, la Commission des oeuvres d'apastolat auprès des non-catholiques (the

Commission of the Works of the Apostolate for non-Catholics) even included a sub-section devoted to the Jewish cause: le Comité St-Paul (St.
Paul Committee). The priests who were active in this committee, including Valiquette, published a brochure in 1946 entitled "Why Work towards
the Conversion of Israel" ("Pourquoi travailler a la conversion d'Israel")
and urged Christians to be more understanding towards the Jews.[23] In
such a context, Ménard's anti-Semitic literature struck a sour note, and the
committee wrote to the members of Le Goglu in February 1947, to ask
them to retract their statements. This was the first time in the modern
history of Quebec that clergymen publicly opposed the spreading of hate
literature against the Jews:

> In its last meeting, the St-Paul Committee examined a few issues of Le
> Goglu and thought it should warn you (Joseph Mènard) that the paper, of
> which you are the director, is proving to be an obstacle in the path of the
> Committee's apostolic work. We are attempting to make Christianity known
> and loved in Jewish circles, in order to make them "see the light" by means
> of this display of kindness. We believe that the general tone of your publica-
> tion and some of its remarks do not conform to the courtesy which is
> customary on the part of journalists, and do not uphold the requirements of
> evangelical charity of which Christians, above all, should be the example.[24]

By protesting against the reappearance of anti-Jewish literature in
Quebec, the Saint-Paul Committee took everyone by surprise. Ménard
responded to the attack by publishing a pamphlet entitled The Clergy and
the Jews (Le clergé et les Juifs), which was directed against the priests who
ran the Saint-Paul Committee. At first, the editor of Le Goglu believed
that Valiquette and his colleagues were acting in isolation, and that it
would be easy to ignore them. However, Mgr. Charbonneau and the high
clergy of the diocese of Montreal had not created the Commission of the
Works of the Apostolate for non-Catholics as a mere formality. The new
atmosphere that the episcopate was seeking to establish with the other
churches and religions of the city was able to withstand the indignity of
this anti-Semitic propaganda: Le Goglu disappeared from circulation in
mid-1947 and Ménard had to cease all public activity directed against the
Jews. As for the Jewish leadership of Montreal, it was quick to grasp the
meaning of this incident, and through it, began to perceive the new dynamics of the relations that were already developing in Montreal between
the Catholic church and the Jews. In his article concerning the state of
anti-Semitism in Quebec, published in May 1947, David Rome referred to
the Goglu affair: "If this cessation is due to this pressure (of the Roman
Catholic committee which deals with Jewish affairs) it represents one of
the few cases where public opinion in Canada was able to stop the publica-

tion of an undesirable periodical without the instrumentality of governmental agencies."[25]

After the war the Catholic clergymen were not the only people in Quebec to feel the need to draw closer to their Jewish compatriots. The surge of liberalism and sympathy also reached lay people, one of whom, Jean Lemoyne, left a detailed account of his efforts to shatter the iron grip of mutual ignorance that embraced the two communities. In 1948 Lemoyne visited Israel and brought back some strong impressions of his voyage, which he described in an article entitled "The Return from Israel" ("Le retour d'Israël"). This is undoubtedly one of the first texts in Québécois literature which allowed the appearance, in lyrical terms, of a thorough knowledge of Jewish history, the Judaic religion and contemporary Zionism. Indeed, in "The Return from Israel," a contradiction to the slanderous writings that had circulated in Quebec during the period between the two wars, the author almost succeeds in identifying himself with the Jewish condition, and even aspires, like the Jewish people, to freedom in the face of long centuries of obstacles: "A people made for apocalypse, those violent meetings of the eternal and the contingent, Israel only stirs by rousing the swirling waters of eternity around it."[26] Lemoyne, who could be considered a mystic Zionist, linked his preoccupation with Israel with the ideal of his Christian faith: "Zionism is an expression of the will of being; it appeals to the right of being, the most urgent and respectable of all rights. Here the exercising of this right corresponds to a providential design, in accordance with our faith."[27]

In his opinion, Catholicism arose directly from the Judaic religion, and he did not know how to detach himself from his roots, without running the risk of drying up and becoming paralysed. It is unnecessary to add that faced with such historical perspectives and the depth of the link he had rediscovered between Christianity and Judaism, any manifestation of anti-Semitism could only arouse Lemoyne's disgust, even more so when the Catholic Church became the accomplice of anti-Semitism through its silence and impotence: "Anti-Semitism, a product of those base, disgraceful and inferior consciences and which knows no other justification than that of the scapegoat, which is in demand, not only symbolically, but literally, presently, in the thick of humanity."[28]

As for Klein, he never participated directly, in the postwar efforts of rapprochement undertaken between the Québécois Jews and the Franco-Catholics. His temperament and his life-style predisposed him to assume a completely different role, less direct but more lasting and, above all, more intangible: the writing of the collection, *The Rocking Chair and Other Poems*. The poet had always been sensitive to current world events as they affected various Jewish communities, particularly his own. One has only to recall, for example, *The Hitleriad*, written in 1942–1943, which was a long pamphlet in poetic form and which represented Klein's entire "war effort." There is also *The Second Scroll*, which finds its dramatic conclusion in Israel after its independence: these two works reveal the depth of the author's historical consciousness. A poet of a certain type of militant Judaism, Klein was also the intimate witness of his Montreal surroundings, of two complementary divisions in his mind, without which his works could never be read and appreciated in their entirety. In such a contradiction in terms lay the foundations of a good part of the dynamics of Klein's writing which culminates in *The Rocking Chair*. For this reason, undoubtedly, the collection became associated with the profound social and ideological changes, which affected all of French Quebec and which would lead to a complete redefinition of its relations with the Montreal Jewish minority.

The Jewish-Catholic rapprochement, which took shape at the end of the forties in Quebec, was rooted in a combination of socio-economic changes that were unprecedented, and whose effects were beginning to be felt by the end of World War Two. The francophone Québécois, like many other peoples, took far too much time to apprehend the impact of the Holocaust upon the Jews of the world for this unimaginable disaster to have influenced their relations with the Montreal Jewish community during the forties. Neither this catastrophe, nor the proclamation of the State of Israel, played any role in the proclivity of francophone Québécois for rapprochement with the Jews living in Canada. In fact, the opening up of all of Quebec to secular and liberal North American influences, the evident prosperity of the new francophone middle classes and their access to a certain occupational mobility began to shatter the visceral mistrust that traditional Québécois society had of everything that did not conform to its cultural and religious ideas. This radically new social climate, largely the result of external influences, led directly to the political events of the sixties and to the ideological ferment known as the Silent Revolution. During the fifteen years from 1945 to 1960, when Quebec society underwent institutional change, such forms of pathological behaviour as the xenophobic rejection of the contemporary world and a withdrawal to the comforting hearth of the past diminished among the francophones, whose anti-Semitism Klein had decried so frequently during the thirties.

Thus, the virulent anti-Semitism of such people as Ménard and Arcand had principally been a particular form of social pathology, produced by a society whose horizons were walled in by a double alienation, born of the economic effects of the Depression and a certain national sclerosis. The fact that a person so highly sensitive to his surroundings as Klein had recognized the dawning of a new day in the relations between francophones and Jews, and that he made himself its hearty propagandist, raises the deeper question of the history of the relations between the two communities since the 1880s. Unfortunately, researchers and historians are more inclined to remember dramatic events, such as the strike of 1934 at the Notre-Dame hospital in Montreal, or the Plamondon affair of 1910, than to dwell on the nature of the daily exchanges which took place between the two communities for more than a century. As for Klein himself, who had so brilliantly depicted the traditional identity of Quebec francophones in poetic tones, a long descent into silence awaited him shortly after, and as of the mid-fifties, his pen became silent. Such a dénouement snatched one of its most magnificent poets away from the Jewish community, and one of its best ambassadors of peace to the francophones of the city.[29]

NOTES

This article was originally published as "A. M. Klein: Du poète et de ses rapports avec le Québec français" in the *Journal of Canadian Studies/Revue d'études canadiennes* 19 (Summer 1984), pp. 114–131, and this translation by Barbara Havercraft is used here by permission.

1. M. W. Steinberg and Seymour Mayne, "A Dialogue on A. M. Klein," *Jewish Dialog* (Passover 1973), p. 16.

2. These poems were "Grain Elevator," "The Cripples," "For the Sisters of the Hotel Dieu," "Air-Map," "The Break-up," "M. Bertrand" and "Frigidaire."

3. At this time, David Rome was the editor of the *Congress Bulletin*. I do not believe that Klein's pamphlets were first published to counter the anti-Semitic influences and opinions in Quebec, but because the social climate had freed itself from this question. I believe that these poems were expected to receive a favourable welcome in francophone circles.

4. This document is kept in the archives of the Canadian Jewish Congress.·

5. Ibid.

6. Ibid.

7. Le Scrutateur (pseud.), "Poems of French Canada," *Les Carnets viatoriens* 8, no. 1 (1948): 62–63.

8. Roger Duhamel, "Courrier des lettres," *L'Action universitaire* 15 (April 1949) pp. 82–83.

9. The Governor General's Award had already been bestowed on Klein in 1949 for the same work.

10. On the subject of anti-Semitism in Quebec, consult Lila-Rose Betcherman's excellent study, *The Swastika and the Maple Leaf* (1975) and *None Is Too Many* by Abella and Troper (1982).

11. M. W. Steinberg and Usher Caplan, eds., *A. M. Klein Beyond Sambation: Selected Essays and Editorials, 1928–1955* (Toronto, 1982).

12. Ibid., p. 230.

13. Although this article is not signed, like many others of similar content, one can assume that they were written by David Rome, because he was the editor of the *Congress Bulletin* at that time.

14. Anon., "The State of Anti-Semitism in French Canada," *Congress Bulletin* 4 (May 1947), pp. 24–25.

15. Louis Benjamin, "The Jews and the French Canadians," *Congress Bulletin* 4 (May 1947), pp. 8, 10.

16. An officially Catholic institution until the sixties, l'Université de Montréal required Catholic students in all disciplines to take courses in Christian ethics which would be suited to their profession.

17. M.-Ceslas Forest, "La Question juive au Canada," *La Revue Dominicaine* 41 (November 1935), pp. 246–277.

18. Ibid., p. 268.

19. M.-Ceslas Forest, "La Question juive chez nous," *La Revue Dominicaine* 41 (December 1935), pp. 329–349.

20. Ibid., p. 268.

21. This is a Yiddish term of Hebrew origin which designates a non-Jewish person who is responsible for certain tasks in a Jewish household or religious establishment. Jews were forbidden by Mosaic law to carry out such tasks. In this case, the young Valiquette's duties probably consisted of extinguishing the candles and turning off the lights after the beginning of the Sabbath.

22. Stéphane Valiquette, "Chronologie autobiographique," 1981.

23. The reader should note that there is a problem of semantics here which is difficult to avoid. Before Vatican II, the Roman Catholic Church was in the habit of maintaining a certain reservation in its relations with representatives of non-Christian religions, including the Jews. At this time, the only path open to a Catholic clergyman eager to associate with believers of other religions was proselytism. The early writings of Valiquette and the St. Paul Committee thus borrowed this language of "the conversion of Israel." However, it should be stated clearly that the number of Québécois Jews who were converted to Catholicism remained extremely low and that Valiquette and his associates did not make apostasy their principal goal in their relations with the Jews. Until the sixties, the regulations of the Catholic Church simply required that the language used in the dialogue with the Jews had to call for their conversion to Catholicism.

24. Joseph Ménard, "Le Clergé et les Juifs," *Le Goglu* (1947), p. 6.

25. Anon., "State of Antisemitism," pp. 24–25.

26. Jean Lemoyne, "Le retour d'Israël," in *Convergences* (Collection Constantes), no. 1 (Montreal, 1961).

27. Ibid., p. 182.

28. Ibid., p. 174.

29. Even today, Klein remains almost totally unknown among Québécois critics, despite the obvious legitimacy of his Montreal roots, and he does not appear in any of the numerous histories or anthologies of Québécois literature that have recently been published in French.

Epilogue

In our time, the urge to endure in some Jewish way, however problematic and attenuated by the prescribed standards of a once-pervasive religious culture, has been a powerful force for Jewish group survival. Constituting the largest agglomeration of Jews in history, however small in proportion to the total population, North America's six million have shown, almost in reflexive response to the fate of that other six million and to the perpetual besiegement of the State of Israel, an undiminished sense of exigency and solidarity. In both Canada and the United States, an all-embracing almost talismanic portmanteau term for encompassing all symptoms of individual no less than of Jewish group consciousness has taken hold. Whether religious or secular, ideological or ceremonial, cultural or artistic, Jewishness, as it has been called, has come to subsume all manifest expressions of Jewish bodies, minds and souls in quest of some larger sense of Jewish connectedness in an open universe of familiar strangers. In so recently secularized a Jewish world, to which one can apply Henry James's observation that the novelist has succeeded to the sacred office of the sages and chroniclers, Jewish novelists suddenly became conspicuous occupants of that office. In the latter half of the twentieth century, to the distress of historians, the novel in the public mind appears to have become the most accessible "modern surrogate" for the chronicle of Jewishness.[1]

In our lamentedly ahistorical post-Holocaust, postindustrial and many would say, post-Judaic and post-Christian eras, the high tribute obliquely accorded to "Jewishness" in the novel and related forms was without parallel. In barely more than a decade, an unprecedented succession of Nobel awards in literature has been conferred upon Jews writing about Jews in both Jewish and non-Jewish idioms—S. J. Agnon in Hebrew, the poet Nelly Sachs in German and Isaac Bashevis Singer in Yiddish—for work which resonated to the totality of the Jewish experience in terms universal. For the Jews of North America, most dramatic of all was the award in the year of the bicentennial to the versa-tongued Montreal-born American, Saul Bellow, whose parents spoke Russian to each other, while their children spoke Yiddish to them, English to one another, French and English on the street, learning Hebrew at afternoon school. Coming shortly after the publication of his *To Jerusalem and Back,* Bellow's Nobel award, and the awards to Agnon, Sachs and Singer, seemed emblematic of the cleaving yet liberating power of the constellation of ancient, medieval and modern languages and cultures, shared historically by the Jews of North America, that has been coextensive with their full humanity and inseparable from their Jewishness.

The North American Jewish ethos, if we may call it that, has been manifested most keenly by Israel's veteran Canadian and American olim. Often referred to by Israelis as Anglo-Saxons or Ha-Americani, for them the diaspora and "Jewishness" were inseparable from their personal commitment to Zion. Ironically, unlike so many Americans and Canadians who rediscovered their "Jewishness" on the eve of the Six Day War when Israel seemed threatened with annihilation, as one of the speakers stressed at the conference's wide-ranging session on Jewishness, an Israeli historian of American birth who had made aliyah shortly after World War Two, saw 1967 as "a very critical year in the history of Israel" for very different reasons. In 1967, maintained Arthur Goren, "maybe we began to lose our Jewishness," a Jewishness that suffused the Zionist ethos and the founding fathers of the State of Israel with a universalistic outlook in which Jews had taken supreme pride. "To maintain and to fill one's Jewishness . . . with broad humanistic values as well as Jewish cultural values," was an ever signal need, insisted Israel's senior American Jewish historian, for only by "trying to be menschen," total human beings, may we hope to approach "the heart of Jewishness."[2]

This first volume devoted to exploring the North American Jewish experience has approached "the heart of Jewishness," or Jewish ethnicity, in its fashion, by provoking interest in the shared past, we trust, no less than in the distinctive histories of the Jews in two neighboring nations with so much in common. The need for extensive historical research in so many areas barely touched on in this volume is self-evident. Yet there seems no question that no two nations better lend themselves to genuine rather than to facile comparisons than do Canada and the United States and that the study of the Jewish experience in these two historically overlapping countries is intrinsically important to Jewish no less than to a wider self-knowledge. The spirited encouragement of Canadian-American studies by the Canadian Studies Center at Duke University and of Canadian-American ethnic studies by the Multicultural History Society of Ontario, along with the vigorous upsurge in the past generation of scholarship in American and Canadian Jewish studies, as evidenced in *The Jews of North America,* has opened the way to a new phase of historical inquiry.[3]

NOTES

1. Josef H. Yerushalmi, *Zakhor: Jewish History and Jewish Memory* (Seattle, 1982), p. 96; also see Oscar Handlin, *Truth in History* (Cambridge, Mass., 1979), pp. 371–382; Cushing Strout, *The Veracious Imagination* (Middletown, Conn., 1981), passim; and Salo W. Baron, *The Contemporary Relevance of History* (New York, 1986), p. 1.

2. See typescript of symposium, pp. 11–12; also see "On Jewishness: A Symposium," *Viewpoints* 12 (May 1983), pp. 1–3, for statements by Louis Greenspan, Morton Weinfeld and Adele Wiseman. See also Dan Miron, "Modern Hebrew Literature: Zionist Perspectives and Israeli Realities," *Prooftexts* 4 (January 1984), p. 67, for a sensitive sharing of Goren's perceptions.

3. See Richard A. Preston, ed., *The Influence of the United States on Canadian Development: Eleven Case Studies* (Durham, N.C., 1972), esp. pp. 3–54; Richard A. Preston, ed., *Perspectives on Revolution and Evolution* (Durham, 1979), esp. John Porter, "Melting Pot or Mosaic: Revolution or Reversion?," pp. 152–179 and the essays by Robin W. Winks, Seymour M. Lipset, Robert Presthus and Andre Raynauld; and Seymour M. Lipset, "Historical Traditions and National Characteristics: A Comparative Analysis of Canada and the United States," *Canadian Journal of Sociology* 11 (1986), pp. 142–144.

Index

Moses Rischin is a professor of history at San Francisco State
University, director of the Western History Center of the Judah L.
Magnes Museum in Berkeley and a past president of the Immigration
History Society. His books include *The Promised City: New York's Jews,
1870–1914*, *The American Gospel of Success, Immigration and the American
Tradition*, *The Jews of the West: The Metropolitan Years* and *Grandma
Never Lived in America: The New Journalism of Abraham Cahan*.

The book was designed by Joanne Elkin Kinney. The typeface for the
text and the display is Galliard. The book is printed on 55-lb. Glatfelter
text paper. The cloth edition is bound in Holliston Mills' Roxite
Vellum over binder's boards.

Manufactured in the United States of America.

The Jews of North
America

$39.95

DATE			